Steven Ungar

Roland Barthes
The Professor of Desire

University of Nebraska Press

Lincoln and London

Publication of this book
was aided by a grant from The
    Andrew W. Mellon Foundation.

The paper in this book meets
the guidelines for
    permanence and durability
of the Committee on
    Production Guidelines for
Book Longevity of the
    Council on Library Resources.

Library of Congress
    Cataloging in Publication Data
Ungar, Steven, 1945–
    Roland Barthes,
the professor of desire.

Bibliography: p.
Includes index.
    1. Barthes, Roland.
2. Linguists – France – Biography.
    3. Critics – France –
Biography. I. Title.
    P85.B33U53 1983ʾ   410ʹ.92ʹ4 [B]
83-6836 ISBN 0-8032-4551-3

For my parents, who first taught me
the pleasures of the

Contents

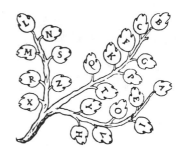

Acknowledgments

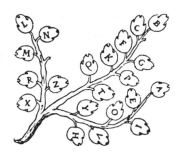

For criticism and encouragement at various stages of this project, I thank Stephen Bonnycastle, Tom Conley, Christophe Gallier, Betty McGraw, Paul Sandro, Gayatri Spivak, and Walter Strauss. In France, Russell Young and Michael Pretina provided the time, space, and atmosphere to work through a long draft of the manuscript at the Camargo Foundation, where conversations with Germaine Brée helped me to locate Barthes within the ongoing histories of literary and critical thinking. For their patience in compiling the bibliography, I thank Victoria Metaxis and Dominique Braud.

A number of sections of the current book have appeared previously in article form. A section of chapter 3 appeared in *Diacritics* 7, no. 1 (1977). Sections of chapter 4 appeared in *The Bulletin of the Midwest Modern Language Association* 14 (1982) and *Studies in Twentieth Century Literature* 5, no. 1 (Spring 1981). Shorter versions of chapters 5, 6, 7, and 8 appeared, respectively, in *Visible Language* 11 (1977); *Enclitic* 2, no. 2 (Fall 1978); *Yale French Studies*, no. 63 (1982); and *L'Esprit Créateur* 22, no. 1 (Spring 1982). I am grateful to the editors for permitting me to reprint material that first appeared in the pages of their journals.

ABBREVIATIONS

These abbreviations refer to Barthes's
books and articles cited frequently in
the body of the text. Page numbers
are for the English translations where
they exist. Full references appear in
sections I and II of the bibliography.

CE	*Essais critiques*
CL	*La Chambre claire (Camera Lucida)*
CV	*Critique et vérité*
E	*Erté*
Emp	*L'Empire des signes*
ES	"Eléments de sémiologie"
FDA	*Fragments d'un discours amoureux*
GV	*Le Grain de la voix*
IMT	*Image-Music-Text*
L	*Leçon*
M	*Mythologies*
MI	*Michelet*
NCE	*New Critical Essays*
OO	*L'Obvie et l'obtus: Essais critiques III*
PT	*Le Plaisir du texte*
R	*Sur Racine*
RB	*Roland Barthes pac Roland Barthes*
SFL	*Sade, Fourier, Loyola*
SZ	*S/Z*
WDZ	*Le Degré zéro de l'écriture*

The work, in its discontinuity, proceeds by means of two movements: *the straight line* (advance, increase, insistence of an idea, a position, a preference, an image) and the *zigzag* (reversal, contradiction, reactive energy, denial, contrariety, the movement of a Z, the letter of deviance).

Roland Barthes

Introduction: Double Figure

This reading of Roland Barthes focuses on the development of his career as writer and critic from the 1940s through 1980, the year of his death. While he is most often seem as a literary critic and advocate of structural analysis, Barthes is more difficult to classify without expanding the tag of literary critic to the more inclusive identity of *writer*. Along with intellectual figures such as Proust, Valéry, Gide, and Sartre, Barthes brings to this wider identity the elements of moralist, autobiographer, and social critic whose rare equivalents in American culture—I am thinking here of Edmund Wilson, Norman Mailer, and Susan Sontag—offer a similar resistance to definitive categories. In the case of Barthes, the resistance to a clear identity or progression was evident in the early 1970s, when *S/Z* and *The Pleasure of the Text* were read as denials of the formalist project Barthes had promoted in the name of structural analysis during the previous decade. By the time the *Roland Barthes* appeared in 1975 as a combination of autobiography, fiction, and literary criticism, "Barthes"—or whomever that signature referred to—seemed too elusive or too playful for those readers who had supported his earlier writings. The fact that he recognized his own development as a series of breaks or zigzags did little to satisfy others who were frustrated by their attempts to bring together the various stages of his career to create a single comprehensive figure.

If, however, we take Barthes at his word and accept the assertion of change and difference against the will to unify, the illusion of a lifelong "career" yields to a plurality of stages or moments first noted by Stephen Heath in his 1974 study, *Vertige du déplacement*. In the wake of Barthes's death, the initial opposition between a career and its various stages takes on a second kind of illusory completeness, a totality that Barthes foresaw prefigured as a woman covered with an endless garment, a weaving of body and garment that fulfills the infinite text produced in and through reading. To end that weaving in the name of totality is, Barthes writes at the close of the *Roland Barthes*, always grotesque. Because he thus hoped to negate in advance the illusion of totality that death would confer on his writings, it is almost as if Barthes were dead before the fact. In this sense, it is (totally) apt to follow Jacques Derrida in writing of the *deaths* of Barthes in contrast to the reality of his passing.

My goal in the chapters that make up this book is to provide an approach to Barthes's writings that deals with the stages of his career in keeping with the broken and reactive movement of the work as a double figure. In so doing, I shall be writing reactively; that is, against the various myths that surround the signature that brings together the work and the man in the act of writing. The portraits of Barthes and his writings set forth in this book took shape between 1975 and 1980 during a period when Barthes no longer fulfilled the expectations of earlier supporters and detractors. At the very moment that he was becoming "difficult"—not just to classify, but also in the sense that a child is described as unruly or unpredictable—Barthes found the harmony of vision and method that had eluded him for so long. From the *Roland Barthes* to *La Chambre claire*, the movement of a paradoxical writing—set against the various conventions of popular doctrine—

projected a new career and a new generation of readers. As I worked to complete this study, the energy of Barthes's change of vision was a constant force. Little did I know at the time that, as Annette Lavers puts it so well, I would have to rewrite my account in the past tense.

The discrepancies between the reception given to Barthes's writings in France and abroad are so great that it is hard to ascribe them to mere cultural misreading or disorientation. One can hardly speak of a dialogue. Ongoing resistance to his writings is so virulent in some quarters that it bears closer examination as a visible form of distortion which transforms critical response into hyperbole and polemics. On occasion, the distortion takes on mythic proportions in which Barthes becomes a foreign agent characterized as threatening so that he can be overcome in the name of a home-grown critical community. The whole affair is quite agonistic and self-serving. It allows the critic to engage in mock heroic encounters without actually running any risk of defeat since his or her opponent has been fabricated out of convenience in order that his fall serve a didactic function. In England and the United States, at least, Barthes is so often the victim of a "bad press" that one might never notice that the portraits in question are caricatures of the 1960s advocate of structural analysis. In the *Times Literary Supplement*, Graham Hough ponders with feigned incredulity the exportation of Barthes's heresies to a gullible foreign public:

"Faut-il brûler Roland Barthes?" Surely not: even ten years ago when the question was first raised no one really wanted an auto-da-fé, and by the time Barthes's heresies fused into a dogma he had become necessary—as the archetype of a left-wing, left-bank, post-Sartrean orthodoxy, rumour of which has spread by now to the plains of Iowa and the slopes of Mount Fuji. Its components are briefly described: three parts Marxism, two parts psychoanalysis, four parts recycled linguistics, and the rest made up of the anti-bourgeois grimaces that the French bourgeois intelligentsia have been frightening their aunts with since 1830.[1]

At a loss for what to do with the author of the *Fragments d'un discours amoureux*, Hough opts for insult by caricature. He uses an ironic attitude to deal with what might otherwise be construed as a veiled compliment at odds with the brief critical encounter he feels obligated to carry on. Characterizing *L'Empire des signes* as a picture book "destined for enlightened coffee-tables," he adds that the book is written "with immense enjoyment, and though I know it is a dreadful thing to say of a French intellectual, Barthes begins to appear in a positively genial light."[2]

More honest about his critical position and its inherent limitations is Philip Thody, who confronts the resistance he brings to his reading. Author of earlier studies on Sartre, Camus, and Genet, Thody is predictably drawn more to Barthes's earlier writings than to what Hough sees as a "post-Sartrean orthodoxy." Of singular interest, however, is a postscript in which Thody states that his attitude toward Barthes's evolution was altered by the appearance of the *Fragments* just as he was completing his own manuscript. Had he seen that book one year sooner, he writes, "the estimate of Barthes put forward in this book would undoubtedly have been far less conservative."[3]

Graham Hough is far from alone in his views. Indeed, it appears at times that almost everyone is saying or writing dreadful things about French intellectuals; so dreadful, in fact, that they are unwilling to account for their views beyond the quip or flippant rejection. This is especially true for those who come to Barthes's writings in English translation and within the context of a (monolithic) structuralism seen either as a "dangerous" methodology—that is, anti-humanistic and foreign—or as a domesticated and innocent scientific project. Ultimately, both versions are misleading because they are based on false assumptions that preclude the possibility of a critical reading open to alternative approaches.

More in keeping with the reflexive elements in Barthes's recent work as I have described it are the comments by Rosalind Coward and John Ellis in *Language and Materialism*. Unwilling to accept the accounts of semiology as an innocent or indifferent activity, they distinguish this "bourgeois" practice as they find it presented by Pierre Guiraud and Jonathan Culler from a semiology they see as devolving from historical change. As part of their argument for a Marxist critique of the sign, they explore the divergence of structuralisms and semiologies as practices of reading. In the *Mythologies*, Barthes had shown how the denotative meaning produced by a first-degree relation of signifier to signified was itself the signifier in a more inclusive sign of ideology operating at the level of connotation. Once the more visible product of denotation is seen as an effect or product of connotation, it is no longer possible for popular myths to circulate as anything other than false images, what Barthes terms "thefts of language." Following Barthes's project in *S/Z*, Coward and Ellis analyze the "natural" practice of reading in search of the ideology connoted within the more visible production of denotative meaning:

> Conventional criticism aims at a closure of the troubling plurality: it aims at an interpretation, fixing a meaning, finding a source (the author), and an ending, a closure (*the* meaning). This form of criticism plays the game that the text proposes: that the text is nothing except what it can denote or describe and the rhetorical grace with which it can do so. Barthes's liberatory criticism intends to discover what the rules of the game are (for writers and readers), in order to enter into a more serious and vital play: to find ideology out in the moment that it is produced.[4]

I have chosen texts by Hough, Thody, Coward, and Ellis because they illustrate the scope of resistance and reception that Barthes elicits at a given moment in his career. Aside from the intransigence of a critical response predetermined by doctrine or temperament, many readers fail to consider the cultural differences which make it all too convenient to say or write such dreadful things about French intellectuals. To be sure, the French are often as hard on themselves as anyone else. Since the mid-nineteenth century, guilt and impotence would appear to be prime traits against which any self-respecting intellectual has had to contend. First, the Paris Commune haunted them as a reminder of the failed passage from ideas toward action. Two decades later, the Dreyfus affair divided French society into numerous factions that were able to penetrate all economic and geographic sectors. Since World War II, the model par excellence — cited on numerous occasions by Barthes himself — has been that of Jean-Paul Sartre. Exemplified by his own changes, Sartre measured his triumphs and failures as a touchstone against which others came to formulate their own positions, even when (especially when) Sartre came to embody what they hoped most to avoid.

As professor since 1961 at the Ecole Pratique des Hautes Etudes and from 1977 to 1980 at the Collège de France, Barthes took an increasingly public stance in his relations to institutions of learning. Never a Marxist in an orthodox sense, his sensitivity to the use and misuse of authority has often suggested a sympathy to left-wing politics.[5] Like Sartre and Gide, Barthes has never claimed to be anything more than a bourgeois whose links with any kind of class struggle could be little more than idealized. At the same time, however, Barthes has upheld a personal commitment in his teaching animated by politics in terms of ethical categories. To the figures of critic and writer, it is necessary to add that of teacher, or master, in the full sense that Barthes derived from the tutor figures of Socrates and Nietzsche in what, in retrospect, was the final period of his evolution.

Chronology

1915	(November 12) Born in Cherbourg, son of Louis Barthes, naval officer, and Henriette Binger.
1916	(October 26) Death of Louis Barthes, in a naval battle on the North Sea.
1916–24	Childhood in Bayonne. Elementary-school classes in the lycée of this city.
1924	Move to Paris, rue Mazarine and rue Jacques-Callot. Henceforth, all school vacations are spent with the Barthes grandparents, in Bayonne.
1924–30	At the Lycée Montaigne, from the eighth form to the fourth.
1930–34	At the Lyccée Louis-le-Grand, from the third form to Philosophy. Baccalaureates: 1933 and
1934	(May 10) Pulmonary tuberculosis. Lesion in the left lung.
1934–35	Treatment in the Pyrenees, at Bedous, in the Aspe valley.
1935–39	Sorbonne: *licence* in classics. Foundation of the Groupe de Théâtre Antique.
1937	Exempted from military service. Reader during the summer at Debreczen (Hungary).
1938	Trip to Greece with the Groupe de Théâtre Antique.
1939–40	Professor of fourth and third forms (rectoral delegate) at the new lycée of Biarritz.
1940–41	Rectoral delegate (tutor and professor) at the lycées Voltaire and Carnot, in Paris. Diplôme d'études supérieures (on Greek tragedy).
1941	(October) Relapse of pulmonary tuberculosis.

1942	First stay in the Sanatorium des Etudiants, at Saint-Hilaire-du-Touvet, in the Isère.
1943	Convalescence at the Post-Cure in the rue Quatrefages, in Paris. Final *licence* (grammar and philology). (July) Relapse in the right lung.
1943–45	Second stay in the Sanatorium des Etudiants. Silence treatment, slope treatment, etc. In the sanatorium, several months of premedical study with the intention of pursuing psychiatric medicine. During treatment, relapse.
1945	(October) Right extra-pleural pneumothorax.
1945–46	Subsequent treatment at Leysin, at the Clinique Alexandre, part of the Sanatorium Universitaire Suisse.
1946–47	Convalescence in Paris. Publishes article in *Combat*, text later incorporated into *Le Degré zéro de l'écriture*.
1948–49	Assistant librarian, then professor at the Institut Français of Bucharest (Rumania), and reader at the university of this city.
1949–50	Reader at the University of Alexandria (Egypt).
1950–52	At the Direction Générale des Relations Culturelles, instruction branch, in Paris.
1952–54	Officer of Instruction at the Centre National de la Recherche Scientifique, in Paris.
1953	*Le Degré zéro de l'écriture*
1954	*Michelet par lui-même*
1954–55	Literary adviser to the Editions de l'Arche.
1955–59	Research attaché at the C.N.R.S. (sociology).
1957	*Mythologies*
1960–62	Chairman of the VIe section at the Ecole Pratique des Hautes Etudes (social and economic sciences).
1962–76	Director of studies at the Ecole Pratique des Hautes Etudes (sociology of signs, symbols, and representations).
1963	*Sur Racine*
1964	*Essais critiques* *La Tour Eiffel*

	"Eléments de Sémiologie"
1966	*Critique et vérité*
	"Introduction à l'analyse structurale des récits"
1970	*S/Z*
	L'Empire des signes
	Erté
1971	*Sade, Fourier, Loyola*
1973	*Le Plaisir du texte*
1974	Trip to China.
1975	*Alors la Chine?*
	Roland Barthes
1977	(January 7) Inaugural lecture, Collège de France (chair of Literary Semiology).
	Fragments d'un discours amoureux
	(June 22–29) "Prétexte: Roland Barthes," Cerisy-la-Salle colloquium.
	(October 25) Death of Henriette Binger, his mother.
1978	*Leçon*
1979	*Sollers écrivain*
1980	*La Chambre claire: Note sur la photographie*
	(February 25) Barthes is struck by a truck as he crosses a street near the Collège de France.
	(March 26) Barthes dies in a Paris hospital.
1981	(February-March) "Roland Barthes: Carte Segni," exhibit of his artwork at the Casino dell' Aurora (Rome).
	Le Grain de la voix: Entretiens 1962–1980
1982	*L'Obvie et l'obtus: Essais critiques III*

I. Questions of Method

Photograph by Arthur W. Wang

The first premise of all human history is, of course, the existence of living human individuals. Thus the first fact to be established is the physical organization of these individuals and their consequent relation to the rest of nature.

Karl Marx and Friedrich Engels,
The German Ideology

CHAPTER ONE

Writing in History

If you have been reading Roland Barthes, you know that attempts to bring together the various moments of his career into any kind of synthesis meet with frustration. Known primarily as a literary critic, Barthes outstrips that particular label and identity with disturbing intensity, to a point where an interviewer describes him in 1977 as "less and less easy to classify" (*GV*, 263).

Along with Derrida, Michel Foucault, and Jacques Lacan, Barthes is often cast in the role of the Parisian guru whose latest pronouncements are marketed abroad with the regularity of seasonal fashions and fads. Faced with an ever-expanding list of new terms and concepts cast in the densest of proses, the reader looking for "useful" information is likely to move from frustration toward anger and fatigue. What many readers identify as the difficult quality of these writings is often an expression of their own inflexibility before the changes of vocabulary and differences in reading these changes impose. The mixing of genres, attitudes, and terminologies in the writings of Derrida, Lacan, Foucault, and Barthes breeds resistance in the most tolerant and curious of would-be converts. Why are these texts so difficult? Whatever happened to the French tradition of clear, rational thinking? Is it really worth all the effort? "Parlez-vous 'French-speak?' And if so, *pourquoi?*"[1]

In 1953, Iris Murdoch wrote that to understand Jean-Paul Sartre was to understand something vital about the then-present age because Sartre's self-conscious attempts to remain contemporary give his writings "the style of their historic moment."[2] The same could be said of Barthes's writings, especially the very first. For although he was born some ten years after Sartre, the opening chapters of his *Writing Degree Zero* can be read as a response to Sartre's call for a committed literature of political activism.

Although the careers of Sartre and Barthes overlap and finish in death within a month of each other in 1980, Barthes's "age" is not identical with that of Sartre. Emerging from an early exposure to writings by Gide, Proust, Valéry, and Anatole France, Barthes passes through his readings of Sartre toward subsequent tutelage in the works of Hjelmslev, Saussure, Lévi-Strauss, Benveniste, and Lacan. In retrospect, it appears that Barthes progresses toward a literary and critical modernity Sartre is unwilling to endorse. To borrow the celebrated Proustian metaphor, the various stages along Sartre's and Barthes's "ways" diverge during the decade following World War II and come together only after their deaths. For Barthes, the progression toward a modernity tied to linguistics is never total; a predilection for premodern and classical writings resurfaces markedly after the appearance of *S/Z* in 1970. Those who caricature Barthes as a mandarin of the avant-garde would do better to note that his writings often resonate with an untimeliness closer in sensibility to Flaubert, Gide, or Proust than to Sollers, Lacan, or Sarduy. In this sense, Barthes remains very much a supporter of modernity and innovation unable to shake off the force of a literary temperament steeped in the classics (not for nothing did he earn a *licence de lettres classiques* at the Sorbonne!). As a result, Barthes often writes as a modernist whose defense of the new is set against more distant modernities of the past. Because he writes consciously for the present age over and against any inclination to fade into untimeliness, Barthes is able to turn the topicality of the "ancients vs. the moderns" polemic into the context for linking contemporary versions of modernity to a critical reflection irreducible to a single dogma, doctrine, or school. Similarly, what some readers see as his failure to maintain a consistent practice as a literary critic is, in fact, less a failure of method or rigor than a way of asserting the ongoing movement and difference of critical thinking within history. An intense polemicist for the cause of modernity in his 1966 *Critique et vérité* tract against Raymond Picard, Barthes can also acknowledge the limits of that defense and admit subsequently: "All of a sudden, it has become a matter of indifference to me whether or not I am modern."[3]

Of the various changes attributed to the structuralist "invasion," vocabulary is the most notorious. Barthes's contribution to that notoriety includes a number of meanings given to the term writing (*écriture*) throughout his own writings (*écrits*). In keeping with his attention to the minor pleasures and ironies of language, it is fitting to see the semantic play between the French terms *écriture* and *écrit* as something more than an embellishment or a pedant's stratagem. Barthes is often accused of coining new terms or lifting others from linguistics or psychoanalysis, allegedly without the competence or license to do so. In response, he points immediately to the pedagogical value of such innovation. New terms call for definition and a rethinking of received ideas which more traditional approaches do not always provide. In this instance, the choice between convention and innovation or change is not difficult to make:

To state matters clearly, between jargon and platitudes, I prefer jargon. To be ironical on this work of license may be easy, but it is not generous. It is unworthy to judge someone on his or her vocabulary, even if it is bothersome. There is no such thing as an innocent vocabulary; everyone has verbal peculiarities ["des tics de langage"]. That doesn't bother me. In an age when psychoanalysis and linguistics teach us to consider man differently from the way Théodule Ribot did, it is normal to say that someone has "semantic problems." (*GV*, 44)

For many American readers, the terms "structuralism" and "structuralist" elicit a visceral response associated with images of crisis, foreign ideas, and influence as influenza. Something of epidemiology sets in at this point to add a touch of clinical authority to the slanted perspective often used to characterize structuralism from a critical stance which is less than innocent. Behind the verbal jousting and inflated rhetorics of such attacks, structuralism serves as a blanket term to designate literary practices deemed hostile to humanistic scholarship. To write today—in early 1982—about structuralism, it is necessary to distinguish between a will to define concepts, principles, or qualities which would constitute the so-called bare facts and a separate but related will to polemicize. We may not always be able to distinguish between these two wills, but few of us fail to recognize the polemic orientation of what purports to be objective or disinterested description.

The link between polemics and the difference or change at stake in critical thinking is visible in the use of language. When, for example, Jonathan Culler writes that structuralism is synonymous with disciplines studying "the world of meaningful objects and actions (as opposed to physical objects themselves),"[4] his claim ascribes a value to linguistics that more traditional students of literature might well reject. In fact, those who doubt the virtues of structural analysis for the study of literature resist the call to rethink behavior in terms of linguistic science, seeing in the proliferation of methodologies and critiques nothing more than updated versions of an avant-garde indebted to the nineteenth-century ghosts of Marx, Nietzsche, and Freud. Barthes is not primarily a political writer—by which I mean that his consideration of social and political institutions is secondary to other concerns with language, literature, and writing. At the same time, however, he tends to see the primacy of language as a historical phenomenon, and the relation to language as political. At various moments in his personal itinerary, that relation surfaces as dominant: neither a repressed truth nor a nemesis of intellectuals, but part of the play of signs tying Barthes to his age in what some readers describe as the liberating factor of his critical vision. In order to see how Barthes's "age" is and is not that of structuralism, it is helpful to start before structuralism or, so to speak, at the zero degree of writing.

In a 1971 interview with Jean Thibaudeau, Barthes describes his early readings and a literary modernity from which he emerged without the slightest exposure to surrealism, Marxism, philosophy, or literary criticism. Political awareness consisted of reading *L'Oeuvre*, a radical socialist journal known for its pacifist and anticlerical views. After an initial bout with tuberculosis ended any serious hopes for a university career, Barthes prepared a *licence* in classics and helped start le groupe du Théâtre Antique at the Sorbonne. Hired as a *lycée* professor in Biarritz and Paris between 1939 and 1941, Barthes spent the better part of the next five years treating his tuberculosis at sanatoriums in France and Switzerland. An article on Gide's journals was his first piece of published writing. Another, on Camus's *L'Etranger*, written during the same period and published in a journal put out by sanatorium patients, led Barthes to the idea of "white writing."[5]

Unlike the more illustrious wartime activities of Malraux, Sartre, and Camus, Barthes's experience of solidarity took the form of conversations with fellow patients:

In Leysin, at the University clinic where 30 of us were undergoing treatment, a friend, Fournié, spoke to me with conviction about Marxism; he was a former typographer, a militant Trotskyite who came out of deportation: the intelligence, grace, and strength of his political analyses, his irony, his wisdom, a kind of moral freedom; in sum, the total success of this personality apparently free of any political arousal whatsoever gave me a high and ideal notion of Marxist dialectics (or rather, what I saw in Marxism, thanks to Fournié, was dialectics); subsequently, I was able to find this seduction only in reading Brecht. Furthermore 1945–46 was the period when Sartre was being discovered. At the time of the Armistice . . . I am therefore a Sartrian and a Marxist; I am trying to "commit" literary form (which I had sensed strongly in Camus's *L'Etranger*) and to marxify Sartrian commitment, or at the very least—and is it not perhaps enough?—to give it a Marxist justification: a double project quite evident in *Writing Degree Zero*.[6]

Through an introduction to Maurice Nadeau, Barthes was able to write for the journal *Combat*—first in 1947 and again beginning in 1950—a number of short texts on "white writing" and the commitment of literary form. These, in turn, became the basis for *Writing Degree Zero*, published in book form by the Editions du Seuil in 1953. In retrospect, the basic argument in this first book reveals some of the polemical and conceptual intensity of his writings after 1970. In *Writing*

Degree Zero, Barthes describes Letters—he uses the singular and capitalized term *Littérature*—as a sequence of writings (*écritures*) without any unifying conception. The initial form of his argument sketches a project in literary history where the transition from absolute to relative conceptions is related to concurrent historical factors. At the same time, the initial distinction between literature and writings(s) becomes the basis for a critique of the values promoting a false image of literature as an unchanging natural phenomenon somehow situated out of history. As early as this first book, Barthes combines literary and historical projects by examining the social values implicit in any theory or practice of literature. In its initial formulation, Barthes's approach derives at least in part from the existentialist practice of demystification (*dévoilement*) set forth during the same period in the writings of Jean-Paul Sartre.

In *What Is Literature?* (1947), Sartre outlines his program for a literature committed to an ongoing critique of injustices perpetuated by a capitalist society built on exploitation of the working classes. In agreement with Sartre on the estrangement of the writer from social groups whose interests conflict with those of the individual, Barthes is less concerned with formulating a specific program of social change than with understanding the historical factors which come to bear on the act of writing: "In front of the virgin sheet of paper, at the moment of choosing the words which must frankly signify his place in History, and testify that he assumes its data, he observes a tragic disparity between what he does and what he sees" (*WDZ*, 86). Because he believes in the force of historical change on the formation of personal identity and self-knowledge, Barthes rejects the existentialist vision of the individual as an integral whole. Instead, he seeks the causes of breakup in order to situate alienation within history: "Barthes will have no truck with oneness, and certainly not with God, the One of Ones; he supports whatever is plural or discontinuous."[7] In another sense, the progression from singular to plural—from LA *Littérature* to DES *écritures*—serves as a theoretical preface to his later critiques of the popular culture of the petite bourgeoisie in the *Mythologies*. In *Writing Degree Zero*, however, the cultural myth to be exploded is that of Letters, and the critical concept employed to explode it is writing (*écriture*).

In *What Is Literature?* Sartre describes prose and poetry as basic attitudes chosen by the writer as a relation to language. Prose is essentially utilitarian, a more or less invisible medium which draws attention to itself only when it ceases to serve a desired end. In daily use, however, prose is almost fully integrated to the body. It is, Sartre concludes, another finger or leg. In short, it is close to a pure function. In contrast to the prose attitude mediating almost invisibly between men and the world, the poetic attitude confronts language in its materiality, with a resulting drop in its pragmatic value. When Sartre asserts that the poet refuses to use language, he means that the poet does not consider words as symbols or signs, dwelling instead on the qualities which make them physical entities in their own right and thus potential barriers to the world of action.

In the opening chapter of *Writing Degree Zero*, Barthes describes language and style as external and internal forms, determinants imposing a number of options out of which a writer chooses a particular writing. Up to this point Barthes upholds Sartre's concern with commitment and responsibility. As it appears in these opening pages, the status of writing is admittedly ambiguous. Both form and practice, it is the result of a confrontation between the writer and society (in the form of language) as well as a return to a primal scene of action and the personal or biological origins of style. When Barthes describes language as a horizon and style as verticality, associations with the paradigms and syntagms of structural linguistics extend the abstractions which put off many readers.

I have never understood this reaction, for the project undertaken in *Writing Degree Zero* strikes me as decidedly historical. And not at all in the sense dismissed by some critics as a naive idealism derived from the "hackneyed Marxist notion that the crucial date in literary history is 1848."[8] The historical project in *Writing Degree Zero* is twofold: Barthes wants to specify the social and historical nature of writing as an activity whose product is the result of the writer's decision of how to use the language which society prescribes as acceptable for literary purposes. In this sense, writing becomes an act of historical necessity and solidarity: "A language and a style are objects; a mode of writing is a function; it is the relationship between creation and society, the literary language transformed by its social finality, form considered as a human intention and thus linked to the great crises of History" (*WDZ*, 14).[9]

In addition, Barthes outlines a study of Literature whose ties with other social institutions he wants to trace historically. Thus, the hypothetical passage from Literature to writings does not occur merely at a conceptual level, but in relation to political and economic changes in nineteenth- and twentieth-century Europe. In contrast to the prescriptive literary program set forth by Sartre, Barthes notes the introspection and self-reflexivity of the modern writer who encounters the paradox of writing without a clearcut and unified notion of Literature. Where Sartre wants to seize the historic moment in the hopes of molding wartime solidarity into a peacetime commitment to change society, Barthes sees the diminished options of the writer to affect any kind of direct social change. As historical awareness increases, it clarifies inevitably the double-bind peculiar to a modernity Barthes inherits from Mallarmé, Valéry, and Gide: "This shows that a modern masterpiece is impossible, since the Writer is forced by his writing into an impass: either the object of the work is naively attuned to the convention of its form, Literature remaining deaf to our present History, and not going beyond the literary myth; or else the writer acknowledges the vast novelty of the present world, but finds that in order to express it he has at his disposal only a language which is splendid but lifeless" (WDZ, 86). Today, an awareness of this double-bind may well be an essential feature of the literary modernity whose origins and development Barthes traces from the initial sketch in Writing Degree Zero through the reflection on classical and modern texts in S/Z, The Pleasure of the Text, and Leçon.

While Barthes is not a political writer in a strict sense, he is also not merely a writer or critic with a casual attitude toward historical and political issues. The encounter with Sartre's postwar writings ties Barthes's earliest views on language, literature, and writing to a specific moment in his own development. It clarifies after the fact what is retained and what is rejected in the later writings. The encounter with Sartre is retained primarily in the discovery of modern writing and a stylistic force in the essay form which Barthes describes as overwhelming. At the same time, What Is Literature? forces Barthes to formulate an initial stand on militancy and a use of language he has never brought into line with his own practice as writer and critic. Consequently, the program of commitment he finds in Sartre's manifesto becomes a source of ambivalence visible throughout Writing Degree Zero. In an interview published shortly after his death, Barthes specifies the extent of that ambivalence:

At the end of the last war, I was quite fascinated intellectually by Sartre, and therefore by the theory of commitment. It corresponded to my adolescence, to my youth, so to speak. But I have never militated and it would be impossible for me to do so for reasons of a personal attitude toward language; I do not like militant language . . . I always try to set forth problems in terms of language. This is my own limit. The intellectual cannot directly attack the established powers but he can inject styles of discourse in order to make things happen. (*GV*, 336)

In view of these rather final words on the subject, a return to the first words can serve to clarify the progression. The convergence of literary and historical questions in *Writing Degree Zero* is marked from the opening prefatory remarks. Barthes begins by invoking the revolutionary figure Jacques Hébert (1757–94), who sprinkled the issues of his *Père Duchêne* with assorted obscenities and invective. For Barthes, these terms do not just signify, but are instead closer to signs, reminders to the reader that they are part of a revolutionary writing or discourse. Used in this way, they furnish evidence that in addition to the functions of expression and communication, writing also points to the values which animate it. In this sense, writing always sets itself in relation to something beyond language—"un au-delà du langage"— which is both history and an attitude toward it.

What Barthes sees in *Le Père Duchêne* he seeks out in LA *Littérature*, recast as an activity built on similar gestures of self-reference defining both an internal limit and external difference. Because limit and difference vary with specific circumstances, they can, in turn, point to a history of Letters as the various attempts to keep it unified, timeless, and thus removed from history. As Barthes concludes, the attempts to refuse history in the name of an eternal Literature only reassert the force of history as an ongoing referent. Ultimately, the repression of history provides the basis for an inquiry to be traced as the shadow or double of more standard literary histories: "It is therefore possible to trace a history of literary expression which is neither that of a particular language, nor that of the various styles, but simply that of the signs of Literature, and we can expect that this purely formal history may manifest, in its far from obscure way, a link with the deeper levels of History" (*WDZ*, 2).

Barthes's attempts to specify the place of writing revise more standard approaches to literary classicism and modernity. Working against the bias of a fixed conception of Literature or Letters, he asserts difference in the plurality of writings such as those he notes in the works of Balzac and Flaubert. At the level of thought, Barthes sees no more than a variation of school or conception. In the writings, however, he finds an essential break or articulation he sets in relation to economic and social changes during the same period. Less sanguine than Sartre about the exact place of the writer in postwar France, Barthes offers no solution to the alienation whose extreme form he terms "the zero degree."

Barthes's divergence from the Sartrian position is cast as a doubt about the prescriptive nature of a program involving direct action. Against the vision of commitment set forth in *What Is Literature?*, Barthes's ambivalence also responds to the essence of any philosophical system as a construct or fiction. Although not formulated in these exact terms, Barthes's argument in *Writing Degree Zero* upholds a perspectival position such as that Barthes acknowledges more recently as derived from Nietzsche and Foucault. To invoke historical perspectivism in this sense is not, however, to suggest the eventual undoing of all systems. Barthes is no nihilist on this point. Instead, the perspectival position sets any single phenomenon within a temporal play and an assertion of difference such as that studied by Hans-Georg Gadamer in the tradition of hermeneutics. Simply put, the program of literary commitment set forth in *What Is Literature?* tends toward an absolute vision which the passage of time has inevitably revised to the point of refutation. One has only to reread the conclusion of *The Words* in order to see Sartre's awareness of this idealism and its impact on his own projects between 1947 and 1963.

The progressive alienation of the writer from society characterized in *Writing Degree Zero* as a solidification is an image consistent with Sartre's poetic attitude. In both cases, language becomes a barrier between its user and the ("real") world. But where Sartre adopts a self-assured attitude toward what the writer ought to do, Barthes remains at the stage of analyzing the conditions leading up to "the zero degree" in the moments of a literary modernity occurring between the mid-nineteenth century and 1947. What he notes as solidification is also the transformation of writing from an open or free function chosen by the writer to an awareness of alienation which all but reduces that function to a fixed form. The "zero degree" or "white writing" Barthes finds in *L'Etranger* and in narratives by Kafka, Blanchot, Queneau, and Cayrol points to that alienation as a silence. The concept of a "zero degree" appears in the writings of the Danish linguist Viggo Brøndal. It refers to a neutral mark or voice irreducible to positive and negative terms.[10] As used by Barthes in *Writing Degree Zero*, it is the product of a historical condition and thus a negative value in a society which sets a premium on utility.

As the writer is set increasingly at the margins of societies geared toward production and profit, the proliferation of writings amounts to what Barthes sees as a flooding of the literary market. When writing disappears as a function and becomes another form alongside language and style, the writer is left with only an awareness of alienation from which Barthes offers no release. No longer under the illusion of a unifying conception of Literature, the writer plays out the consequences of an alienation Barthes explores in subsequent approaches to modernity. *Writing Degree Zero* casts those consequences as tragic because awareness alone cannot overcome or erase the conditions of alienation. Between Sartre's call to mobilize the writer to social activism and the complete paralysis of a radical nihilism, Barthes's attitude toward the place of the writer in history remains tentative, elliptical, and problematic. Barthes formulates questions and outlines future investigations which, in retrospect, suffer from a lack of theoretical or conceptual support. When, for example, he describes the "zero degree" in terms of silence, one can note a prototype of the archeology of silence studied by Foucault in *Madness and Civilization* as the phenomenon of madness imposed by a so-called discourse of reason. Likewise, the self-referring quality of the literary sign only promotes a future study of the phenomenon of connotation.

In sum, what Barthes sets forth in *Writing Degree Zero* as an introduction to the history of writing(s) calls for a more rigorous theoretical formulation than he provides at the time. In part, his reluctance to do more than sketch a future investigation can be explained by his aversion to the prescriptive aspects of the argument in *What Is Literature?* At the same time, the alienated condition referred to as the "zero degree" comes from a level of understanding in which traditional conceptions no longer suffice to contend with the literary and historical modernity encountered through Sartre's writings. Responding to Stephen Heath in a 1971 interview, Barthes clarifies the project undertaken in *Writing Degree Zero* from the perspective of its later reformulations through the "heroic" period of Parisian structuralism:

The problem is that at the time of *Writing Degree Zero* I was thinking in terms of a more traditional history. I was thinking vaguely of a history of writing which ultimately might follow the model of a history of literature, by simply displacing its object. Since that time, obviously, things have changed. The difficulty is that now it seems that historical discourse meets another need, and this is probably one of the more censored problems of contemporary thought, even of avant-garde thought which tries to confront history without rethinking historical discourse in a serious way. Is there a historical discourse today—I do not mean a concept of history, but a historical discourse—which does not account for itself as such? What might it be? What kinds of resistance might it encounter? These are the questions which must be asked. (*GV*, 133)

Writing Degree Zero remains a disturbing text because the convergence of literature, history, and writing it points to is not fully drawn out and explained. Hence its "problematic" status and its tendency to resurface throughout Barthes's writings. From the start, Barthes embarks on his critical project aware of its ties to the discourses of literature and history. In the pages which follow, I want to trace the development of that inquiry in two series of writings on history and modernity spanning the period between 1954 and 1970. Where *Writing Degree Zero* sketches a history of writing, Barthes's first variation on that theme is animated by a figure of reversibility. His *Michelet par lui-même*, published in 1954, is a text fully concerned with the writing of history.

The readers who progress directly from *Writing Degree Zero* to the *Mythologies* neglect a text Barthes considers one of his favorites. Why Jules Michelet (1798–1874)? Why write a monograph on a nineteenth-century historian so clearly removed from the "zero degree" of modern writing? In 1972, Barthes stated that what had attracted him to write on Michelet some twenty years earlier was the thematic insistence of the *oeuvre*: "Each figure returns without end with the same epithets, from a reading that is both corporeal and moral."[11] In retrospect, the reference to these figures situates the *Michelet* as a forerunner of the orientation toward autobiography and utterance evident in the 1975 *Roland Barthes*. Both texts were, in fact, written for the same "Ecrivains de Toujours" series whose titles used to appear as "X par lui-même." (Barthes was the first in the series to write "on" himself, a subtlety he uses to full stylistic and rhetorical advantage.) The *Michelet*

also appears in the wake of *Writing Degree Zero* and just as Barthes began the series of texts later to become the *Mythologies*. In this sense, the *Michelet* extends the project announced in the first book. It studies the convergence of literary and historical inquiries by an approach to history as discourse and writing.

Against those who might equate this approach with attempts to perceive history as a (mere) text or effect of writing, Barthes's focus in the *Michelet* is on a writing on history whose peculiarities compose an attitude or relation to history in their own right. What draws Barthes to write on Michelet is a specific use of language: a "certain problem of discursivity" such as that identified in *Writing Degree Zero* as the alienated condition of the modern writer. At the time of the Michelet study, Barthes is still formulating his own attitude toward literary and historical inquiries coming out of his readings of Gide, Sartre, and Marx. In fact, the pivotal date of 1848, often dismissed as a banality of Marxist rhetoric, appears in *Writing Degree Zero* as imposing on the writer the role of "unhappy consciousness," a concept lifted straight out of Hegel's *Phenomenology of Mind* and the vision of dialectics Marx later claims to have stood on its head. Likewise, the passage from *The German Ideology* quoted at the beginning of this section appears on page 80 of the *Michelet*. It supports the dual concerns of Barthes's attempts to account for writing as a point of contact between the individual and his or her place in history. The initial question set forth by Marx in the passage splits immediately into two. For in order to specify what the individual is in terms of corporeal organization, it is necessary to insert that corporeal organization within a wider context. Marx uses the term "nature" to designate that context, but it is easy enough to see how "nature" points to history and change.

Ultimately, the project undertaken by Marx restates questions of identity and knowledge within a wider logic of meaning and history. In order to know who or what an individual is, it is necessary to state the very presuppositions—to say what always goes without saying—which allow the individual to become intelligible within the historical process. In the early 1950s, Barthes's concern for the individual is a holdover from his readings of Gide and Sartre. But the focus on the place of the individual within a logic of historical writing also serves as a minimal unit of meaning or function such as that set forth later as a prime object of structural analysis. As with *Writing Degree Zero*, the Michelet study does not provide the theoretical framework necessary to resolve the problems it proposes to deal with, deferring the force of a theoretical formulation until a more consistent position is achieved in the *Mythologies*.

Unlike the first book, however, the *Michelet* supplies a first glimpse at the methods of inquiry which resurface some twenty years later in the wake of Barthes's disillusionment with structural analysis. A prime interest of the *Michelet* is that of any essay in method written during a period of transition. Within the total corpus of Barthes's writings, the *Michelet* is the single most ambitious project, coming close to the totalizing approach undertaken by Sartre in his three-volume study of Flaubert. The *Michelet* combines a number of critical perspectives with comments on the presuppositions of critical and biographic inquiry. Barthes writes on Michelet in order to clarify the singularity of the individual much along the lines projected in the quote from *The German Ideology*: that of the corporeal organization found in the writings, and that of the received figure of the nineteenth-century historian of the Revolution and author of *La Sorcière*. In addition, Barthes breaks up the continuity of his study by alternating between extended passages quoted from Michelet's writings and short commentaries of his own focusing on questions of method. As he writes in his preface, the *Michelet* should be read as an essay in pre-criticism:

The reader will find in this little book neither a history of Michelet's thought nor a history of his life, and much less an explanation of one by the other. I am convinced that the writings of Michelet, like all objects of criticism, are the products of a history. But there is an order of tasks: it is first necessary to give this man his coherence. That has been my intention: to relocate the structure of an existence (not that of a life), a thematics, so to speak, or better yet: an organized network of obsessions. Afterward may follow the real criticisms, historical or psychoanalytic (Freudian, Bachelardian, or existential). What follows is only a pre-criticism; I have tried only to describe a unity, not to explore its roots in history or biography. (*MI*, 5)

There can be little doubt that Barthes is drawn to write on Michelet as a case in point of a singular existence and a writing irreducible to standard critical approaches. Early in the book, Barthes writes that Michelet was so smitten with his work that he felt forever on the point of a delicious and sensual death: "He dies from History as one dies— or rather as one does not die—from love" (*MI*, 19). In this reading of *Michelet*, the historian's passion for accumulating facts becomes an obsession for relating them to each other in what Barthes comes to see as a practice of writing on a par with that of the novelist. The decision to write *on* Michelet projects the task of the historian/writer to a second degree. Barthes sets out to trace the very relations between the practice of writing and the identity of the writer posited by that practice as a historical and biographic fact. At stake in this project are a number of critical questions concerning the status of biographic criticism and the "psychological value of description"[12] confronted more openly some twenty years later in the *Roland Barthes*.

In 1954, however, the prevailing question of method points to the hegemony of a critical approach derived from the latter half of the nineteenth century. In the writings of Sainte-Beuve and Gustave Lanson, literary studies became a monumental activity grounding interpretation in the life of the writer. Voluminous dissertations on "the man and the life" supplied fact after fact for a universal archive like those described by Jorge Luis Borges.

The trouble with Jules Michelet is that his writings upset the standard categories. They promote a general uneasiness about his status as a historian suffering from a literary excess he is all too willing to indulge: "Hasn't it been written everywhere that I was a historian plagued by a happy imagination?" (*MI*, 89). Pushing this quality to its logical extreme, Barthes writes that what is judged unfitting for a historian is, in fact, an attitude toward language which flouts the conventional belief in the representative function of historiography. And not merely in terms of stylistic license; but in a deliberate attempt to show how historical thinking tends to assert as timeless—and thus "outside" or removed from history—what Barthes studies as the "Imaginary Museum" of Michelet.

By approaching the historian's activity from the perspectives of writing and discourse, Barthes sees Michelet as an operator of texts who opposes the will to truth of historical knowledge with an awareness of the force of language. As he does more pointedly when dealing with mass culture in the *Mythologies*, Barthes locates in Michelet's writings a second level of signification always at work in the more accessible processes of denotation and factual evidence. And what Barthes finds at the second or connotative level is a practice of writing which undermines the status of the facts on which historical knowledge is constructed: "Furthermore, and this is perhaps even more upsetting, it is not only the association of facts which vacillates in

Michelet's writings, but the facts themselves. *What is a fact*? That is a philosophical banality of historical epistemology, a problem which Michelet, for one, accepts."[13]

From questioning the status of the fact in the discourse of historical writings, it is only one more logical step to questioning the significant unit at work in Barthes's own project of writing. The problem of method acknowledged by Barthes in dealing with Michelet complements his portrait of the alienated writer at the end of *Writing Degree Zero*. After suggesting that his reading of Michelet ought to be seen as clarifying an organized network of obsessions, Barthes characterizes his portrait of the writer/historian as constituting a fiction or artifice. These recurrent figures suggest a natural order which is more properly an order of language and writing. Once he specifies the artifice of the "natural" vision in Michelet's writings, Barthes's own project doubles that vision by seeking to place it within its appropriate historical context: "The historical mass is not for Michelet a puzzle to be put back together; it is a body to grasp. The historian exists only to know again a singular warmth" (*MI*, 73).

The consistent repertory of themes and figures uncovered by Barthes also reveals an attraction to formalized analysis and interpretation such as that called into question in *S/Z*; that is, after the 1966–70 break with structural analysis: "It is therefore not excessive to speak of a true hermeneutic of the Michelet text. Michelet cannot be read in a linear manner, one must give back to his text its founding network of themes. Michelet's discourse is a true cryptogram that needs a grid, for it is the very structure of the work. It follows that no reading of Michelet is possible unless it is total; it is necessary to place oneself resolutely within this limitation" (*MI*, 180).

The figure of Jules Michelet located by Barthes in his 1954 study clarifies the inner division in his own orientation between critical method and personal predilection. He is obviously drawn to the marginality of a cultural persona whose notoriety as a historian seduced by "literary" tendencies serves to make him a tutor figure. The fragmentary nature of the book and the abundant use of photographs support this attraction to the figures of the individual. At the same time, however, the choice of a historical writing as object of an extended study reverts to the project described in *Writing Degree Zero* to trace the self-reflexive signs of writing. To be sure, the *Michelet* provides no full articulation of the project, as Barthes's flirtation with the phenomenological approaches of Gaston Bachelard, Georges Poulet, and Jean-Pierre Richard supports the primacy of a literary orientation.

As a result, the question of how best to relate literary and historical inquiries extends into the *Mythologies* as a reading of popular culture. Barthes's continued concern with historical writing during the 1947–57 period is best summarized in a 1967 statement which allows for a theoretical reassessment of what he had originally undertaken in more pragmatic terms: "Historical discourse is presumably the only kind which aims at a referent 'outside' itself that can in fact never be reached. We must therefore ask ourselves again: What is the place of 'reality' in the structure of discourse?"[14]

However, is myth always
depoliticized speech?
In other words, is reality
always political?

Barthes, "Myth Today"

The *Mythologies* provide a first balance between what *Writing Degree Zero* and the Michelet study imply as a critical position toward literature and history in the decade following World War II and what "Historical Discourse" reformulates theoretically in 1967. Taken out of a strict context—that is, out of their place within Barthes's corpus of writings—the *Mythologies* are a disarming *tour de force* of topical studies. In book form, they include short texts on films, advertising, women's magazines, food, striptease, Billy Graham, the Tour de France, automobiles, and plastic. The charm of the individual pieces is deceptive, especially so once one discerns the method at work in Barthes's approach to popular culture. Beyond the cleverness of describing an advertising campaign in terms of military strategy, the imposed metaphor reveals the logic at work in producing false images of human "nature" marketed by commercial interests. The critical project of the *Mythologies* ties a reflection on the essence of mythic activities to analyses of how these "operations" of meaning and writing purvey false values in a society adapted to portray itself in collective images. Because Barthes wants, in part, to expose the economic

nature of a society held together via class hierarchies and an exploitation of labor, he tends increasingly to view the products of mythic
activity as an illusion which always supplies more—which is also, in
this instance, to say less—than is apparent.

Today, the social values explored twenty-five years ago in the
Mythologies resonate with the minor truths of daily existence blasted by
media messages and assorted types of hard or software. The historical
project of defining the essence of mythic activity in the lower middle-
class of postwar France begs comparison with similar approaches to
the social determinants in other historical and cultural conditions. In
addition, the *Mythologies* mark Barthes's first attempt to couple a
revised practice of Sartrian demystification with an analytic method
adapted from structural linguistics. Although it is admittedly deriva-
tive of Saussure and Hjelmslev, this first excursus into semiology
recasts the project set forth in *Writing Degree Zero* in the terms of
linguistic science, which remain essential to Barthes's thinking and
writing hereafter.

The impact of this first linguistic model on the *Mythologies* is such
that a cautionary note is in order. As they appear in the current French
and American editions, the individual mythologies are enclosed at
both ends, giving the total book a neatness and homogeneity which
are deceptive. As with the first two books, the *Mythologies* are written
in and about passage. Consequently, their consistency at the theoretical level is belied by a number of factors only partly masked by the book
form. In this sense, the long 1956 epilogue "Myth Today" reads at
times like a theoretical justification after the fact, as though the will to
theory was a necessary supplement to the demonstrations provided by
the analyses. In view of Barthes's earlier misgivings about the systema-
ticity of Sartre's program in *What Is Literature?*, it is curious that he
should be drawn toward a similar system at the level of method and
theory. Likewise, his preface to the 1970 French edition appears glib in
what it suggests about the nature of the inquiry undertaken some
fifteen years earlier. As Barthes states in the same preface, differences
in personal and historical circumstances would prevent him from
writing new mythologies or rewriting the old ones.[15] But when he
asserts in 1970 that no semiology is possible without the self-reflexive
dimension of a semioclasm to break up the signs to be studied, what
intervenes is the unacknowledged factor of historical difference crys-
tallized in the events and aftermath of *printemps '68*. Even though these

internal breaks are glossed over in the current image of the *Mythologies* as Barthes's first *book* of semiology, they are necessary to any understanding of his place in the structuralist adventure.

The inaccurate approach to the *Mythologies* described above tends also to falsify their critical orientation into what is mistaken for a political semiology. The cause of this false approach derives, in large part, from the changes in Barthes's critical practice between 1954 and 1970. After the period of his involvement with and defense of structural analysis, Barthes could not in good conscience but follow through the implications of his dissociation. After 1968—that is, after the "Eléments de sémiologie," *Critique et vérité*, and *Système de la mode*—Barthes can more readily identify the presuppositions at work in his earlier conceptions of semiology. By that point in his own evolution—in 1970 he publishes *S/Z* and *L'Empire des signes*—he also appears to have arrived at a critical stance capable of resolving the problems inherent in his practice since *Writing Degree Zero*. Because vision and method did not yet complement the evident political orientation of the *Mythologies*, the reference to a political semiology is misleading. It assumes a denial of the initial formulation which is a prerequisite to understanding his subsequent practice in the period beginning with *S/Z*.

In their evocation of the social values at work in popular myths of the French petite bourgeoisie, the *Mythologies* do not simply denounce or expose collective images as false or misleading. Instead of concentrating on the objective forms of such images, Barthes analyzes how they are produced, circulated, and exchanged—in other words, how myths manipulate the processes of meaning in order to create what purport to reflect collective conceptions of reality and "human nature." The impetus for such a project is undoubtedly political, with a focus on what others would term ideology and the processes of representation. Like Marx and Sartre, Barthes is out to expose the inversion essential to mythic invention. Like these two, he wants to expose these kinds of mythic activity as the objective forms of alienation promoting class division. Critical method is the link Barthes later identifies between literature and history. This moment of insight occurs after the 1966–70 break with structural analysis; it is apparent in *S/Z* and "Change the Object Itself." In order to see that later insight in its full difference from earlier practices, I shall discuss a number of *Mythologies* dealing with literary criticism before turning to the theoretical statements in "Myth Today."

"Blind and Dumb Criticism" is a first example of how Barthes animates the short text or cultural "item" into an analysis of popular myth as a production of meaning. In *Writing Degree Zero*, that production would have been seen as a kind of writing. By the mid-1950s, that writing would more likely be cast in Saussurean terms as a language. Barthes begins in good journalistic practice with a short explanation of his title. The explanation also ripostes the tendentious avowals of confusion and incomprehension voiced by literary critics. Whenever a critic begins with such a claim, Barthes notes the gesture of a rhetorical strategy whose goal is to undermine and reject the text it only appears to confront. The means of accomplishing this inversion is a complicity between the critic and his or her reader against the author of the text in question. To this end, the initial statement soon passes for a more dramatic display which, in turn, suggests a more complex use of language and production of meaning. In this case, the lack of understanding denoted in the initial statement asserts an excess of meaning Barthes identifies as a separate system of signs. It is, in fact, this second system which, via connotation, serves as the site of mythic writing.

In order to be convincing—in order to make the critical "operation" a success—the initial display of incomprehension must also hide or displace the connotative system. For if it fails to do so, the initial statement is revealed as dependent on an assumed superiority and a strategy Barthes deemed worthy of the Verdurin salon in Proust's *Remembrance of Things Past*. Because what purports to be an initial statement is, in fact, dependent on a system of connotation it displaces, Barthes must demonstrate the essence of mythic utterance as a simultaneous assertion of the denotative system and denial of the connotative system. In "Myth Today" Barthes takes apart the process of utterance via linguistic models which clarify its dynamics. In "Blind and Dumb Criticism," his analysis is limited to an example of that dynamics as an appropriation or theft of language.

Within the "opening" statement of incomprehension, Barthes locates a deeply rooted mistrust of novelty and difference. The critical "operation" aims at excluding whatever fails to support the values of sound argumentation it projects as the prime virtue of thought. Was it not Descartes who claimed in the *Discourse on Method* that reason is, of all things in the world, the most universally shared among men? Yes, and that is why Barthes sees the avowal of incomprehension as a ploy against those whose "new ideas" threaten whatever calls itself *le bon sens*.

Rather than take on what is new or different at the level of concept or polemics, it proves more self-serving to skirt open dismissal by covering a will to incomprehension by setting up a complicitous front between critic and reader against the author of the text in question. By turning critical activity into a judgment of the figure of author, the ploy of incomprehension effectively neglects the text for an attack *ad hominem*. As a result of this displacement, blindness and silence appear justified, the only possible responses . . . within reason. The text under review is a piece on Kierkegaard by Henri Lefebvre. Noting that the invocation of *le bons sens* amounts to nothing more than an appeal to mediocrity, Barthes describes its logic of exclusion as an operation fully geared to the anti-intellectual element of the petite bourgeoisie. Since the critic does not question the possible causes of his or her incomprehension, the initial statement asserts a tacit superiority over a critical object seemingly unworthy of suitable analysis: "To be a critic by profession and to proclaim that one understands nothing about existentialism or Marxism (as it happens, it is these two philosophies particularly that one confesses to be unable to understand) is to elevate one's blindness or dumbness to a universal rule of perception, and to reject from the world Marxism and existentialism: 'I don't understand, therefore you are idiots'" (*M*, 35).

A variant of this intellectual "operation" against the new or the different mobilizes a logic of tautology in the cause of a know-nothing chauvinism. Where a false image of common sense in "Blind and Dumb Criticism" barely conceals its xenophobia—Kierkegaard the Dane versus Descartes the pride of French rationality—a mythology entitled "Racine Is Racine" brings home the full force of a cultural heritage animated by an inverted patriotism straight out of Drumont, Maurras, and *L'Action Française*. And not for nothing does Barthes invoke Racine, a second cultural figure from the seventeenth-century period and the center of Barthes's subsequent notoriety in the mid-1960s debate with Raymond Picard.

As in "Blind and Dumb Criticism," Barthes focuses on a strategic gesture cast as an ostensible display of common sense thinking. This time, however, an epigraph from Flaubert's *Bouvard et Pécuchet*—"Good taste is good taste"—reveals the emptiness in the apparent logic of identity. Tautology of this sort is, as Barthes concludes, another instance of the hostility toward thinking at the core of the petit bourgeois vision of France: "We know that the war against intelligence is always waged in the name of *good sense*, and here we are essentially applying to Racine that kind of Poujadist 'understanding' I have already spoken about" (*M*, 97).[16]

A third piece takes up the analyses of writing which make up the first half of *Writing Degree Zero*. Barthes begins "Neither-Nor Criticism" by noting how the stylistic practice of double exclusion displays the signs of common sense thought, once again invoking the ghost of Descartes to serve a more dubious deformation of meaning: "One reckons all the methods with scales, one piles them up on each side as one thinks best, so as to appear oneself as an imponderable arbiter endowed with a spirituality which is ideal and thereby *just*, like the beam which is the judge in the weighing" (*M*, 81).

Since each of the three analyses cited exposes a dual system of meaning, its revelation calls, in turn, for a more rigorous distinction between the dynamics of connotation and the ideology it serves. To this end, Barthes's discovery of Saussure's *Course in General Linguistics* supplies a new model of analysis and a way out of the bind of method evident in *Writing Degree Zero* and the *Michelet*. Via Saussure and Hjelmslev, Barthes formulates a new set of terms visibly removed—in method—from the practice of demystification. And so where Sartre was, shall Saussure be. It is 1956, structuralism exists in France primarily in the writings of Lévi-Strauss, and most of the future demonstrators of May-June '68 are at the low end of the primary school system. It is, in a well-traveled but evocative expression, the *printemps des philosophes* and Barthes makes his entrance with "Myth Today."

Since the linguistic model inspired by Saussure's *Course* has passed—for better or worse—toward the realm of received knowledge, I want to review a small number of points to specify the nature of Barthes's initial excursus into semiology. Between the appearance of the *Mythologies* and the present, the status of Saussure's investigations has been revised in the wake of the discovery of an extended study of anagrams in classical Latin poetry. The period of that investigation in Saussure's career and its basis in the uniqueness of poetic language oppose the more standard identity of the Swiss linguist as founding father of structural analysis. The discovery also suggests that the doubts cast after the mid-1960s concerning a future science of literature revert to the internal paradoxes of Saussure's practice. A second revision of Saussure's place in the history of structural analysis was prompted by the appearance of a new edition of the *Course*, whose original version was published under the direction of his former students Bally and Sechehaye in 1916, three years after his death. By studying course notes taken by students during the three years Saussure gave the course, the editors of the new edition have found a number of discrepancies between Saussure's lectures and the posthumous book published under his name.[17]

Among the discrepancies is that of the relation between language and speech (*langue* and *parole*, respectively, in French). For most readers of the *Course*, the primary focus of inquiry is on language, the abstract system and social concept which contains the totality of speech acts or utterances intelligible within a fixed time and place. The question of primal focus in the *Course* was debated even before the appearance of the new edition. On the side of *langue*, it led to the glossomatics developed by Louis Hjelmslev and the Copenhagen school. On the side of *parole*, there was the thesis set forth by Mikhail Bakhtin that the theoretical fiction of *langue* was dependent on the more immediate phenomena of individual utterances. There is no evidence to suggest that Barthes came to the *Course* aware of the possible discrepancies mentioned above. (He has stated that A. J. Greimas was among the first to acquaint him with Saussure's writings and that this occurred while both were at the University of Alexandria in the early 1950s.) It is all the more surprising, then, that one of Barthes's opening statements in "Myth Today" is fully consistent with the revised reading and focus on utterance adopted in the wake of the new edition. After defining myth as a message, utterance, and finally, a system of communication, Barthes writes that it can be defined less by its object than by its manner of transmitting a message: "We are no longer dealing here with a theoretical mode of representation: we are dealing with *this* particular image, which is given for *this* particular signification" (*M*, 110).

In opposition to the adaptation of the *langue*/*parole* dichotomy from Saussure's *Course*, the focus on individual utterance is consistent with the model of communication set forth against Saussure by Bakhtin and Vološinov in *Marxism and the Philosophy of Language*.[18] Without, once again, suggesting that Barthes writes "Myth Today" aware of a 1929 text that remained out of print for the better part of forty years, the common focus on utterance over language inscribes even this first excursus into semiology within the historical orientation present as early as *Writing Degree Zero*. Even when set against the abstract semantic system adopted from Hjelmslev to schematize the dual process of mythic utterance, Barthes's initial deviance from the Saussurian canon set forth in the *Course* helps to explain how utterance resurfaces after the break with structural analysis as a prime theme in *Roland Barthes* and *A Lover's Discourse*.

A second noteworthy feature of Barthes's initial semiology is the system of double signification derived from Louis Hjelmslev to characterize myth as a metalanguage. This system amounts, in effect, to a game of hide-and-seek in which a connotative meaning is displaced by a more accessible denotative sense. The primacy of the denotative system is an illusion, an effect of the inversion Barthes finds at work in mythic activity. Set into schematic form, the double system holds together only as long as the ("deeper") system of connotation does not reveal itself as the metalanguage dominating the language object of denotative sense. The dual system of mythic activity is represented by Barthes in the following schema:

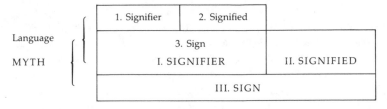

An example can clarify the nature of this double system as well as the pertinence of the schema. Barthes writes about a cover of *Paris-Match* showing a young Negro in military uniform saluting the French *tri-colore*. This immediate image forms the denotative system, but it does not account for something more Barthes sees taking place. Through the immediate message he perceives a second system of connoted messages emitting values of patriotism, French-ness (*francité*), and militarism. Although it seems to depend on denotation, the connotative message is neither parasitical nor destructive. Instead, it formalizes denotation ("reifies it"), makes it a means to the connotative system and the essence of mythic activity. This is why Barthes comes to see myth as a continuous deformation of denotation (*sens*), what he also terms a theft of language:

But the essential point in all this is that the form does not suppress the meaning, it only impoverishes it, puts it at a distance, it holds it at one's disposal. One believes that the meaning is going to die, but it is a death with reprieve; the meaning loses its value, but keeps its life, from which the form of the myth will draw its nourishment. The meaning will be for the form like an instantaneous reserve of history, a tamed richness, which it is possible to call and dismiss in a sort of rapid alternation: the form must constantly be able to be rooted again in the meaning and to get there what nature it needs for its nutriment; above all, it must be able to hide there. It is this constant game of hide-and-seek between the meaning and the form which defines myth. The form of myth is not a symbol: the Negro who salutes is not the symbol of the French Empire: he has too much presence, he appears as a rich, fully experienced, spontaneous, innocent, *indisputable* image. But at the same time this present is tamed, put at a distance, made almost transparent: it recedes a little, it becomes the accomplice of a concept which comes to it fully armed, French imperiality: once made use of, it becomes artificial. (*M*, 118)

Myth is the product of an alternation between the two systems of meaning, a complex message which tends to formalize denotation to the point of subverting ("alienating") its normal function. Seemingly more immediate than the system of connotation, denotative sense plays the role of decoy to inflect a process of signification and appropriate it in the cause of commercial interests. This deformation of sense also constitutes the inversion Barthes traces throughout the *Mythologies* as the replacement of historical and economic realities with false images of "nature" necessary to maintain capitalist institutions at peak efficiency. The result, as Barthes sees it, is a repertoire of stock images which simulate the purportedly universal values of what amounts to a faceless and anonymous society. (*Société anonyme* is the French expression whose abbreviated form, *S.A.*, is commonly used to designate a commercial corporation!)

When Barthes unpacks the double system of mythic writing, the object of his analysis is the attempt to enclose and reduce the reality of historical struggles within a simplified narrative form. Myth does not deny history as much as banalize it. By promoting values and images which seemingly transcend the minor conflicts of daily life, mythic activity circulates as the antithesis of a politicized language! That antithesis is itself political, especially so when a strategy of inversion uses systems of denotation to fabricate the illusion of a depoliticized utterance: "It is now possible to complete the semiological definition of myth in a bourgeois society: *myth is depoliticized speech*. One must naturally understand *political* in its deeper meaning, as describing the whole of human relations in their real, social structure, in their power of making the world; one must above all give an active role to the prefix *de-*: here it represents an operational movement, it permanently embodies a defaulting" (*M*, 143).

The illusory sense of world fabricated by mythic activity projects a simulacrum of "natural" values Barthes terms a *pseudo-physis*. Because he approaches this phony "nature" as the product of inverted meanings, Barthes looks to semiology for an analytic model to describe its dynamics. In so doing, he moves beyond the simple denunciation of myth toward a more systematic access to the banality of myth promoted in various modern societies. At the same time, however, this first elaboration of semiology points to a conceptual weakness Barthes does not identify and try to correct until some fifteen years later in the *Système de la mode* and *S/Z*. The weakness in question is closer to a reservation or gesture of explanation so disarming that it is necessary to insist on its incompletion as something less than innocent. After discussing the differences between myth in terms of "left" and "right" political visions, Barthes turns the universality of mythic activity toward the values he sees at work in his own analyses: "I must, in conclusion, say a few words about the mythologist himself" (*M*, 156). The final words are those of self-reflexivity: the critic acknowledges his or her involvement beyond or within the preceding analysis. It is, so to speak, a gesture of presence and indication modeled on the Cartesian *Larvatus prodeo*. Admirable, perhaps, but insufficient. For Barthes goes on to limit the extent of that presence to a neat question of method, leaving room for an implied separation — between method and matter or object — it will take the next decade for him to accept as illusory. As with his own reservations about Sartre's vision in *What Is Literature?*, Barthes sees the necessary task but fails to attain it. In this case, it appears that his awareness of the writer/mythologist's alienation is undercut by an inability to follow through militantly the action implied by his own vision. At this point in his own theoretical statement, one wonders whether the alienation is not to some degree channeled through self-exclusion. When Barthes describes the mythologist's link to the world as sarcastic and his sociality as theoretical, he knows that something more is needed. That knowledge does not, however, make it any easier for him to act: "One must go even further: in a sense, the mythologist is excluded from this history in the name of which he professes to act. The havoc which he wreaks in the language of the community is absolute for him, it fills his assignment to the brim: he must live this assignment without any hope of going back or any assumption of payment" (M, 157).

Having tried to demonstrate the systematic production of inverted values at the expense of the petite bourgeoisie and working class, Barthes has also asserted his own alienation as an intellectual removed from the processes of myth he reveals. The effect of that recognition leads to an unstable grasp of his own function Barthes locates—mistakenly—in method rather than in the more personal and less militant scope of value and affect. As he comes to state his alienation, its very measure is duplicitous and self-serving because it allows the mythologist to defer a more decisive commitment to social change in full awareness of what that deferral might risk:

The fact that we cannot manage to achieve more than an unstable grasp of reality doubtless gives the measure of our present alienation: we constantly drift between the object and its demystification, powerless to render its wholeness. For if we penetrate the object, we liberate it but we destroy it; and if we acknowledge its full weight, we respect it, but we restore it to a state which is still mystified. It would seem that we are condemned for some time yet always to speak *excessively* about reality. This is probably because ideologism and its opposite are types of behavior which are still magical, terrorized, blinded and fascinated by the split in the social world. And yet, this is what we must seek: a reconciliation between reality and men, between description and explanation, between object and knowledge. (M, 159)

The period between the *Mythologies* and *S/Z* tends to be seen by many as heroic or revolutionary, a decade of innovation when Barthes supports and defends modernist theory in the name of structural analysis and *la nouvelle critique*. Yet within the scope of the initial project outlined in the 1947–57 period, this heroic period is closer to a displacement whose intensity finally yields to a break with the avant-garde after the 1966 "Introduction to the Structural Analysis of Narratives." For those who see the mid-1960s period as the height of Barthes's contribution as theoretician and practical critic, the interruption marked by his disenchantment needs to be seen as a necessary radical break growing out of a conflict between the project of a literary science and a more personal recognition Barthes works out in stages between *S/Z* and *Camera Lucida*.

It is of prime importance to examine how Barthes comes to this eventual break between 1966 and 1970. We need to think hard about the economy of discourses circulating in Barthes's writings which allow for that break to occur when it does. Once that is made clear, we need to insert that insight into our own approaches to Barthes's itinerary, to understand exactly what allows us to invoke him in a particular context or make him an exemplary case study of how difference and repetition are embodied in the figure of the writer. Because Barthes turns critical writing into a self-reflexive activity, his pursuit of change serves as the constant factor around which a number of interpretations can be organized. Where Stephen Heath opts for vertiginous displacement, Jonathan Culler locates a preeminent critical project.

Before I can attempt such a synthesis or overview based on what is now a complete chronology, at least one more account—set forth by Barthes himself in a 1971 interview with Heath—should be considered to set biography and chronology against what Barthes sees as a banalized history of semiology:

Semiology as I live it now is no longer the one I saw, imagined, and practiced at the start. The break, in regard to literary semiology, is quite acute and can be located exactly between the "Introduction to the Structural Analysis of Narratives" and *S/Z*: these two texts correspond to two semiologies. The causes of this mutation (since it is a matter of mutation rather than evolution) could be tracked down first in the recent history of France—why not?—and then in the intertext: in the text surrounding and accompanying me, those that precede or follow me, and with which I continue to communicate. (*GV*, 123)

Between the *Mythologies* and *S/Z*, the mutation of Barthes's semiology from practical analysis to self-reflexive writing complicates simple chronology because the practice of writing breaks up in much the same way LA *Littérature* yields to DES *écritures* in *Writing Degree Zero*. Not only does the revised 1971 semiology analyze signs, it actively pursues and produces them by a focus on the production of the text. As a result, the political dimension of this revised practice replaces the question of the referent with that of how meaning is produced. An afterthought to the *Mythologies* from the 1971 period asserts a similar change along the lines of historical and personal difference. In

"Change the Object Itself: Mythology Today," Barthes admits that the question of method at the end of "Myth Today" had been false or incomplete as long as it failed to encompass its object of inquiry. In the wake of positions taken in texts such as the 1964 "Structuralist Activity," Barthes writes in 1971 that a change in method carries with it a change in the object itself. If and when such a change is achieved in this more complex sense—and Barthes is only somewhat closer to it in 1971 than in 1957—a liberatory practice of reading can become viable. Because it amounts to a long theoretical pause from which the possibility of this future practice follows, the interim between 1957 and 1971 supplies the impetus for Barthes's evolution toward and beyond a straightforward structuralist activity. Even after the search for a method is revised to coordinate method and object, the pursuit of a more stable practice continues in a polemical defense of the new and the modern that Barthes has since termed his "heroic" period.

Scientific advances often come from
uncovering some previously unseen
aspect of things, not so much as a
result of using some new instrument,
but rather of looking at objects
from a new angle. This look is
necessarily guided by a certain idea
of what so-called reality might be.

François Jacob,
The Possible and the Actual

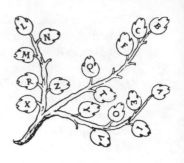

CHAPTER TWO

Linguistics and the Dream
of a Science of Literature

The decade following the *Mythologies* marks the
period of Barthes's active participation in the
Parisian version of the structuralist adventure. In
France, the same period overlaps with a wide-
spread reform of critical thinking that began after
World War II as an updated battle of ancients and
moderns. To see the wave of innovation as a
unified front or movement—as the blanket label
of *la nouvelle critique* implies—is somehow to
misrepresent the plurality of approaches found
in the writings of Sartre, Bachelard, Poulet,
Mauron, and Starobinski. In this sense, the notion of a monolithic *nouvelle critique* is as misleading as those of *nouveau roman* and *nouvelle vague*
commonly used to designate a similar practice of

innovation in the novel and cinema. Ultimately, the notoriety of structuralism derives in large part from the imprecision that accommodates a desire for instant access at the cost of reducing change to an ineffectual variation of convention. Outside France, the tensions between reform and convention took on the appearance of a battle of books that obscured substantive issues within a barrage of accusations, denials, and counteraccusations from most parties concerned. In retrospect, such polemics are easier to account for today as an offshoot of the self-consciousness essential to any critical activity that takes the impulse to change seriously. As Robert Scholes sees it, the effects are close to programmatic: "An age of criticism is a self-conscious age. Its tendency is to formulate rules, to attempt the reduction of art to science, to classify, to categorize, and finally to prescribe and proscribe."[1] Today it is not unusual to look back on this period as a historical curiosity or interval during which formalism made one of its infrequent incursions into literary thinking. Barthes himself encourages this attitude when he states—in the 1971 interview published in *Tel Quel* no. 47—that structuralism was nothing more than a "dream of scientism" from which he awoke in the late 1960s.

The 1971 dismissal is clearcut and strong; so strong, in fact, that it attests to the intensity of an earlier involvement that made the Barthes of 1959 through 1966 a staunch and articulate advocate of structural analysis. How exactly are we to relate the positions surrounding the 1965–67 period? At a distance of some twenty years, the various statements of support and rejection of structuralism tend to be glossed over in favor of a standardized account. Writing in 1974, Robert Scholes provides a portrait of Barthes's transition that asserts difference to the point of contradiction:

Roland Barthes is a literary critic, an advocate of *le nouveau roman* and a practitioner of *la nouvelle critique*, a student of popular culture, a scholar of Racine, a brilliant polemicist, a formidable rhetorician, an ingenious, mercurial man of letters. He is an essentially unsystematic writer who loves system, a structuralist who dislikes structure, a literary man who despises "literature." He loves to take up the outrageous position on any question and defend it until it becomes plausible, or—better still—attack the other views until they seem inferior.[2]

In many accounts of structuralism, it is Barthes who lands the role of literary figure to complement Lévi-Strauss as anthropologist, Lacan as psychoanalyst, and Foucault as historian. The duplicity Barthes notes in the caricature that he tends to become for others is an effect of a different kind of structural analysis, one that by 1975 already turns the linguistic model of ten years earlier into a tool of personal knowledge. If, by 1975, Barthes becomes the textual object of a revised structural analysis, how might we retrace the various moments of his previous practice and specify his involvement with the scientific project?

Once the primitive linguistic model set forth in the *Mythologies* tied Barthes to the *nouvelle critique* inspired by Saussure and structural linguistics, his practice also became part of a critical stance that set him at odds with the established literary critics of the Sorbonne and the French university system. Since Barthes taught during this period at one of the *Grandes Ecoles* parallel to but technically outside the university system, the potential for personal and professional polemics was difficult to avoid. Among Barthes's many pronouncements in defense of structural analysis, few (if any at all) skirted polemics. As a result, the rhetorical force of individual statements serves as an indication of the level of debate in which it occurs. "The Structuralist Activity" appeared in a February, 1963, issue of *Les Lettres Nouvelles*, in the same year that his *On Racine* sparked an extended polemic with the Sorbonnard, Raymond Picard.[3] Of particular interest in this short text is Barthes's attempt to acknowledge the resistance to structuralism as part of a view that its focus on structure tends to neglect historical factors with a resulting immobilization of time. Akin to charges leveled at structuralists by dissenters such as Sartre and Henri Lefebvre, this view looks to nomenclature in order to seek what it perceives as the distinguishing mark of a structuralist practice: "Watch who uses *signifier* and *signified*, synchronic and *diachronic*, and you will know whether the Structuralist vision is constituted."[4]

Barthes is unwilling to accept the standard view that structuralism is a school or movement. Instead, he prefers to describe it as an activity with a common exercise of structure rather than a shared vocabulary. At one remove from the notion of structuralism in its subsequent literary form as a science of language, Barthes nonetheless sets forth an argument upholding a distinctive experience and imagination defined less by ideas or language than by a mental experience of structure. Thus he arrives at the notion of a common practice that he terms the structuralist *activity*, defined as "the controlled succession of a number of mental operations." The goal of that activity is to reconstruct an object in a way that clarifies its operation or function. The result is no longer the original object, but its simulacrum, what Barthes terms a "directed, *interested* simulacrum" that fulfills the function of model as essential to scientific method: "Structural man takes the real, decomposes it, then recomposes it."[5] Where the Barthes of *A Lover's Discourse* stages the production of meaning as an ongoing process, his position in this earlier text focuses on the simulacrum that process produces.

Having identified the structuralist activity as an operation or work of understanding removed from strictly literary concerns, Barthes returns to the nature of the simulacrum in order to answer the allegations that structuralism ignores history in favor of structure and function. For once the simulacrum is constructed, it creates what Barthes sees as a new object that highlights the human processes by which meaning is created: "Ultimately, one might say that the object of Structuralism is not man endowed with meanings, but man fabricating meanings, as if it could not be the *content* of meanings which exhausted the semantic goals of humanity, but only the act by which these meanings, historical and contingent variables, are produced. *Homo significans*: such would be the new man of structural inquiry."[6]

As in the *Mythologies*, but more consistently and with greater success, Barthes borrows from Saussurian linguistics in order to show how structuralism as a practice or activity supports a revision of history focused on the diachronic axis of time and change. This is so because the activity of constructing the simulacrum occurs both within time and specifically as the creation of new objects and new meanings. As in the *Mythologies*, the focal point of Barthes's critique is the notion of the *natural* as a created meaning whose fabrication is more important than the meaning itself. Because the fabrication of *nature* or the *natural* varies according to historical, geographical, and cultural factors, Barthes argues that the specific features of individual simulacra elucidate a notion of function with distinct historical referents: "Structuralism does not withdraw history from the world: it seeks to link to history not only certain contents (this has been done a thousand times) but also certain forms, not only material but also the intelligible, not only the ideological but also the esthetic."[7] Because he finds participation in the fabrication of such intelligible forms to impose a sense of responsibility, Barthes ties the structuralist activity to a process of change and a future language that will, in turn, specify its historical specificity.

The questions of critical method and polemics that set structuralism against norms of established critical practice converged in 1963 when Barthes's *On Racine* became the focal point around which students, critics, and scholars took sides, either for or against *la nouvelle critique.*[8] In addition to this specific tract—which Barthes later described as a commissioned work he had accepted despite a dislike of Racine's tragedies—the critical positions taken on Racine spawned a number of shorter statements that develop the view of critical practice set forth in "The Structuralist Activity." The first of these supplements is "The Two Criticisms," first published in the United States in *MLN*, the journal edited by the Department of Romance Languages at Johns Hopkins, whose chairman, the late Georges Poulet, was himself a prime figure in the debate between traditional and *nouveaux critiques.* Barthes acknowledges this debate at the outset of his article by aligning Poulet with various representatives of an interpretive criticism—other names included here are those of Sartre, Bachelard, Goldmann, Starobinski, Girard and Richard—against an academic criticism he describes as positivist in the tradition of scholarship inherited from Gustave Lanson. Between the two criticisms lies a practice of teaching that objectifies questions of value and method into social phenomena that we identify in the institutions of learning and culture. For while Barthes admits that the two criticisms are inevitably linked, he also argues that their differences are real.

The point of difference between the two criticisms is that of value or ideology. For where those critics whom Barthes describes loosely as interpretive can be seen as proponents of ideological movements such as existentialism, psychoanalysis or phenomenology, the academic critics reject the real or perceived link to ideology, claiming instead to base their practice on an objective method. When the heat of debate forces them to uphold a clear position or attitude, the loose positivism taken from Lanson yields to the more hallowed invocation of humanism. Barthes's first insight into the two criticisms look at positivism as the visible form of a commitment whose supporters fail to recognize that the discovery of "facts" is anything but value-free. By claiming to investigate the sources of a work via external reference, positivist critics reduce it to a type. In so doing, they fail to account for the very questions that an accumulation of facts ought to promote: "And yet, what is literature? Why does one write? Did Racine write for the same reasons as Proust? Not to ask these questions is also to answer them, for it is to adopt the traditional notion of common sense (which is anything but historical) that a writer writes quite simply *to express himself,* and that the Being of literature is in the 'translation' of sensibility and the passions."[9] By focusing on a genetics of literary detail, the positivist critic seeks outside the work the basis of explanation that Barthes sees located fully inside it.

By abstaining from asking the fundamental questions such as why Racine wrote (and why he later stopped writing), the positivist critic eventually denies the very historical scope of inquiry that has been the ostensible support of his or her practice. By failing to establish its focus within the text it claims to explain via external facts, the positivist approach resists not just the truths of historical specificity, but those of function as well:

Which brings us to one of the gravest responsibilities of academic criticism: focused on a genetics of literary detail, it risks missing the detail's functional meaning, which is its truth: to expend prodigies of ingenuity, rigor, and tenacity to discover whether Oreste was Racine, or whether the Baron de Charlus was the Count de Montesquiou is thereby to deny that Oreste and Charlus are essentially the terms of a functional system of figures, a system whose operation can be grasped only within the work; the homologue of Oreste is not Racine but Pyrrhus; the homologue of Charlus is not Montesquiou but the narrator precisely insofar as the narrator is *not* Proust. In short, it is the work which is its own model; its truth is not to be sought in depth, but in extent.[10]

Because it adheres to a determinist view of the literary work as the product of an external cause, the so-called historical practice inspired by Lanson is incapable of dealing specifically with the internal aspects of function whose analysis Barthes wants to promote. In addition, the object of Barthes's critique is not simply the critical practice or ideology of positivism, but the institutions of teaching, study, and research that it supports in France.

The place of critical practice in social institutions is the object of another short article, "What Is Criticism?" published around the same period. As with "The Two Criticisms," it is noteworthy that this piece first appeared outside of France, in the *Times Literary Supplement*. In this text, however, Barthes returns to a question of logic whose implications for practice and ideology are strong enough that they resurface some fifteen years later in the opening statements of *A Lover's Discourse*. The question is that of the relation between critical discourse or language and its object. Borrowing a set of terms from formal logic, Barthes characterizes criticism as discourse upon discourse, a *metalanguage* that operates on a first language (or *language object*). Where

Barthes drops the claim to a metalanguage distinct from the language object in *A Lover's Discourse,* his earlier reference to the notion already softens any formal counterdistinction into an interdependence of function. Within the polemic context of the earlier piece, it is not surprising that this interdependence is described as a "friction" relating the metalanguage to two additional terms: "It follows that the critical language must deal with two kinds of relations: the relation of the critical language to the language of the author studied, and the relation of this language object to the world."[11] The two sets of relations bring together the topicality of Barthes's position in support of structuralist practice against the Lansonian tradition and the scope of that support in ideological questions set forth from *Writing Degree Zero* through the *Mythologies.* Because the positivist critics refuse to recognize that criticism is a language (or metalanguage) akin to the languages it claims to study, they cultivate a narrow practice based on a notion of scientism that is illusory and an accumulation of facts that Barthes sees as something other than objective. Furthermore, the erection of this positivist practice into an academic criticism allows it to proscribe as well as prescribe. And what it proscribes is the immanent description of functions or structure that Barthes sees as a necessary supplement to the patient knowledge that positivist criticism never, in fact, attains.

A second phase in Barthes's involvement with structuralism is found in the "Elements of Semiology" and "Introduction to the Structural Analysis of Narratives," published, respectively, in 1964 and 1966. While *On Racine* provoked a polemic that led to the programmatic support of modernity and innovation set forth in the 1966 *Critique et vérité,* Barthes was also working during the same period to apply the various descriptive systems of Saussure, Lévi-Strauss, Propp, and Greimas to the study of literature. Before the definitive break with the "dream of scientism" between 1966 and 1970, this middle period of Barthes's structuralist activities upheld the expansion of the linguistic model in a movement toward literary semiology. Thus, despite his subsequent rejection of scientism in the wake of *Critique et Vérité,* there is every reason to believe that the project of a literary science remained viable from the "Elements of Semiology" through the "Introduction to the Structural Analysis of Narratives." At the same time, however, it is possible today to note in these pivotal texts the early forms of disaffection that were to redirect Barthes's semiology from science toward figuration.

The sole aim of the "Elements" was to provide a clear set of analytic terms from linguistics in order to start research on what

Saussure had described in the *Course in General Linguistics* as semiology: the future or tentative science that studies the life of signs in society. But before he can proceed to elaborate Saussure's sketch, Barthes finds himself drawn to question how the extension of Saussure's linguistic model would call for it to be altered. In order to see social phenomena as elements in systems of meaning that often go beyond the model of verbal language, Saussure felt that linguistics had to be seen as yielding to the study of nonverbal systems that semiology would describe within the context of a mass or social psychology. Barthes, on the other hand, believes at this point in the extension of a revised linguistic model that would, in effect, invert Saussure's view. For Barthes, linguistics would not be seen as part of a general science of signs. Instead, semiology would remain part of linguistics: "To be precise, it is that part covered by the *great signifying unities* of discourse."[12] Although he does not supply the limiting principle that allows his reader to identify the specific discourse or discourses to be studied by his semiology, Barthes seems here to straddle the two sets of relations referred to in "What Is Criticism?" as situating the critic between his object of study and the (historical) world beyond that study. In 1964, however, the place of the critic is less secure than one might expect. For, less than seven years after the section on connotation in the closing text of the *Mythologies,* Barthes's attempts to set forth critical writing as a metalanguage distinct from the language object to be studied collapse under his inability to detach that first relation from the historical relation in which it takes place. As a result, nothing would prevent a metalanguage from becoming the language object of a new metalanguage, "spoken" by another science within a vision of relativity on which Barthes's dream of scientism ultimately shatters.

Where the first invocations of the distinction between metalanguage and literary object had come from mathematics and logic, Barthes can no longer support the absolute break between the two beyond the relativity he sees in the evolution of metalanguages as historical entities:

This relativity, which is an inherent part of the general system of metalanguages, allows us to qualify the image we might at first form, of a semiologist over-confident in the face of connotation; the whole of a semiological analysis usually requires, in addition to the studied system and the (denoted) language which in most cases takes it over, a system of connotation and the metalanguage of the analysis which is applied to it. (ES, 93–94)

Because Barthes sees connotation as operating at a social or collective level rather than emanating from the individual, the task of the semiologist changes from that of deciphering a fixed and objective meaning to that of noting how objective meaning is made provisional by the historical processes that renew metalanguages.

The "Elements" prefigures the shift from objective to relative perception that animates Barthes's later evolution from a semiology based on scientism to something more intimately bound up with the assertion of personal value Barthes derives from the tutor-text of Nietzsche. (This is the sense in which Nietzsche and Lacan supplant Saussure, according to the chart appearing on page 145 of the *Roland Barthes*.) But before that break with scientism occurs, Barthes's "Introduction to the Structural Analysis of Narratives" provides the outline for a semiology of literature that—ironically—Barthes revised in what became a parting of ways with structural analysis as he conceived it between 1957 and 1966. In contrast to the elliptical remarks at the close of the 1964 "Elements," Barthes's tone in the 1966 "Introduction" is assertive and close to programmatic. Faced with what he describes as the numberless narratives of the world, he sees the task of the semiologist as that of creating a common model to master the infinity of utterances by describing the language which generates them. Following the emphasis in Saussure's *Course* on collective language over individual utterance, Barthes appears to uphold the priority of *langue* as the semiologist's principal object of study. Yet the impact of this theoretical position is not borne out by Barthes's own practice of semiology in texts such as *S/Z*, *L'Empire des signes*, and *The Pleasure of the Text*. Thus the theoretical problem of finding the suitable vocabulary for extending the language/speech notion acquires a more practical dimension in the "Introduction" as Barthes studies how an extended linguistic model might be used in a semiology of literature.

The immediate question set forth in the "Introduction" is that of how to mobilize a linguistic model capable of accounting for units of literary discourse beyond the sentence. To be sure, the matter of extending the linguistic model beyond the sentence is still a problem linked to classification and the scientific approach evident in the "Elements." But when he looks to linguistics for help in making the transition from the sentence to literary discourse, he finds it only at the stage of tentative postulation. Similarly, when he looks to traditional rhetoric, he finds only a limited scope of application to belles-lettres more or less removed from the study of language he wants to undertake. The specific problem that neither linguistics nor rhetoric appears to resolve is that of using the language/speech distinction to study literary discourse in a way that accounts both for its singularity and its status as one "language" among others. Because the primary source for this proposed linguistics of literary discourse is Saussure's *Course*, Barthes finds it necessary to posit a relation of similarity or analogy—he uses the term "homology"—between language and literary discourse. Thus, the practical study of the individual narratives that constitute the body of literary discourse can proceed only after the relation between (Saussurian) language and narrative has been understood:

> The general language (*langue*) of narrative is one (and clearly only one) of the idioms apt for consideration by the linguistics of discourse and it accordingly comes under the homological hypothesis. Structurally, narrative shares the characteristics of the sentence without ever being reducible to the simple sum of its sentences: a narrative is a long sentence, just as every constative sentence is in a way the rough outline of a short narrative. (*IMT*, 84)

Departing from both Saussure's *Course* and the model of actantial types proposed by A. J. Greimas, Barthes explores the homology between language and literature as a problem of logic that ultimately removes his literary semiology from structural analysis toward the demonstrations of textuality set forth in *S/Z* and the "Textual Analysis of Poe's 'Valdemar.'" In this sense, the "Introduction" needs to be seen as pivotal in Barthes's evolution. For while the emphases on questions of method and terminology still uphold the preeminence of a scientific model, Barthes is unable to formulate a satisfactory approach to narrative based on an extended linguistic model derived from Saussure's *Course*. That inability is not at all provisional, not a momentary condition to be overcome at a later point. For when Barthes returns to the study of narrative in *S/Z* some two to three years after the "Introduction," his notion of structural analysis will have evolved to accommodate a nonscientific approach that asserts the mobile structuration of meaning in the text. As he will quip in 1973—after the break with structural analysis—"No reader, no subject, no science can arrest the text."[13]

While they serve to restate questions of vocabulary, method, and ideology that preserve the scientific dimension of Barthes's literary semiology, the "Elements" and "Introduction" also extend the linguistic model to a point where the critical practice it legitimates in a text such as *S/Z* can no longer be seen as consonant with a science of literature. To restate the point somewhat differently, these two texts extend the theory of a literary semiology toward a general poetics whose demonstration in the close analysis of specific texts yields a model of reading whose rigor is no longer that of scientism. Or, as Thomas Sebeok puts it, "Barthes's extended, fascinating essay (*Elements of Semiology*) . . . set in motion a new inquiry and debate in a personal idiom or, if you will, reopened Pandora's box of semiotic tricks."[14] From a science of literature to something more like a phenomenology of reading, the practice of semiology that followed the 1964–66 period could no longer be assimilated to the values of scientific inquiry set forth in the decade following the *Mythologies*. As a demonstration of that change, *S/Z* made it clear that Barthes's break with structural analysis was irrevocable.

To read in any real way, then, is to enter
into connotation. Futile maneuver: in
dealing with the denoted meaning, positivist
linguistics deals with a meaning so extenuated
that it has become obscure, improbable, unreal.

Barthes, *Roland Barthes*

A brief cautionary digression: in keeping with the early application of a metalanguage in the social critique set forth in the *Mythologies*, the recourse to linguistics and to linguistic models in Barthes's writings derives from a generalized or monolithic notion of science that breaks up on closer inspection. Similarly, to characterize Barthes as a "structuralist" or as someone associated with "structural analysis" is to think in blanket terms that are not merely imprecise, but misleading. In order to approach those blanket terms and define them, it is necessary to confront the very distinction between connotation and denotation Barthes refers to in the above quotation. For if we do not always know with certainty what these terms denote, it is often easier to sense the connotations that accompany them. Taking this distinction seriously is, then, a first step in understanding the change of values at work during this period of Barthes's career. The initial exploration of linguistic models in the *Mythologies* is part of Barthes's search for a method that would provide a consistent and respectable means of support for his critique of popular myths. In order to show ideology at work in the production of meaning, Barthes needs to come up with a more rigorous account of the interplay between denotation and connotation. This is, in fact, the project he begins in *S/Z* and develops in *The Pleasure of the Text* in his "slow-motion" analyses of the reading process. The trouble Barthes encounters in the 1964–66 writings comes from the fact that his search for a critical method is based on an instrumentalist view of language that, under the name of *écrivance*, becomes the object of critique in *S/Z*. Through the "Introduction to the Structural Analysis of Narratives," the application of a linguistic model proceeds in the name of a future poetics of literary discourse. Thus, what begins in *Writing Degree Zero* and the *Mythologies* as an inquiry into the social institutions of literature and popular culture looks very much by the mid-1960s to be depoliticized in the name of a scientism seemingly removed from social issues. Because it was based in a view of language that valued the fixity and closure of denotation over the more elusive phenomena of connotation, the positivist linguistics Barthes fashioned from the work of Saussure, Lévi-Strauss, and Greimas proved to be less and less suitable to what Barthes saw as the production of meaning. For all practical purposes, then, method came to conflict increasingly with the original end. By the time Barthes understood the implications of the linguistic model at work in the "Elements of Semiology" and the "Introduction to the Structural Analysis of Narratives," a revision of the model called for something closer to a radical break. For what had evolved into a project of devising a superior formal method asserted a vision of scientism and mastery Barthes saw in conflict with the critical project he had formerly sought to execute.

A final version of Barthes's views on literary science appears in the latter half of *Critique et vérité* in a three-part distinction between science, criticism, and reading. Written at about the same period as the "Introduction" and the collective effort in *Communications* no. 8 to found a literary semiology, these statements are both programmatic and polemical. Unlike the earlier attempts to set forth the working model for a future inquiry, *Critique et vérité* serves as a position paper that forces the reader to side for or against it. Because Barthes states his views with concision, they serve to recapitulate the evolution from *Mythologies* toward the openly nonscientific orientation in *S/Z*. In addition, the manifesto-like tone makes it clear that Barthes's relation to the science of literature is founded on values and conventions that were the evident objects of debate between himself and academic critics such as Picard.

In keeping with the position taken in the "Introduction to the Structural Analysis of Narratives," Barthes begins by defining the science of literature as a general inquiry (he uses the term *discours*) into the plurality of meanings that make up the literary work (*oeuvre*). Close to what Todorov and Genette pursue as a poetics of literature, this general inquiry becomes an attempt to formulate the conditions or principles at work in classifying literary works according to genre, form, and type. In terms of method, such a project falls completely within the realm of scientific inquiry, as a close study of a limited number of data is used to examine a more general range of data for purposes of comparison and prediction. In this sense, a literary science would seem to share with its academic adversary a common commitment to positivism. But where the scientific project projects a system for classifying texts, it does so according to a linguistic model that Barthes characterizes as generative: not what the meaning should be, but how it comes to be:

The science of literature will therefore have as its object neither why a particular meaning should be accepted, nor why it has been (this, once again, is a matter for the historian), but why it is *acceptable*, not in terms of philological rules of the letter, but in terms of the linguistic rules of the symbol. Here is found, transposed onto the scale of a science of discourse, the task of recent linguistics, which is to describe the grammaticality of sentences, not their meaning. In the same way, one will try to describe the *acceptability* of works, not their meaning. The set of meanings will not be cast as an immobile order, but as the traces of an immense "operational" arrangement (since it allows works to be made), expanded from author to society. (*CV*, 59)

Once its scope is agreed upon, the initial project of a descriptive science of literature can proceed from a hypothetical poetics toward the study of individual works that Barthes sees as the task of literary criticism. Or as he states it with aplomb: "How could science speak of *an* author?" (*CV*, 59).

Against the scientific project of a generalized poetics, Barthes sets the activities of the criticism and reading that deal with specific works. While both involve the production of meaning as a phenomenon occurring within the text, Barthes sees critical activity as mediated by its own considerations and the questions derived from the linguistic model. Thus the critic neither clarifies nor "translates" the work. Instead, he or she traces the production of meaning within a specific form. The critic creates a second language unfolded from the text as a coherence of signs, an activity Barthes compares to anamorphosis.

Where the critic creates a second language to be superimposed over the work, the formal nature of that second language relegates it to the status of commentary and a redistribution of the work akin to what Barthes had described in 1963 in "The Structuralist Activity.' Because the critic contends with critical writing as an intermediate element, he or she cannot attain the direct experience of intimacy that Barthes finds only in reading: "Only reading loves the work, maintains with it a relation of desire. To read is to desire the work, to want to be the work, to refuse to double the work outside any word other than that of the work itself. The only commentary that a true reader could produce and that would remain so, is the pastiche (as would be indicated by the example of Proust, lover of both readings and pastiches)" (CV, 78–79). From science through criticism toward reading, such is the progression Barthes outlines in *Critique et vérité* as a prelude to the extended reflections on reading and writing in *The Pleasure of the Text*. In addition, the three-part distinction prefigures the pendulum swing from the object of critical writing toward its subject and the notion of intertexuality: not a "full" subject that operates language with mastery, but something closer to an emptiness around which the critic weaves an utterance capable of infinite transformation.[15]

By 1968, the linguistic model Barthes had set forth in the "Elements" and the "Introduction" had become a kind of monster, the product of scientism that Barthes saw as an aspect of the popular values he had sought to expose in his earlier writings. Thus, a revised linguistic model could only continue to assert the values that were at odds with his undertaking. Barthes's only choice was to break with the orthodoxy of a structural analysis based on an instrumentalist view of language. It meant that Barthes had to turn the model against itself in what amounted to a double tactic of asserting the "new" meaning of connotation beyond the orthodoxy of a linguistic model and science that suppress connotation in favor of denotation:

It is not a question of recovering a pre-meaning, an origin of the world, of life, of facts, anterior to meaning, but rather to imagine a post-meaning: one must traverse, as though the length of an initiatic way, the whole meaning, in order to be able to extenuate it, to exempt it. Whence a double tactic: against *Doxa*, one must come out in favor of meaning, for meaning is the product of History, not of Nature; but against Science (paranoiac discourse), one must maintain the utopia of suppressed meaning. *(RB, 87)*

Where linguistics had once offered the promise of approaching meaning as a social product of denotation and connotation, Barthes came to see that promise as blocked by the values of a scientism unable (and ultimately unwilling) to account for meaning as anything more than denotation. Against this fantasy of clear meaning, Barthes will move from structural analysis to the more open analysis of the text whose first and most notorious demonstration appears in *S/Z*.

II. The Break: From Criticism to Figuration

In the West, the mirror is an essentially narcissistic object: man thinks the mirror only in order to see himself in it. But in the East, so it seems, the mirror is empty.

Barthes, *L'Empire des signes*

CHAPTER THREE

On the Subject of Loss

Toward the end of the *Roland Barthes*, Barthes uses the device of an imaginary self-interview to answer (in the third-person singular) that he re-reads "himself" in the various texts of his writing, judging each according to its success and failure. The confession is straightforward: part apology for rereading as a play of repetition and difference, part demonstration of how the materialist subject seeks its coherence in and through language. Unwilling at first to think in anything other than terms of relative success and failure, Barthes prods himself toward a more forceful assertion. Asking himself whether no book is successful throughout, he states, "Probably the book on Japan" (*RB*, 156). After the fact, one can

insert the "book on Japan" within the chronology of Barthes's disenchantment with structural analysis. Thus, *L'Empire des signes*, which
appeared in 1970 along with *S/Z* and the commentary on Erté's
alphabet, may appear at first glance to be nothing more than a secondary work, an offshoot of the travel literature that Barthes writes on
elsewhere in connection with the images of Pierre Loti's Orient and
Stendhal's Italy.[1]

But Japan is less the subject of this account of Barthes's trip abroad
than its pretext or point of departure. As in the early text on the
vacationing writer (reprinted in the French edition of the *Mythologies*,
30–33), Barthes acknowledges the inevitable gap between what he
sees and the fiction of that experience that surrounds it in his expectations and afterthoughts. The true subject of the book on Japan is the
activity of writing that the trip provides as the possibility of a difference
Barthes seeks both to assert and master in his writing. In this sense, the
concept or notion of "Japan" before and after the fact of his visit to the
country is inevitably linked to the cultural perceptions he brings with
him. The title of his account refers not merely to the "empire of signs"
as a site or geographic location. It emphasizes the sense of the term
"empire" as dominance or mastery. For as much as this trip abroad
takes the form of a search for difference, its account is very much the
account of the impossibility of shaking the dominance of cultural
values and habits that appropriate difference into sameness. Consequently, *L'Empire des signes* demonstrates a self-reflexive quality that
collapses the conventions of travel narrative into something more
personal that ties Barthes to Japan with a self-consciousness focused
on what becomes the writing of "Japan" into an unlimited text of sorts.
Thus, to return to the answer Barthes gives himself about the success
of the "book on Japan," he rereads this account looking for how the
transition from one culture to another forces a change in perception
that Barthes responds to in a desire to write. As he states at the start of
L'Empire, the images Japan provides are not those of the country, but
rather those of himself displaced—dis-Oriented?—by the loss of
meaning that a foreign culture sends back to him. It is this loss—and
its impact on Barthes as the writer/semiologist on vacation—that he
recasts in *L'Empire des signes* as a momentary exemption from the
mastery of signs he had sought to write out in earlier texts such as the
"Introduction to the Structural Analysis of Narratives" and the "Elements of Semiology." Because the "book on Japan" asserts loss against

mastery, it becomes for Barthes the single success—the "happy mythology"—he acknowledges in the *Roland Barthes*.

The result of the self-reflexivity Barthes develops is a textual account that transforms Japan into a composite of image and physical encounter:

> The Orient and the Occident cannot therefore be understood here as "realities" to be approached and opposed historically, philosophically, culturally or politically. I do not look lovingly toward an Oriental essence. The Orient is indifferent to me, it simply provides me with a stock of features whose formality and invented play allow me to "caress" the idea of an unheard of symbolic system entirely separate from our own. What can be aimed at in a consideration of the Orient is not other symbols, another metaphysics or another wisdom (although the latter appears quite desirable); it is the possibility of a difference, of a mutation or revolution in the propriety of symbolic systems. (*Emp*, 7)

Once again, the pretext of the trip abroad inscribes the factor of travel literature within an activity of writing that oscillates between text and image. As *L'Empire* first appeared in the series published by the Swiss art house Skira on the "Ways of Creation" ("Les Sentiers de la création"), it should be noted that the abundant use of illustrations provides Barthes with the suitable interplay of word and image he describes as text. Because he uses the trip abroad as a pretext to write out the signs of habit and value he brings along as a kind of cultural baggage, Barthes's "book on Japan" is the textual account of how meaning simultaneously dominates and disperses when it is projected within a foreign setting. Thus, *L'Empire des signes* is a happy mythology because it deflates the myth of mastery that semiology had become for Barthes by the late 1960s. Because that loss of mastery is desirable as a personal remedy, Barthes can assert it openly while he writes it out in the new form of text that is to become his preferred mode during the final decade of his career: "The text does not 'comment' on the images. The images do not 'illustrate' the text. . . . Text and image, in their intertwining, promote the circulation and exchange of these signifiers: the body, the face, writing, and read therein the retreat of signs" (*Emp*, 5).

Despite his earnest attempts to set his cultural biases into clear outline as the bases for outstripping a stereotype of Japan, Barthes's desire to write out emptiness is, at best, something he can only hope to simulate. When, for example, he describes his writing in the context of Zen practice, the references to *satori* and the empty sign, *Mu*, do not escape the reappropriation into Western sign systems that Barthes had hoped to avoid. At best, the retreat of signs he experiences and transcribes in his account makes for a counterstatement to the claims he had made several years earlier for a semiology he was coming to see as culturally bound. As a result, the invocation of Zen concepts relativizes the standard notions of writing into something less predictable than the myth of the European vacationing in the Orient. In this sense, Barthes can hope at best to account for the impact of his cultural displacement by writing a text that breaks up the mastery of a semiology capable of appropriating difference in the cause of Western hegemony. To write out loss of mastery is, consequently, to assert a different kind of mastery, much as the so-called absurdist playwrights such as Ionesco and Beckett have made careers out of their abilities to communicate a universal inability to communicate! What Barthes succeeds in doing in *L'Empire*—and what makes "the book on Japan" into a singular success—is the shift from a straightforward application of semiology to a looser account that supplements analysis with personal narrative, photographs, and images. The result is a text in the revised sense of a mixed and uneven construct: neither criticism nor fiction, but with elements of both. As in *A Lover's Discourse* and *Camera Lucida* to follow, the appropriate designation of genre is less helpful in approaching the specific text than a looser reading in which multiple forms animate an activity of writing in terms that become increasingly personal. Still some six to ten years from the more open recognition scenes staged in his final writings, Barthes nonetheless moves toward a drama of writing in *L'Empire des signes* by setting the pretext of the trip to Japan against his semiology as a practice of writing.

If *L'Empire des signes* is a book about writing that uses the trip to Japan as a point of departure, the practice of writing it describes and demonstrates is appropriately self-reflexive in a strict sense. To return to the passage from the *Roland Barthes* referred to at the start of this section, Barthes writes on Japan in order to locate (or relocate) the image of self that appears in his account. This is not, however, quite the same as writing oneself into an account as a kind of fictional character. For the nature of the text mixes word and image beyond the clear product of intention and will. Rereading his account, Barthes thus comes up with the primary image of himself not only in Japan, but always within language: "There are no longer distinct moments or places: he becomes decentered, like an uninterrupted text" (*Emp*, 33). Similarly, the account serves a more intimate analysis than that found in Barthes's earlier semiology. It reveals the writer to himself in the act of writing, not simply a materialist subject made of words, but something more akin to Lacan's interplay between the Imaginary, the Symbolic, and the Real. As if to prevent a neat equation between the materialist subject and language, Barthes emphasizes the role of the Imaginary in language by means of metalepsis, the figure of exchange that, in this instance, works against the myth of the vacationing writer: "The writer has never, in any sense, photographed Japan. Rather, it is closer to the contrary: Japan has starred him with multiple flashes; or better yet, Japan has put him into a situation of writing" (*Emp*, 10).

To write the self as reflected in the loss of confidence encountered in a foreign setting provides Barthes with the search for the ultimate sign of emptiness and a Zen practice that counteracts the fuller sense of self he associates with fixed and definitive meaning. To this end, the signs of difference Barthes notes in his account characterize writing via figures of the self and body that he interprets in textual terms. Thus, he comments on the city of Tokyo, whose concentric form follows that to be found in most Western cities. But where the center of the Western city is, as in the case of Paris, a full site of origin, Tokyo's central area is an empty area, a "sacred 'nothing'" around which daily life is re-routed. Using this example of cartography to relate urban space to a sense of self, Barthes sees the map as a figure of writing. The city becomes an ideogram, continuing the text in word and image: "In this way, it is said, the imaginary is spread out as in a circle, by deviations, twists and turns around a empty subject" (*Emp*, 46). Similarly, what appeals to Barthes in the Zen garden is the apparent absence of the subject except for the trace of the rake in the sand or the placement of the rocks . . . as in a text. Once again, the haiku projects a figure of the self dispersed along the reading of the text.

Two other forms of writing associated by Barthes with figures of the self are those of packaging and the Bunraku puppet theater. The text of the package is the product of mixing various materials—paper, cardboard, ribbon, wood—to displace the centrality of the object contained within toward the envelope itself. In the Bunraku theater, the text of dramatic representation is the result of what Barthes sees as three writings acted out, respectively, by the puppet, the person working the puppet's movements, and a second person who recites a text as the voice of the puppet. Because the Bunraku theater separates act and gesture by an openly representational relay, it fulfills the self-reflexivity that Barthes wants to attain by dramatizing his own writing. In addition, this self-reflexivity attains the alienation effect set forth by Bertolt Brecht in order to have the body on stage remind us beyond its gestures that it is also a figure of representation, the "voice" of ideology. For Barthes, the Bunraku theater thus fulfills the notion of a total spectacle that multiplies the line of writing by the intertwining of word, image, and cultural codes that Barthes is to describe in the texts of modernity he studies in *S/Z* and *The Pleasure of the Text*. As in these two other texts, the critical question of how meaning is produced becomes the setting for a more intimate inquiry into exactly how the acts of reading and writing construct the materialist subject in and through language. In *L'Empire des signes*, the loss of self is unsuccessful beyond the force of a willful transposition. Because it simulates the image of loss that gives form to his phantasy, Barthes includes the clipping from a Japanese newspaper that announces his visit. In a photograph that accompanies the announcement Barthes sees himself turning Japanese, his eyes elongated and darkened, no longer Roland Barthes, but Monsieur Baruto.[2] As if to show that the transposition is reversible, Barthes notes soon after that he reads the face of a young Japanese actor as a loss of Asian features that he models on the American actor Anthony Perkins. As the privileged metonymy, the face thus becomes a text to be read and understood not merely for what it may or may not be, but for the image of self it reflects back toward the perceiver. Across from a photograph of a wooden statue of a monk whose face splits open to reveal another face, Barthes resumes the essence of his account when he writes that the sign is a fracture that never opens except onto another sign. Ultimately, there is no escape from the dominance of signs because meaning is projected out of a need to assume mastery and appropriate difference. Likewise, if the sense of self cannot be totally lost or undone, the dislocation of meaning in a foreign context can simulate a momentary loss of self that Barthes will explore in terms of the materialist subject he sets forth in *The Pleasure of the Text* and the *Roland Barthes*.

You say "I" and you are proud of this
word. But greater than this—although
you will not believe in it—is your body,
which does not say "I" but performs "I."

Nietzsche, *Thus Spoke Zarathustra*

The lead article in issue no. 205 (1–15 March 1975) of *La Quinzaine Littéraire* featured a review of *Roland Barthes par Roland Barthes*. What distinguished the new book from the others in the collection was the fact that Barthes himself was author of his own text, turning the former "par lui-même" designation from commercial to literal reference. But after the novelty of the enterprise had passed, many readers harbored a suspicion that this thinly veiled autobiography was just another turn of the screw, one more virtuoso performance by the writer who, as much as any other individual, had come to represent the strengths and weaknesses of the French new criticism of the 1960s. The review in the *Quinzaine* gives us much to ponder: "I suppose that if one were to ask Barthes to criticize his own book he would simply decline. Doubtless he would have little difficulty accounting for the shortcomings of his performance; but this would not in itself go beyond what the writer might tell us in personal conversation. For anything more, since criticism is traditionally nothing more than a hermeneutics, how could he accept to give meaning to a book which is so completely a refusal of meaning."[3] If we are struck by the candor with which the reviewer allows himself to speak for Barthes, it should be added that he is none other than Barthes himself, or rather none other than someone who signs the name Roland Barthes to a text entitled "Barthes puissance trois." Barthes to the third power? Barthes cubed? What kind of third degree is this and what might it tell us about reading Barthes today?

Along with Lévi-Strauss, Foucault, and Lacan, Barthes is most often cast as one of the prime movers in an enterprise which we might situate in France as beginning in 1955 with the appearance of Lévi-Strauss's *Tristes Tropiques* and ending with the events and repercussions of May–June 1968. But while he is most readily associated with the structuralist period, Barthes's personal itinerary includes links at an earlier moment with existentialism and Marxism and at a later time with textuality and reading. Structuralism is but one of a number of phases in his writings. As he quips in the *Roland Barthes*, "Structuraliste, qui l'est encore?"

And that brings me to what I really want to examine: Barthes and the body. As he attempts to disenfranchise himself from a scientific approach to criticism, Barthes moves increasingly toward self-scrutiny and introspection in the guise of an anatomical discourse. But even after the critical break, Barthes still remains somewhat of a structuralist—*un structuraliste encore*—who seeks self-knowledge by trying to make himself into a kind of text: a body to be observed, analyzed, and ultimately understood. Beyond questions of method, the classical nature of this quest for self-knowledge posits a most unexpected image: Roland Barthes, the pariah of French academic criticism only a decade earlier, writes a personal testament as he approaches the age of sixty and submits his candidacy in the hopes of joining his chosen literary pantheon: "Tel qu'en lui-même enfin l'éternité le change." Concurrent with the shift away from a scientific stance is a reversion to values of modernity in which Flaubert, Nietzsche, Gide, and Proust are invoked to support a critical position which would be blatantly reactionary if Barthes did not temper these references with others to Sollers, Kristeva, Derrida, and Lacan. While it should not stand as a last word or ultimate statement of views on the subject, the *Roland Barthes* examines points of contact between critical and anatomical discourses and offers new material to chart the development of Barthes's critical practice in the wake of structural analysis.

The prefatory statement of method in *Sade, Fourier, Loyola* is a hybrid of structural analysis and something else: "From Sade to Fourier, sadism is lost: from Loyola to Sade, divine interlocution. Otherwise the same writing: the same enumerative obsession, the same language practice, the same erotic fantasmatic fashioning of the social system" (*SFL*, 3). Despite the evident overriding differences, Barthes shows little reluctance about affirming convergence and centrality around the ways in which the writings in question participate in a common process of language production, what he terms *logothesis:* "The language they found is obviously not linguistic, a language of communication. It is a new language, traversed by (or traversing) natural language, but open only to the semiological definition of the text" (*SFL*, 3). This is structuralism with a difference. The individual studies in the book expand a vision of the reading whose deviation from a scientific project is most apparent in the increased value ascribed to notions of pleasure. Henceforth the text is to be experienced as an object of pleasure. Nothing is more depressing, Barthes asserts repeatedly, than to im-

agine it as an intellectual entity. With an image that may have remained dormant for the better part of thirty years, he characterizes the
pleasure of the text in existential terms as a transmigration into the life
of the reader, a coexistence in which the text "succeeds in writing
fragments of our own daily lives" (*SFL*, 7). If this recalls the phenomenological readings of Bachelard and Richard, the implications for
Barthes's critical practice are more immediate. Alongside his invocation of existential modes of reading, Barthes applies structural
methods to divide, classify, and reconstruct the specific in question.
While he wants to use pleasure as a wedge against science, Barthes
retains a critic's mania for comparison and measurement. Admittedly,
this is a critical practice of paradox. Antonin Artaud wrote in *L'Ombilic
des limbes* (1925) that his poems expressed sensations whose impact he
was able to record only by transforming writing into a kind of neuro-
meter (*pèse-nerfs*). At this moment in his liberation from structuralism,
Barthes turns to a phenomenon of pleasure—literally the degree to
which pleasure hits him—which he cannot help but try to quantify. Is
there an eroteme, a discrete unit of measure analogous to the
phoneme, morpheme, and mytheme? And if so, can pleasure become
a viable criterion for making critical statements? Such questions, not
nearly as rhetorical as I have made them sound, expand the consideration of pleasure and inscribe the texts discussed in *Sade, Fourier, Loyola*
within a wider investigation whose objective is a fuller understanding
of the interplay between the bodies of classical and modern writings:

Faced with the old text, therefore, I try to efface the false sociological, historical,
or subjective efflorescence of determinations, visions, projections; I listen to the
message's transport, not the message. . . . The social intervention of a text (not
necessarily achieved at the time the text appears) is measured not by the
popularity of its audience or by the fidelity of the socioeconomic reflection it
contains or projects to a few eager sociologists, but rather by the violence that
enables it to exceed the laws that a society, an ideology, a philosophy establish
for themselves in order to agree among themselves in a fine surge of historical
intelligibility. This excess is called: writing. (*SFL*, 10)

With the turn toward a view of writing as excess, Barthes's critical
vision is clearly opposed to the orthodoxy of a structural analysis.
Where one of the tenets of that practice was to stay within the text,
Barthes expresses a tacit rejection by looking for a way out. In "Les

Sorties du texte," first read in July 1972 at the Artaud/Bataille collo-quium organized at Cerisy-la-Salle by the *Tel Quel* group, Barthes spoke on "Le Gros Orteil" by Georges Bataille and offered further evidence of a desire to disintricate himself from his former activities. Rather than explicate Bataille's text, Barthes prefers to string together a series of excursuses whose discontinuity he embellishes by means of individual titles and alphabetical order, simultaneously order and disorder, the zero degree of order: "I am not going to explicate this text. I shall only utter a number of fragments, which will be so many departures [*sorties*] from the text."[4] The presupposition supporting such a disclaimer, already implicit in *Sade, Fourier, Loyola*, is that a text is irreducible to the various discourses (*codes du savoir*) commonly employed to describe and explain it. Barthes writes that he chose to speak on this particular text because Bataille's interests in ethnology exceeded the imposed limits of a single cultural system (that of the journal *Documents*, in which "Le Gros Orteil" first appeared in 1929). The excess produced a friction (*frottement*) of codes which Barthes deems useful as a weapon against the monolith of scientific knowl-edge. More likely, he also chose the text because it allowed him to return to the question of the body—*le sens du corps*, an expression in which *sens* refers both to meaning and movement. It is the reversibility of the two—mobility of meaning and meaning of mobility—which Barthes goes on to qualify when he links meaning to Nietzsche's inquiry into personal value: "Knowledge [*le savoir*] says of everything, 'What is this? What is the big toe? What is this text? Who is Bataille?'— But value, following the Nietzschean expression, extends the ques-tion, 'What is this for me?' Bataille's text offers a Nietzschean answer to the question: *'What is the big toe, for me, Bataille?'*—and by displacement; what is this text, *for me*, as I read it?"[5]

In order to implement this turn toward value, Barthes provides a working notion of the first-person subject which precludes reducing value to subjectivism. He refers to a certain kind of subject which, far from being itself a certainty (*subjectivité certaine*), functions as a wedge against the margin of indifference maintained by the so-called scien-tific claims to objective knowledge. Once again, Barthes is less in search of a new paradigm for criticism than on the lookout for the rub, the friction and points of contact implied by any tentative distinction between knowledge and value: "In sum, knowledge is retained as a force but is opposed as tediousness; value is not that which scorns, relativizes, or rejects knowledge, but that which amuses it, rests within it; value does not oppose knowledge from a polemical perspective, but in a structural sense; there is an alternance of knowledge and value, an arrest of one by the other following a kind of *amorous rhythm*. And that, in sum, is what writing is, and in particular the writing of the essay (I refer here to Bataille): the amorous rhythm of science and value: heterology, bliss."[6]

In *The Pleasure of the Text*, the links to Nietzsche's inquiry into value develop as Barthes removes himself from judgmental distinctions between "good" and "bad" texts, opting instead to chart the boundaries of critical response as an activity which exceeds the capabilities of objective knowledge. As a result, when Barthes wants to explore pleasure as a possible criterion for evaluating modern texts, he goes as far as possible into verbal articulation and then enters a second mode he designates differentially as an excess or supplement to the first. Using the interplay of likeness and difference between pleasure and bliss, Barthes again seeks out the verbal contours of pleasure and their impact on critical reading and textuality:

As textual theory has it, the language is redistributed. Now *such redistribution is always achieved by cutting*. Two edges are created: an obedient, conformist plagiarizing edge (the language is to be copied in its canonical state, as it has been established by schooling, good usage, literature, culture), and *another edge*, mobile, blank (ready to assume any contours), which is never anything but the site of its effect: the place where the death of language is glimpsed. These two edges, *the compromise they bring about*, are necessary. Neither culture nor its destruction are erotic; it is the seam between them, the fault, the flaw, which becomes so. . . . Whence, perhaps, a means of evaluating the works of our modernity: their value would proceed from their duplicity. By which it must be understood that they always have two edges. The subversive edge may seem privileged because it is the edge of violence; but it is not violence which affects pleasure; destruction does not concern it; what pleasure wants is the site of a loss, the seam, the cut, the deflation, the *dissolve* which seizes the subject in the midst of bliss. Culture thus recurs as an edge: in no matter what form. (*PT*, 6–7)

Edges, seams, joints, and flaws promote a metaphoric equivalence of text and body which removes reading from science and resituates it in pleasure, a transition discernible in the fragmentary nature of Barthes's own texts. But what, exactly, is the "nature" of the artifice termed text? Are we to read *The Pleasure of the Text* as though it were a body, a textual *corpus?* The text itself allows us to follow through the metaphor and see how far Barthes pushes the implied equivalence:

Apparently Arab scholars, when speaking of the text, use this admirable expression: *the certain body.* What body? We have several of them; the body of anatomists and physiologists, the one science sees or discusses: this is the text of grammarians, critics, commentators, philologists (the pheno-text). But we also have a body of bliss consisting solely of erotic relations, utterly distinct from the first body: it is another contour, another nomination. Thus with the text: it is no more than the open list of the fires of language. . . . Does the text have a human form, is it a figure, an anagram of the body? Yes, but of our erotic body. The pleasure of the text is irreducible to physiological need. (*PT*, 16–17)

A number of factors point to the *Roland Barthes* as a text fully devoted to exploring the body by elaborating on the wordplay at the close of *The Pleasure of the Text* which blends Ça (French term for the Freudian notion of id) and Sa (common French abbreviation for signifier) into homonymic equivalents denoting body and word. The *Barthes* begins with forty pages of annotated photos, a nostalgic review of Barthes's prehistory and a visual staging of his past. Images are the dividend of pleasure Barthes allows himself in order to keep scientific pretense at bay and regain contact with himself ("avec le ça de mon corps"). Autobiography poses traditional problems which Barthes confronts in a number of ways. By alternating between first-, second-, and third-person narrations, he upsets the continuity of his critical discourse to a point where even the documentary status of photographs is suffused by a personal myth. Placing side by side on a single page two photo portraits dating from 1942 and 1970, Barthes comments in the form of a mock dialogue: "'But I never looked like that!'—How do you know? What is the 'you' you might or might not look like? Where do you find it—by what morphological or expressive calibration? Where is your authentic body? You are the only one who can never see yourself except as an image; you never see your eyes unless they are dulled by the gaze they rest upon the mirror or the lens. (I am interested in seeing my eyes only when they look at you): even and especially for your own body, you are condemned to the repertoire of its images" (*RB*, 40).

Can one escape from the body and see oneself from the outside? In studies on Baudelaire, Genet, and Flaubert (and on himself in *The*

Words), Sartre deals with a similar set of problems. In Gide's *The Immoralist*, Michel's recovery from a near-fatal disease serves as pretext for an attempted recreation of the self founded in large part on physical gratification. While the problematics are traditional, Barthes outstrips his predecessors by assuming an approach to autobiography which accounts for mythopoeisis, the capacity for self-delusion and untruth which is all too often a byproduct of introspection and hyperconsciousness. Rather than attempt the impossible task of self-analysis, Barthes strips his writing of positivistic aspirations and acknowledges his undertaking obliquely as various sets of edges (*bords*) between pleasure and bliss, science and value, criticism and fiction. In so doing, he both indicates how we might read his book and formulates the presuppositions of his current critical practice. Having chosen to articulate an extended metaphor of the body as the impersonal third-person entity of the *Ça*, Barthes approaches himself from the side of value when, in a fragment entitled "Le Livre du moi," he advises his reader to read the new book as though it were a set of utterances voiced by a character in a novel:

All this must be considered as if spoken by a character in a novel—or rather by several characters. For the image-repertoire, fatal substance of the novel and labyrinth of levels in which anyone who speaks about himself gets lost—the image-repertoire is taken over by several masks (personae), distributed according to the depths of the stage (and no one—*personne*, as we say in French—is behind them). . . . The substance of this book, ultimately, is therefore totally fictive. The intrusion, into the discourse of the essay, of a third person who nonetheless refers to no fictive creatures, marks the necessity of remodeling the genres: let the essay avow itself almost a novel: a novel without proper names. (*RB*, 119–20)

In his *Structuralist Poetics*, Jonathan Culler questions the degree to which Barthes's invocations of Nietzsche and Derrida deviate from his earlier interests in the full development of codes and systems. To cite the obstacles to analysis posed by plurality and dispersion of meaning does not, Culler maintains, preclude or deny the existence of systems or their possible analysis. The point is doubtless well taken (and it should be added that Culler was not in a position to account for the *Barthes* in his own study). Yet it becomes increasingly important to determine the nature and intended application of the Nietzschean elements which find expression at this particular moment in Barthes's writings. To formulate the question in its simplest terms, we might ask: who is Nietzsche for Barthes?

In the light of the active controversies surrounding current Nietzsche criticism in France, a preliminary task involves separating an individual reading from a general intellectual environment in which both philosophers and literary critics draw on Nietzschean terms and categories where they formerly worked within a Hegelian context. The two are, of course, not without their own points of contact. Yet it is the Nietzschean connection which prevails for now and which needs to be explored and clarified. In Barthes's writings from 1970 on, that factor proceeds from a transition in his practice of interpretation from an activity with scientific aspirations to a meditation on the personal values which underlie it. It is a shift which has long attracted French readers, initially as part of an existential inquiry (the sense and value of a phenomenon or act for an individual at a specific time and place) and more recently in the frontal attack on interpretation whose origins date from the writings of Bataille and Maurice Blanchot during the 1940s.[7]

In *Nietzsche et la métaphore*, Sarah Kofman analyzes the effects of metaphor to support what she sees as an alternance between science and art in Nietzsche's writings. Arriving at a similar position, Paul de Man writes that "On Truth and Lie in an Extra-Moral Sense" and the notes for a course Nietzsche gave at the University of Basel project a notion of rhetoric that moves away from the study of eloquence and persuasion toward a theory of speech or tropes. Rather than a secondary or aberrant form of language, the trope becomes the linguistic paradigm par excellence. Consequently, language is equated with rhetoric in the sense that it conveys opinion (*doxa*) rather than truth (*epistēmē*). But despite this insight into the rhetorical function of language, de Man argues convincingly that Nietzsche does not avoid falling into metalepsis, the exchange or substitution of cause and effect that characterizes the figure of metonymy in the notes for his 1872–73 course: "The deconstruction of the self as a metaphor does not end in the vigorous separation of the two categories (self and figure) from each other but ends instead in an exchange of properties that allows for their mutual persistence at the expense of literal truth."[8] Nietzsche's inability to break the pattern of substitution in his own writing illustrates the lie of language that, for de Man, leads to an equation of subject and text.

As he places the self onto the figure of the body, Barthes follows this Nietzschean turn from concept to metaphor to an extent which calls for adjustment on the part of the reader. When metaphor is used as the cohesive element within a text—as it is in writings as disjointed as *The Pleasure of the Text* and the *Barthes*—it can all too easily acquire referential dimensions to which it might otherwise have no claim. Reliance on metaphor has long been disparaged by philosophers as a literary quality incompatible with rigorous thinking. It is a charge often leveled against Nietzsche and one which Barthes is likely to encounter. In this sense, there is little doubt that the body metaphor fulfills utopian and fetishistic functions for Barthes, who, since *Sade, Fourier, Loyola,* had seen the erotic textual body as a verbal construct predicated on simile and metaphor and an implied alternative to traditional literary conventions. Consequently, the practice here appropriates a component of Nietzsche's attack on the language of philosophical thinking which devolves less from a specific set of problems than from a wider style or strategy. By granting privilege to the metaphor of the textual body, Barthes takes a critical stance which animates the impact of his own transition to a degree which, I believe, responds to Culler and points to the implications of that transition for Barthes's brand of post-structuralist criticism.

Given this centrality of metaphor, the *Barthes* appears to support a prejudice in favor of unreality. The book is less an autobiography or confessional essay than a critical fiction on a par with Sartre's reference to his mammoth study of Flaubert as a true novel. But is this really the case? What, after all, is more real than a body? Whatever value one might ascribe to the metaphor of the body, it is undeniably true that a body is also . . . a body. Despite the prevailing reservations concerning the status and usage of metaphor in general, the seriousness with which Barthes treats metaphorical focus—the expression is used by Max Black—calls for increased attention to its intended application as part of Barthes's reassessment of critical activity. It should come as no surprise that the abstract of that reassessment toward the end of the *Barthes* should be formulated under the aegis of Nietzsche. Referring to himself in the third-person singular (third degree or rhetorical voice of removal), Barthes describes a number of misgivings:

He suspected Science, reproaching it for what Nietzsche calls its adiaphoria, its in-difference, erected into a Law by the scientists who constituted themselves its procurators. Yet his condemnation dissolved each time it was possible to *dramatize* Science (to restore to it a power of difference, a textual effect); he liked the scientists in whom he could discern a disturbance, a vacillation, a mania, a delirium, an inflection; he had learned a great deal from Saussure's *Cours*, but Saussure had come to mean infinitely more to him since he discovered the man's desperate pursuit of the Anagrams; in many scientists, he suspected a similar kind of happy flaw, but for the most part, they dared not proceed to the point of making a whole work out of such a thing: their utterance remained choked, stiff, indifferent.

Thus, he thought, it was because it could not be *carried away* that semiological science had not turned out well: it was so often no more than a murmur of indifferent labors, each of which made no differentiation among object, text, body. Yet how could it be forgotten that semiology has some relation with the passion of meaning: its apocalypse and/or its utopia?

The *corpus:* what a splendid idea! Provided one was willing to read the *body* in the corpus: either because in the group of texts reserved for study (and which form the corpus) the pursuit is no longer of structure alone, but of the figures of the utterance; or because one has a certain erotic relation with this group of texts (without which the corpus is merely a scientific *image-repertoire*). Always remember Nietzsche: we are scientific out of a lack of subtlety.—I can conceive, on the contrary, as a kind of utopia, a dramatic and subtle science, seeking the festive reversal of the Aristotelian proposition and which would dare to think, at least in a flash: *There is no science except of differences.* (*RB*, 160–61)

Is the structuralist designation (still) valid for Barthes after the *Roland Barthes?* Even if we admit the scope and pronouncements in the mid-1960s period, there remain discernible limits to Barthes's practice of structural analysis. For all its wealth of detail, *Système de la mode* (1967) fails as an application of semiology to the phenomenon of fashion. And *S/Z* is no longer in the same mold as the previous studies, with an ironic distance pervading the masterful reading of Balzac's "Sarrasine." In retrospect, Barthes's contribution is greater as a theoretician than as applied critic. He is, as Robert Scholes puts it in *Structuralism in Literature*, a "high structuralist" whose meditations on models of critical reading hold an intrinsic value which is likely to outlast the codes and taxonomies of low (applied) structuralists. No matter how convenient it might prove to maintain the delusions of paranoia in certain quarters, Barthes, post–*Roland Barthes*, is no longer a suitable straw man for critics of structuralism.

While it is plausible to question the prevailing American view of Barthes as key figure in an ongoing structuralist invasion, there are those whose views are extreme from an opposite perspective. For the French linguist and critic Georges Mounin, there is cause to argue that

Barthes's analyses have less to do with linguistics or semiology than with sociology. For Mounin, Barthes is a social critic of the middle class who appropriates and misuses linguistic notions to promote a personal discourse: "What Barthes studies are never signs in the Saussurian sense of the term; they are more often symbols (whose systems—if systems they are—are never analyzed, although their functioning ought to be quite different from a language)."[9] If Barthes is no longer the structuralist he may never have been, where does that leave him and where does that leave his readers? Who, in other words, is Barthes *for us?* Beneath the various guises of critical strategy and fashion, the essential feature of the *Roland Barthes* involves the implementation of an autobiographical mode as a ploy against false objectivity, a move which recalls Nietzsche's conclusion that the objective is, in fact, merely a form of the subjective.

From *The Pleasure of the Text* to the *Barthes*, the cleaving of con- sciousness into contiguous entities of self and body provides the working model for Barthes's transition from science to art, a move which he justifies in the cause of eros. As early as *Critique et vérité* (1966)—which contains his most receptive appreciation of a structural- ist revision of critical reading—Barthes rejects the stable polarity be- tween the old and the new, a binary opposition which he prefers to characterize as a variable consequence of what a critical community does and does not tolerate at a specific moment. In *The Pleasure of the Text*, that view is updated when Barthes questions the myth of the "versus" which semiologists invoke in claiming to distinguish white from black. To avoid this binary bind, Barthes promotes imbalance and a continuous flow of duplicity between the terms of his own argu- ments: "Both sides of the paradigm are glued together in an ultimately complicitous fashion: there is a structural agreement between the contesting and contested forms" (*PT*, 55).

In the *Barthes*, duplicity and instability are evident in the reliance on metaphor as a double-sided figure which loosens the science of literature into something more pleasurable. In *Vertige du déplacement*, Heath argues that metaphor acts primarily as a force to open the text and displace fixed meaning and reference. In the *Barthes*, that force can be seen to posit a neutral relation between active and passive terms which is less a discrete third term than a tension or oscillation which replaces contradiction and antinomy with plurality and dispersion of meaning. Metaphor is an illustration *in* the text of the intermittent proximity and distance between the terms of figurative expression, a verbal analogue of the play of contact and release (akin to the *Fort / Da* of Freud's *Beyond the Pleasure Principle*) described in *The Pleasure of the Text* as a privileged site of eros. It also recalls the surrealist game of *l'un dans l'autre*, in which the terms of an analogous comparison are reversed in order to generate new images and expose the artifice of analogy. In both instances, reversibility is the essential point: neither term receives priority and metaphorical focus remains intentionally ambiguous and mobile.

The obvious difficulty with the writings that come after *The Pleasure of the Text* lies in the impossibility of determining whether they are to be read as texts of pleasure or bliss. To the extent that they succeed in transmitting a set of messages to a public of readers, they function within the mode of articulate pleasure and rely on determinable norms such as those of verbal meaning and implicit genre referred to by E. D. Hirsch in *Validity in Interpretation*. The mixture of critical, autobiographical, and fictional narratives acts at the level of genre to dislodge clear and precise meaning in favor of the kind of continuous instability promoted elsewhere by metaphor. Those who come to the *Barthes* with expectations of finding a self-evident and unironic text—I am thinking here of the gap between the *Barthes* and Wayne C. Booth's *A Rhetoric of Irony*—will no doubt be frustrated by the irresolvable play between the two pleasures and its implications for critical practice.

The *Barthes* ends with a fragment entitled "The Monster of Totality" and a sequence of statements which upholds the hypothesis of vertiginous displacement set forth by Heath. It also affirms that Barthes has come almost full circle, at least momentarily, to a concern for interpersonal relations and an ethical approach to communications not unrelated to that which he proposed more than twenty years earlier in *Writing Degree Zero*. Returning to the anatomical discourse to formulate the last fragment, Barthes reasserts the doublesidedness of metaphor as a final clue on how to read the book. He encourages an approach to it as a textual corpus with equal focus on both terms. Figurative reversibility—text as body, body as text—is the definitive sign of Barthes's removal from a scientific project, particularly when such removal is seen in relation to the autobiographical factor and its incipient notion of the critical subject.

Already in *S/Z*, The plenitude of the self had been seen as deceptive; the "I" which approaches a text devolves from previous acts ("intertextuality," as Kristeva might term it). Shades of Freud and Sartre: plenitude is an illusion, monstrous and unnatural because it is founded on a false determinism which also precludes subsequent change. Such fixity and determinism are precisely what Barthes tries to avoid when he questions the self as a complete (or "full") system. They also suggest the ultimate import of the Nietzschean connection. The incomplete nature of the critical subject negates the possibility of an indifference to or removal from its discourse; there is no metalanguage or privileged perspective "outside" the *Barthes*. Consequently, those who see the model of the two pleasures as leading to a critical paradigm of unbridled subjectivism should not fail to observe that this nihilistic moment in Nietzsche's meditations on interpretation yields to a subsequent yes-saying to the subjective nature of truth as a human (all too human) valuation. Nietzsche thus upholds a vision of the truth which contains error—"not the error which has been overcome in a new truth, not the error which those who lie to themselves accept, but the inescapable error which is present even in the new truth."[10]

On a more personal level, the juggling of narrative voices in the *Barthes* extends the donning and doffing of masks as a virtuoso performance by a great pretender who, although identifiable by name, is not yet either a complete or "full" entity. From the side of the conscious self, the *Barthes* continues the search for a personal identity (*nom propre*) which has been heretofore simulated retrospectively as a succession of masks. From the side of the body, the homonymic play of *Ça* and *Sa* yields to the recurrent image of the Argo, the mythological ship in which Jason sailed in quest of the Golden Fleece. For Barthes, the ship serves as allegory of the structural object: it is a body created out of substitution and denomination. Since the Argonauts were said to have rebuilt the ship piece by piece while at sea, the myth leaves us with a parting metaphor of the writer as Argo: a protean body whose continuous self-transformations add a novel dimension to one of the oldest of self-evident truths: *Plus ça change, plus c'est la même chose.*"

He thought that the
Tropes were a people.

Dumarsais,
Des Tropes (1730)

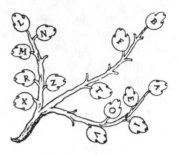

CHAPTER FOUR

Figuration, Musicality, and Discourse

What is figuration and what does it mean when we say that it functions *in the text*? In common usage, the term refers to the creating or supplying of figures, either as allegorical representations or the elucidations of form, outline, or pattern. Depending on material and context, figuration can occur in graphic or plastic form: in language, painting, and sculpture as well as in mathematics or music. In such cases, figuration as process, production, or movement is set against its object, result, or effect, an emphasis well rendered by the German term *Gebildschrift* and translated loosely as "image writing." In relation to language, the term refers to the creation of verbal patterns or structures whose meaning cannot be determined by a direct coordination of signifier and signified such as that described by Saussure as the association of acoustic image and concept. As in the traditional use of tropes, figuration involves a turning, bending, or deflecting of meaning, replacing it with a mobile space or field of action better understood as the site of metaphoric or metonymic activity. Attempts to account for figuration in spatial terms are often figurative in themselves, a peculiarity Erich Auerbach attributes to its dynamic and radiant qualities.[1]

In view of his former involvement in literary activities based on scientific inquiries, Barthes's disillusionment with semiology after the 1966–70 break coincides with a revised attitude toward the experiences of reading and writing as they relate to figuration and the dynamics of figuration. Those who balked at the overwrought vocabulary of *On Racine* might be surprised at the return to traditional questions of interpretation reanimated in *S/Z* in terms of personal value. Where Barthes's reputation as a structuralist had earned him a notoriety as a critic concerned with how a text produces meaning, the orientation of the writings that follow *S/Z* is toward meaning. Always a lover of language and inventor of new terms, Barthes demonstrates repeatedly in his verbal play that the terms themselves are less important than their roles in the ongoing process of figuration. The pursuit of novelty as an end in itself is no longer the mark of Barthes's modernist or post-modernist stance, not when his defection from the rearguard of the avant-garde culminates in recognition scenes whose settings are unabashedly literary.

Responding in 1973 to a question by Maurice Nadeau on whether writing was made up of anything other than combinatory elements, Barthes reveals a distance from the values of an avant-garde vision he no longer supports as he did, for example, during his mid-1960s polemic with Raymond Picard:

NADEAU: Are there then nothing but combinatory elements?
BARTHES: Yes, although this formula belongs to the heroic period of Structuralism. What we might perhaps do at present is to perceive the specifically current aspects of literature (keeping in mind that the word "critical" is the adjective associated with the noun "crisis").[2]

In order to see how this later position evolves from an earlier image of Barthes as an advocate of the modern and the *nouveau roman*, it should be recalled that his 1962 review of Michel Butor's *Mobile* was, in part, a defense of writing as a purely functional assemblage of disparate materials without psychological or rhetorical value. As a demonstration *in the text* of its links to a theory of the novel, Butor's text pursues mobility as variety without variation, a perpetual movement compared by Barthes to mathematics and music where an illusion of thematic unity is structured on the basis of contiguity: "The example of music is useful here, because the most connected of the arts actually possesses only the most discontinuous of raw materials; in music—at least in our music—there are only thresholds, relations of difference and constellations of these differences ('routines,' one might say)" (*CE*, 181).

Where Barthes locates unity in the "grand corps animé" of the Butor text, his subsequent practice asserts a literary or textual value to figuration at odds with the perpetual mobilization of *Mobile*. While he continues to see thematic consistency as unstable, figuration operates *in the text* as a process imposing a movement toward interpretation . . . along lines not yet formulated by the terms of structural analysis. Evidence of the differences between figuration and open structuring is visible in *S/Z*, where the symbolic code used to read Balzac's "Sarrasine" produces a new text which is less a copy of the original than its simulacrum rewritten via the breakdown and reassembly (*découpage et agencement*) of the structuralist activity. But the Barthes who writes *S/Z* during 1968–69 is no longer the same kind of structuralist he had been some years earlier. As a result, the reconstitution of the text formerly inscribed within an approach to the production of meaning is now directed more toward questions of interpretation. Where Barthes had formerly treated the simulacrum as an intellectual invention or novelty, he moves in *S/Z* to see how the simulacrum is produced in the process of writing animated by figuration. In this sense, the end product of figuration is of less interest in itself than in its impact on the constitution of the materialist subject.

As I have suggested in earlier chapters, the transition from structural analysis toward a practice of figuration is neither clearcut nor complete. Even the initial project set forth throughout the *Critical Essays* between 1954 and 1964 is marked by an imbalance between theory and practice pointing to the revisions undertaken in the wake of the "Introduction to the Structural Analysis of Narratives" and *Critique et vérité*. In terms of the theory / practice dichotomy visible in the *Critical Essays*, Barthes tends to assert a theoretical impulse to the detriment of specific texts. When he treats individual works, he often chooses them from the *nouveaux romans* by Robbe-Grillet and Butor, which reveal a similar orientation toward theory. Even the close reading of "Sarrasine" disperses the text in question by inscribing it within a wider approach to classical and modern texts and a problematics of literary history set forth as early as *Writing Degree Zero*. Until the mid-1960s, Barthes is still very much the "high structuralist" of theory whose primary concerns are organized around concepts such as writing and text.

Only after *S/Z* are these former concepts and concerns revised by a practice of figuration that achieves its full force in the final decade of Barthes's life. Where *Critique et vérité* promotes a battle of books over Racine and what Barthes describes in *On Racine* as the grounding of critical practice in theory, *S/Z* inverts the relation and rejects the project of a literary science in favor of "another semiotics" set forth in *Communications* no. 8. The successive appearances of *S/Z*, *Sade, Fourier, Loyola*, and *The Pleasure of the Text* point to the active figuration that is undeniably a prime feature of the *Roland Barthes, A Lover's Discourse*, and *Camera Lucida*. To steal a turn of phrase from Freud's comment on the ego and the id, where the text of theory had been, that of figuration should come to be.

Concurrent with Barthes's movement toward dramatizing theory within writing is the frequency of references to voice and musicality, initially as elements in a wider semiology and later as textual qualities linked to utterance and figuration. From the side of theory, Barthes's inquiry begins as an attempt to relate verbal and musical signs. As that inquiry proceeds, it is focused increasingly on utterance, less as a problem of theory to be resolved than as a phenomenon of meaning and intensity in figuration. Barthes adapts this phenomenon in his writing to a degree where intertextuality is described in the *Roland Barthes* as "a music of figures" and the fragment as "a high condensation neither of thought, wisdom or truth (as in the Maxim) but of music" (*RB*, 94).

In *Camera Lucida*, Barthes's reflections on photography dramatize a personal narrative of discovery within a wider approach to images and what Lacan terms the imaginary. Shortly after the death of his mother in the fall of 1977, Barthes finds a photo of his mother in a winter garden at the age of five. Moved inwardly by the illusion of stasis which seemingly lifts a single moment from the passage of a uniform and linear temporality, he writes:

Or again (for I am trying to express this truth) this Winter Garden photograph was for me like the last music Schumann wrote before collapsing, that first *Gesang der Frühe* which accords with both my mother's being and my grief at her death; I could not express this accord except by an infinite series of adjectives, which I omit, convinced however, that this photograph collected all the possible predicates from which my mother's being was constituted and whose suppression or partial alteration, conversely, had sent me back to these photographs of her which had left me so unsatisfied. These same photographs, which phenomenology would call "ordinary" objects, were merely analogical, provoking only her identity, not her truth; but the Winter Garden photograph was indeed essential, it achieved for me, utopically, *the impossible science of the unique being.* (*Cl,* 70–71)

While understandably reluctant to reduce his mother to an object or mere function, Barthes is nonetheless drawn to the photo as to the Schumann piece for the affective responses they elicit from him. As they appear in the passage above, photography and music are not simply artistic languages to be analyzed as objects of a semiology. And while it is true to cast Barthes as a practitioner of structural analysis and semiology, the final stages in his critical evolution—from *The Pleasure of the Text* through *Camera Lucida*—go beyond the more conventional critical project he supported through the mid-1960s.

Rather than cast his revised practice as a straightforward critical discourse, Barthes has mixed critical and narrative elements. When he sketches the *plaisir/jouissance* binary in *The Pleasure of the Text,* the conceptual links between the two elements are set within a more substantive discontinuity of expression and utterance. And while it is possible to classify this discontinuity as instances of anacoluthon, asyndeton, and tmesis, to do so would be to neglect figuration and its textual function beyond the concerns of theory. When Barthes refers to Schumann's *Gesänge der Frühe* in *Camera Lucida,* he does so less to set forth thematic resemblance than in terms of a process of expressivity he links to voice and body.

In a 1972 text written for an issue of *La Musique en jeu* devoted to psychoanalysis, Barthes contends with how to treat music as a system of signs via verbal categories which seemingly limit responses to the adjective as an emotive predicate. The resulting drawback is that music thus becomes either predicable or ineffable. Looking for a way to overcome the bind of the predicable/ineffable dichotomy, Barthes approaches the musical sign as part of a wider inquiry into the function of the imaginary in symbolic processes. Where his 1964 "Elements of Semiology" draws mainly from the linguistics of Saussure and Hjelm-slev, Barthes bases his comments on musicality and voice on systems of symbolic expression set forth by Freud and Lacan. The alternative model he thus proposes involves musical text and voice in a dual production of meaning he links to the body:

Something is there, manifest and stubborn (one hears only *that*), beyond (or before) the meaning of the words, their form (litany), the melisma, and even the style of execution: something which is directly the cantor's body, brought to your ears in one and the same movement from deep down in the cavities, the muscles, the membranes, the cartilages, from deep down in the Slavonic language, as though a single skin lined the inner flesh of the performer and the music he sings. The voice is not personal; it expresses nothing of the cantor, of his soul; it is not original (all Russian cantors have roughly the same voice), and at the same time it is individual: it has us hear a body which has no civil identity, no personality, but which is nevertheless a separate body. (*IMT*, 181–82)

Beyond the semantic, logical, and rhetorical functions associated with a semiological analysis of musical expression, the irreducible presence referred to above is what Barthes terms "the grain of the voice." This "grain" is not synonymous with vocal tone or timbre; instead, it refers to the materiality of a movement or expressivity Barthes associates with figuration. Borrowing from a vocabulary developed by Julia Kristeva, Barthes coins the expressions *pheno-song* and *geno-song* to mark the differences in vocal artistry between Dietrich Fischer-Dieskau and Charles Panzera, lamenting in the former the absence of corporeal diction and quality of grain he admires in Panzera's performance: "With FD, I seem only to hear the lungs, never the tongue, the glottis, the teeth, the mucous membrances, the nose" (*IMT*, 183).

The quality of grain is not always discernible, not unless it forces the listener into the more active role of an operator who participates in what Barthes describes in another text as *musica practica*. Transposing this time from the vocabulary of *S/Z*, Barthes reinvokes the differences between readerly and writerly texts (*texte lisible* and *texte scriptible*, respectively) to extend the figuration of body images he had noted earlier as composing the symbolic code. Going beyond vocal music, Barthes cites compositions for the piano by Beethoven and Schumann setting forth two musics — one of listening, the other of playing — each with its own history, erotics, sociology, and esthetic. He claims that standard histories of music have imposed a definitive image of "the Romantic Beethoven" as a composer of complex structural features. Consequently, he sees them as neglecting the physicality of playing which, for Barthes, persists only in the isolated *amateur* who makes no claim to the technical competence presumably required to interpret and execute the music correctly. Against this doctrine of mastery and the illusion of plenitude it confers on the expert, Barthes pits the *amateur* who plays lovingly and whose lack of expertise heightens the physicality of performance.

The *amateur* who operates a Beethoven score does not simply read or receive it passively. Performance as operation of the text involves structuring, displacing, and recombining its parts in what amounts to a process of rewriting such as that Barthes had seen in *The Pleasure of the Text* as imposed by modern ("writerly") texts: "Just as the reading of the modern text (such as it may be postulated) consists not in receiving, in knowing or in feeling that text, but in writing it anew, in crossing its writing with a fresh inscription, so too this reading Beethoven is *to operate* his music, to draw it (it is willing to be drawn) into an unknown *praxis*" (*IMT*, 153).

Musica practica is primarily a descriptive concept. Barthes makes no claims to serious musicology, using the concept instead to distinguish the idealist values of "soul" and "heart" personified in the standard image of romantic music from the interplay between tongue, hands, lips, nose, and legs he finds in the *amateur*'s performance. As a result, the "grain" of the voice is not at all the condensation via synecdoche of a unified whole, but the movement of various parts of the body toward utterance, what Benveniste terms *signifiance*. The convergence of the "grain" and *musica practica* clarifies the differences between conventional voice and the wider symbolic processes Barthes brings to the practice of music in performance and active reading as part of a figuration based on corporeal images. As an immediate consequence of figuration, voice is increasingly overdetermined, both as irreducible presence of the body and as figure of the process of *signifiance* evoked for Barthes in the musical notation *quasi parlando*. Which brings us back—almost full circle—to *Camera Lucida*, the photo of the winter garden, and Schumann's final compositions:

Quasi parlando (I take the indication from a Bagatelle by Beethoven): it is the movement of the body *which is going to speak*. This *quasi parlando* rules an enormous portion of Schumann's work; it extends far beyond vocal works (which can, ironically, have nothing at all to do with it); the instrument (the piano) speaks without meaning ["parle sans rien dire"] in the manner of a mute who has his face express all the inarticulable power of the word.[3]

The metaphor suggested by the expression *quasi parlando* extends the figuration set forth in the "grain" of the voice and *musica practica*. The piece of music is to be played *as if* spoken, with the phenomenon of voice no longer synonymous with vocality and thereby less a discrete entity linked to a reduced or condensed self than a quality of singing — "Comme cela chante!" The same quality also transcends the convention of vocal "families" in which bass, tenor, alto, and soprano designate the respective figures of father, son, mother, and daughter. After he claims the breakup of this Oedipalized voice in romantic song, Barthes again relates it to the illusions of plenitude at odds with his view of musical performance as an operation of the text: "It is precisely these four voice families that Romantic song, in a sense, *forgets:* it does not account for the sexual marks of voice, because the same song can be sung without difference by a man or a woman; no vocal 'family,' nothing but a human subject, *unisex* (one might say) in the sense that it is in love: because love — passionate, romantic love — accounts for neither gender nor social roles."[4]

The implied body of romantic song evoked as processes of *significance* and figuration is described by Barthes as that of a loss. Whether as performer or listener, the operator of romantic song sings the loss of totality brought on by the absence of the other, symbolized as a sense of self Barthes sees as asocial and internalized: "I address myself inwardly to an image, that of the loved one in which I lose myself and which sends back to me my own image, abandoned. The song supposes a rigorous address to the other, but that address is imaginary, enclosed in my deepest intimacy."[5] What *speaks* in this mode of address — and what illustrates the diction beyond vocality Barthes also finds in Schumann's *Kreisleriana* — is the declaration of irreparable loss and absence whose resulting images of a broken and incomplete self serve as the uncanny doubler of a former plenitude. Something akin to Lacan's mirror stage enters here, although Barthes appears less concerned with a decisive misapprehension than with an irreparable loss and its recurrence in the phantasm — *Fantasieren* is the appropriate German term — described as the incandescent kernel of romantic song.

Not merely expressions of nostalgia for a lost origin or plenitude, the *Lieder* by Schubert and Schumann are seen by Barthes as pointing to a symbolic activity that is ongoing and thus without a fixed object or end: "Even the song cycles recount no love story, but only a voyage whose every moment is turned back upon itself, blind, closed in every general sense to every notion of destiny, to every spiritual transcendence. In sum, it is a pure essence, a becoming without end: time as much as it can, from a single moment to infinity, start again."[6]

The truth sought in the photograph of the mother in the winter garden—present, heard, perhaps even visible in the values of brilliance linking the diffuse light of the winter garden to the dawn in Schumann's piece—is that of a death to come. The affective impact of the photo is akin to that of the *Gesänge der Frühe* in the sense that both evoke a staging Barthes describes as catastrophic and which appears to be a variant of dramatic irony. When Barthes sees the photograph of the winter garden or "operates" the Schumann piece as player or listener, he asserts a temporal advantage over the fate of what will have occurred, going so far as to specify this advantage as a dramatic aspect of the future anterior and illusion of stasis essential to the photographic image. Knowing that his mother has died or that the *Gesänge der Frühe* were composed shortly before Schumann's death, Barthes cannot stop himself from seeking the signs of future catastrophe, in full recognition that this particular pursuit of signs only heightens his affective attachment to the figures and process of figuration he comes to see.

Barthes's attraction to romantic *Lieder* as exemplary practice of figuration derives in large part from his decision to stage writing as an action (or "drama" in the Greek sense) combining disparate materials into an uneven and discontinuous process. Of importance is the quality of instability enhanced by the use of fragmentary forms and alphabetical orders to counteract the will to posit a whole or unified text. One way to specify this instability would be to perceive the text as a symbolic space or field of interaction whose totality is belied by the complexity of its components. When, in *The Theater and Its Double*, Artaud redefines dramatic space in the name of a physical and concrete language, he refers to the unexplored potentials of lighting, sound, and gesture to serve as bases of a staging removed from the conventional priority given to the text as origin or point of departure. The possibility of that future language is also the possibility of a future dramatic sign whose functions Artaud explored more as processes of staging than as finished product.

In the writings on voice, grain, and musicality, Barthes adopts a similar attitude toward the text as a field of interaction. As with Artaud's notes for staging cruelty in the theater, the interaction between a number of individual actions is deliberately dissonant and uneven, in clear opposition to integrations of the *Gesamtkunstwerk* and symbolist theater. In place of convergence and harmony, Barthes's writings sketch a musicality of dispersion and breaks, less a commentary on music or voice than a repeated assertion of their intensity and function within a drama of personal catastrophe. In *A Lover's Discourse*, the lover/narrator places under the *argumentum* of love's obscenity a memory from the Marx brothers' *A Night at the Opera* in which an incompetent tenor appears on stage and declares his love for the woman standing at his side. The narrator comments: "I am this tenor: like a huge animal, obscene and stupid, brightly lighted as in a shop window, I declaim an elaborately coded aria, without looking at the one I love, to whom I am supposed to be addressing myself" (*FDA*, 175).

The recalled image is doubly obscene: it exposes the emotion of the "very bad tenor" as that of an *amateur* whose public declaration also reveals his vocal inadequacies. It is also curious that the scene recalled by the lover/narrator sets the declaration against its object. Description of the utterance all but overshadows the loved one to whom the tenor is supposedly singing. What exactly is going on here? And what might an amateur tenor and details of displacement have to tell us about figuration, musicality, and Barthes? One way to deal with such questions would be to specify the individual writings whose diversity makes the resulting "text" irreducible to a single genre or even a consistent alternation between a fixed number of writings. While I have suggested that Barthes's evolution works against a critical practice removed from the more immediate intensities of writing as process, "Rasch" and "Le Chant romantique" in particular point to this evolution because they are no longer critical texts as such. They cannot be assimilated—except via difference—to a semiology of music such as that developed by Nicolas Ruwet or Jean-Jacques Nattiez in the wake of Saussure's *Course* and Barthes's 1964 "Elements of Semiology."

A second approach to the writings on music is biographic, recalling Barthes's voice lessons as a child as well as the numerous references in *Roland Barthes* and *A Lover's Discourse* to the physicality of singing as complement to the practices of writing and *signifiance*. For all the insistence on an antitheoretical stance, the writings on music imply a theoretical position in the status of the musical sign within the wider relationship between text and music. Where, for example, Barthes's 1962 review of Butor's *Mobile* invoked musicality as a structural principle of predetermined movement and repetition, he tends in the more recent texts to set musicality within a dramatic context of figuration, as in the fragment on love's obscenity analyzed above.

Finally, Barthes's choice of romantic song provides not merely a *topos* of writing but a narrative setting which seems to fulfill his growing predilection toward dramatic address and discursivity apparent from *The Pleasure of the Text* through *Camera Lucida*. Simply stated, romantic song invokes the very mode of figuration—fictional writing outside the novel—which frustrates those who no longer find it possible to "use" his later writings as they might have tried mistakenly to "use" *S/Z* to explicate or interpret Balzac's "Sarrasine." Figuration as a practice of writing subverts the distinction between so-called primary and secondary texts as the basis of critical writing as a metalanguage. The term is borrowed from logic and refers to the artificial language used to investigate an ostensible object of inquiry. In 1959, Barthes had already noted the fragility of attempts to distinguish between the two in the name of a literary criticism inevitably removed from literature "itself." By the time he writes *A Lover's Discourse* some twenty years later, that distinction and removal have disappeared: no metalanguage, no critical discourse *on* writing, literature, or love. In their place, writing and figuration as a text(ure) of polyvalence and as an affirmation of the materialist subject (as is said) . . . *in the text*.

To the degree that figuration works against the status of Barthes's practice as a critical writing predicated on a metalanguage distinct from its object of inquiry, it promotes the dramatic force Barthes finds in musicality and in the fragments of *A Lover's Discourse*. Removed from the illusion of mastery associated with his earlier critical projects, Barthes sets his writing into the very text of discourse; as with Benveniste, the use of language rather than its mere forms. For the world of romantic song is also that of the lover whose discourse of fragmented speech stages critical and theoretical questions in a blatantly dramatic mode of address: "These figures are not persons but little pictures, each of which is made out of a memory, a countryside, a walk, a mood, out of anything at all that points to a wound, a nostalgia, a happiness, a project, an anguish; in sum, a reverberation."

Love is, among other things, a discourse; that is, something written or spoken, cast into words and circulated. In this sense, love displays all the outward signs of a commonplace, so universal that its proliferation as a *topos* of recent critical thinking makes one wonder whether Lacan's *Encore*, Derrida's *Carte postale*, Foucault's *History of Sexuality*, or Barthes's *Discourse* can be saying anything new or different, anything we might not already know, sense, or live in the (real) world outside the text. In fact, the untimeliness of a recycled discourse on love is a decoy whose charm only heightens the subversion of a nostalgia we are hesitant to acknowledge but somehow willing to defend. Because it is such a commonplace, "love" as concept and discourse can reanimate the more tedious aspects of critical practice in the name of a revisionary attack on values we tend to protect over and above what we admit to. Because it is no longer possible—after Freud—to think about love unselfconsciously, love becomes a discourse, a battle of words to assert (or reassert) mastery over a *terrain vague* (no man's land) over which we have neither privilege nor right. Because language plays a vital role in love, the possibility of a discourse on love approaches its object as a possession disputed and fought over rather than shared. That battle over what goes by the name of love and in the name of love thus works to promote a dramatic function of discourse along the very lines set forth by Benveniste and followed in various ways by Lacan, Derrida, Foucault, and Barthes.

In letter 29 of *Les Liaisons dangereuses*, the young Cécile Volanges writes to her correspondent, Sophie Carnay, how Madame de Merteuil has agreed to tutor her in the preliminary lessons of love and courtship. Unsuspecting of what might motivate this offer of tutelage, Volanges is equally unaware that the education she is about to begin bears all the signs of an apprenticeship in rhetoric, dialectics, and stylistics: "Madame de Merteuil said too that she would lend me books which speak about all this and will teach me how to conduct myself and how to write better than I do; for, you see, she tells me all my faults, which is a proof of how much she loves me; she only advised me not to say anything to Mamma about these books because it would look as if she had neglected my education and that might make her angry. Oh! I shall say nothing to her about them."[8] If we limit the practical aspect of this projected sentimental education to what is described above, the use of language as discursive address—stated or withheld in order to reveal or dissimulate according to interlocutor, moment, and motive—acquires a strategic function that tempers emotion with calculation. Outstripping any concern to communicate is a more immediate objective of self-protection, seemingly at the expense of the other. As a statement addressed to an interlocutor, the letter from Volanges to Carnay is already an account at one remove from the statements it claims to report. And to the degree that these statements are accepted as serious—that is, at "face value" and without irony—they call for a closer analysis that questions the possibility of a "face value" while promoting a mode of reading patterned on the very strategy and calculation they attribute to discursive address. Taken seriously—as I believe they should be—the reported statements cannot serve as metastatements, cannot explain the "original" statements or be detached from them in any way whatsoever. At the very least, they reaffirm by demonstration that discursive address functions in amorous relations as a means of tactical confrontation.

Referring in *A Lover's Discourse* to letter 105 from the Marquise de Merteuil to Cécile Volanges, Barthes's lover/narrator finds only the signs of strategy and self-protection. From a theoretical discourse on love to epistolary narration, the transition toward dramatic address draws attention to the simulacra equated by Benveniste with *prosopa* and *personae*.[9] As a case in point, Laclos's 1782 novel stages discourse as a *liaison dangereuse* in which any statement serves a function of self-protection. As Barthes's lover/narrator observes, the Marquise is *not* in love and the address she forwards is merely a *correspondence*, "i.e., a tactical enterprise to defend positions, make conquests" (*FDA*, 158). In contrast to the *correspondence*, the lover/narrator affirms a *relation*, an address that is primarily expressive and that reveals its dependence on the other in the expectation of a reciprocal exchange of roles. As dramatic address, the love letter relies on the ambiguity tying *correspondence* and *relation* more closely than the lover/narrator suggests. In the terms of the Laclos novel, semantic ambiguity adds to any *liaison* the elements of risk, value, and danger which complicate the neat distinction suggested above. To the extent that it is forwarded in the expectation of a reciprocal address, amorous discourse is always calculated and tendentious. Yet because that tendentiousness also reveals vulnerability in its mode of address, it cannot be equated with the more masterful ploys of a seducer (*dragueur*).

The love letter is also a noteworthy instance of dramatic address because the interplay between correspondence and relation simulates the other as a variant of prosopopeia. In the *argumentum* of a fragment entitled "Love Letter," the lover/narrator reasserts the force of language capable of "staging" discourse and distributing the roles of lover and loved one as verbal constructs, nothing more or other than language. As the initial distinction between correspondence and relation collapses, so the use of language in dramatic address involves something more than the ostensible function of direct communication: "LETTER: This figure refers to the special dialectic of the love letter, both blank (encoded) and expressive (charged with longing to signify desire)" (*FDA*, 157). To the degree that it reiterates the encoded banalities that make its message impersonal and "empty," the love letter functions as tactical correspondence. Yet if we consider that this emptiness can also serve as the manifest element or signifier of a second sign system, the ambiguity and glibness of discreet address also function as litotes. This, in turn, remains consistent with the complexities of amorous discourse so long as litotes is the ploy of a strategy whose goal is more relation than correspondence. As a result, the artifice of a blatantly tactical model can simultaneously reveal and hide, making the danger of the *liaison dangereuse* into a semiological matter of knowing how to recognize the signs of love in their essential ambiguity. The more blatant the artifice, the more dramatically the address approaches a self-reflexive activity on the order of a wordly game of hide-and-seek: "The hiding must be seen: *I want you to know that I am hiding something from you*, that is an active paradox I must resolve: *at one and the same time*, it must be known and not known: I want you to know that I don't want to show my feelings; that is the message I address to the other. *Larvatus prodeo:* I advance pointing to my mask: I set a mask upon my passion, but with a discreet (and wily) finger I designate this mask" (*FDA*, 42–43; see also *DZE*, 40).

The Latin expression is a motto of Descartes cited by Barthes as a gesture of self-reflexivity and an early instance of figuration. The reference also reminds us that amorous discourse involves both word and image. When the lover/narrator uses the term relation to designate the exchange of roles between lover and loved one, he invokes a category of intersubjectivity studied by Jacques Lacan as the various links between the Imaginary, the Symbolic, and the Real.[10] Beyond playful references to the mirror stage in the *Roland Barthes* and *A Lover's Discourse*, substantive ties between Barthes and Lacan go back at least as far as *S/Z* and a "politics of the Imaginary" that emerged in France in the wake of events in the spring and summer of 1968.[11] At the same time, Lacan is undeniably a contemporary and critic of Sartre with a similar concern for questions of existence, being, and value. When Barthes invokes categories of the Symbolic and Imaginary, we need also to recall that the culmination of the analytic process as Lacan sees it is, in fact, never achieved: "The point toward which the progress of analysis moves, the extreme point of the dialectic of existential recognition is, *'You are this.'* This ideal is, in fact, never attained."[12] This sounds very much like Sartre's claim in *Being and Nothingness* that reciprocity between individuals is impossible because of an irrevocable discrepancy between the modes of being he terms "for-itself" and "in-itself."

But where Sartre locates the source of interpersonal conflict in an ontology of fixed images of self and other, Lacan studies the relation to the image as part of the insertion of the subject into language and discourse. The clinical context thus stages discourse of a different sort, touching on Sartre's existential psychoanalysis only in the common topics of conflict, identity, and being. For Lacan, the ongoing problem of the self—often termed the "problematics of the subject"—is that of its insertion into symbolic systems it posits and encounters as the "real" world. The trouble with this "real" world is that it comes to be seen as a series of traps or illusions complicating any notion of reality with the additional orders Lacan terms the Imaginary and the Symbolic. Adding his own inquiry into the processes of meaning to Sartre's exploration of being, Lacan recasts the problem of the subject as that of knowing what, if anything (or any thing) at all, is designated by the use of language by he or she who says "I." Because the use of the first person singular directs language toward others, any sense of self invariably confronts discourse as a basic mode of intersubjectivity. As an intense staging of that mode, love is caught up in the problem of the subject as the exchange of language and symbols which, for Lacan, is designated by the very term of relation used in *A Lover's Discourse*:

Love is caught up and stuck in this imaginary intersubjectivity on which to focus your attention. In its developed form, it requires participation in the register of the symbolic, free exchange embodied in utterance. A zone is built up where one can see areas of identification, as we say in our often imprecise language, and an entire scale of subtleties, a web of forms between the Imaginary and the Symbolic.[13]

For both Lacan and the lover/narrator of *A Lover's Discourse*, the amorous relation occurs in language as a dialogue ideally predicated on exchange and mobility of roles. At the same time, the spatial values suggested by the terms register, zone, scale, areas, and web limit such interactions to something inherent in language. In this sense, the spatial vocabulary employed by Lacan again points to the metaphoric equivalence of *prosopa, personae,* and figurations in Benveniste's 1946 article. Where Lacan alludes to the paradoxes and illusions of amorous discourse in terms of ties or bonds of an imaginary intersubjectivity, Benveniste approaches them as language used pragmatically. Unsatisfied with the attempts to account for the self via questions of being, Benveniste limits his comments to the differences between ideal conditions and the more specific uses he describes as instances of discourse. Sense of self, he writes, is experienced mainly as the differences of "person" projected by the first-person singular. As Benveniste quips, whoever says "ego" is "ego," which also suggests that the abstract notion of dialogue posits a polarity between "I" and "you" that is seldom reciprocal in pragmatic usage: "This polarity does not mean either equality or symmetry: 'ego' always has a position of transcendence with regard to *you.* Nevertheless, neither of the terms can be conceived of without the other; they are complementary, although according to an 'interior/exterior' opposition, and, at the same time, they are reversible."[14] As Benveniste concludes, the lack of a parallel or equivalent to this opposition in other forms of communication underlines the unique condition of human language.

Playing on what is implied in Benveniste's studies, Barthes writes the amorous address of *A Lover's Discourse* to heighten textual and thematic effects by the very differences between linguistic forms and figuration. Within what Benveniste calls the mechanism of utterance, the loved one is not simply a silent figure in the text. The detail is important, for the figures in question are those of the lover/narrator who addresses the other fully aware that the onesidedness of the discourse would overwhelm the loved one were it not given in expectation of a future address in kind: "Whence the cruel paradox of the dedication: I seek at all costs to give you what smothers you" (*FDA,* 79). The loved one present in the amorous discourse is neither figure nor fetish, but the product of a discursive force which, following Benveniste's studies, is irreducible to the standard categories of linguistic analysis. Because he sees that irreducibility in its potential for dramatic expression, Barthes also succeeds in drawing the reader into the discursive relation via the structures of desire he describes at the start of *The Pleasure of the Text.* By affirming a discourse of love over and against purely theoretical considerations, the lover/narrator addresses an other whose function—the absent/present quality of the *prosopa*—implicates the reader within a process of progressive identification. Because that identification derives from both the structure and use of language described by Benveniste, the amorous discourse acquires completion as it is directed toward a reader who is a double or supplement, as an effect of the onesidedness of the lover/narrator's address. Were *A Lover's Discourse* simply a variant of fictional narrative, that completion would fall well within the scope of epistolary writing. Yet since a theoretical question also animates *A Lover's Discourse*, the complication of fictional and critical writings leaves its specific mode of address as something other than suitable to straightforward analysis by genre. And therein the displacement Barthes uses to stage the implied absence/presence of the reader as supplement to the *prosopa*, an effect combining theory and practice in a demonstration occurring and intelligible fully *in the text*.

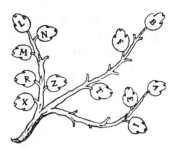

The alphabet is a useful system for manual retrieval of stored information and a useful memory device. Anything that has been named or can be placed in a category can be alphabetized. The alphabet assumes spoken language and is the basic code for written language, although in English phoneticism is chaotic.

John Perrault

CHAPTER FIVE

Alphabetese

The progression from theory to figuration covers a period in Barthes's itinerary which can also be approached by looking more closely into the process and materials of writing. What might be the discourse of a frustrated artist? It is almost as if in order to write, Barthes has had to repress a predilection for graphic and plastic invention. When the Casino dell'Aurora in Rome held an exhibit of Barthes's painting and sketches in early 1981,[1] it was the culmination of a creative activity Barthes acknowledged openly in the interplay between word and image evident throughout the photos, sketches, and fragments of the *Roland Barthes*. When he admits in that text that he cannot help but *see* language where others might simply hear it, we really ought to take his statement literally, or, as the French say, *à la lettre*. In a sense both literal and figurative, Barthes is *pris aux lettres;* that is, "taken" with letters as one is smitten or infatuated. The initial point of reference for Barthes's attitude toward the physicality of writing is the distinction set forth in *Writing Degree Zero* between literature and writing(s). When Barthes describes the isolation of the writer in front of the virgin sheet of paper, the historical context of that isolation yields to a staging and decor of the act itself recalling the personal setting of Mallarmé's "Brise marine."

From the early model of literary practice as a social language set forth in *Writing Degree Zero* and the *Mythologies*, Barthes's inquiry into writing develops toward the setting of literary practice within social and historical categories. Through the mid-1960s, the linguistic model used to characterize writing continues to function as a critical tool used to expose the historicity of literary institutions. *On Racine* (1963) is, in part, an attempt to disentangle the tragedies of Jean Racine from what has been written about them in the name of literary tradition. Taking pains to polemicize this issue, Barthes goes to great lengths in order to show how a modern understanding of the plays—what he describes as their intelligibility and meaning *for us*—needs to be distinguished from a history of critical writing which has paralyzed their specificity in the name of a timeless classicism. Beyond the polemics against Picard and other academic scholars, Barthes's characterization of literary conventions as a social practice inscribed within history adds a moral dimension to the linguistic model. In *Système de la mode* (1967), the model takes on an added significance when Barthes studies fashion in clothing design. As in the book on Racine, what Barthes explores in *Système de la mode* consists less of the material objects of fashion clothing than the ways they are verbalized and *written* as cultural signs. For Lucette Finas, the resulting object of inquiry as a cultural system is a hybrid located between words and things: "The object of analysis is feminine clothing as fashion magazines describe it. . . . True fashion clothing does not exist, in fact, without the word [*parole*] which institutes it."[2] By probing the metaphoric equivalence between word and garment, Barthes is able to study fashion as an ongoing process where the garment participates in a collective activity dictated by changing norms commonly known as "taste."

Barthes's 1970 text on the alphabet composed by fashion designer Romain de Tirtoff (better known under the pseudonym of Erté) seems very much to follow up the context and argument of *Système de la mode*.

The linguistic model is still in full force as Barthes explores the language of fashion by transposing onto it the vocabulary and emphasis of Saussure's *Course in General Linguistics*. What distinguishes the *Erté* from Barthes's other studies in semiology is the choice of a sign system that literally incorporates characters—dramatic as well as alphabetical—as the signifying units of a sign system "composed of elaborate silhouettes of female figures draped in flowing outfits" (*E*, 22). As they appear in Erté's alphabet, these figures—neither letters nor women in a stable sense—furnish Barthes with another example of the ambiguity and polyvalence he had explored in *S/Z*. To be sure, the mixture of eros and misapprehension in Balzac's "Sarrasine" may well fascinate Barthes for personal reasons. Unlike the figures of Erté's alphabet, the object of desire in "Sarrasine" turns out to be something more (or less) than a *femme fatale*.

The ambiguity explored in the *Erté* is that of letters which can be joined to compose either words or alphabets. Following the Danish linguist Hjelmslev, Barthes treats each letter as a *figura*, Hjelmslev's term for the minimal elements—without meaning or individual content—which articulate a theoretical language via combination. Barthes's reading of the alphabet is suitably twofold. Primarily, he wants to describe the production of meaning in a sign system whose discrete functional units are both letter and female figure. But rather than isolating a dominant factor from the two possibilities, Barthes shows how alternation and ambiguity are essential to the production of meaning. The adaptation of a linguistic model should not be misconstrued as a direct appropriation of analytic tools in the name of a scientific project. Barthes has never viewed his writings as value-free or devoid of ideology. When, for example, he describes Erté's alphabet as a closed system of signification, he adds that it is pervaded by an underlying mythology of Woman whose historicity he emphasizes by treating it as a kind of narrative written sketch by sketch, letter by letter. Near the start of his commentary, Barthes writes that the coherence of the alphabet is dependent on the image of Woman as a cultural sign designating femininity in a specific time and place. Each letter functions as a morpheme, a minimal unit of grammar allowing us "to speak that period" (*E*, 22). In this semiological function, Erté's female figures are inscribed within systems of social exchange perpetuated by an ability to disentangle the female body from the sequence of letters forming the sign system.

The coherence of the female sign/figure is possible only on the condition that the body is sacrificed to writing. The uniqueness of the individual body is reduced to stereotypes which, in turn, point to the violence inherent in this cultural phenomenon. Even in a strict philological sense, the concept of writing preserves in European and Semitic cultures its early sense of incising or marking with a pointed instrument.[3] As Barthes sees it, the sacrifice of the body to writing occurs in one of two possible forms: either as the fetishistic cutting of a single part from the whole, or as the reductive movement of a three-dimensional body to a two-dimensional silhouette.

Neither body nor dress, Erté's silhouettes impose a new relationship in which body and dress become a composite sign capable of multiple (and unstable) readings. From the side of the letter, Erté's figures inscribe the human body into an updated chimera: the mythological creature made up of animal and human forms. From the side of the female body, Erté's gynecography inscribes the body into a system of cultural innovation in dress which Barthes approaches via reference to Saussure. In the *Course in General Linguistics*, Saussure sets forth the program for a future inquiry into social activities to be studied in terms of exchange:

A science that studies the life of signs within society is conceivable; it would be part of social psychology and consequently of general psychology; I shall call it *semiology* (from the Greek *semeion*, "sign"). Semiology would show what constitutes signs, what laws govern them. Since the science does not yet exist, no one can say what it would be; but it has a right to existence, a place staked out in advance. Linguistics is only a part of the general science of semiology; the laws discovered by semiology will be applicable to linguistics, and the latter will circumscribe a well-defined area within the mass of anthropological facts.[4]

The initial conception of semiology is based on a future expansion of linguistics to incorporate social signs in terms of what has since come to be seen—by Culler, Jameson, Hawkes, Pettit, and others—as the linguistic model. And particularly because of the various ways the expanded linguistic model has been interpreted since Saussure, it is worth recalling that its original formulation projected scientific values and methods Barthes initially upholds but later rejects. Here is the initial statement from the 1916 *Course:* "If we are to discover the true natures of language we must learn what it has in common with all other semiological systems. . . . By studying rites, customs, etc. as signs, I believe that we shall throw new light on the facts and point up the need for including them in a science of semiology and explaining them by its laws."[5]

To see the alphabet as an autonomous signifying system requires an extension of Saussure's semiology to what has been described as a third-order system in which the direct and stable communication in first-order systems such as traffic lights and semaphore and Morse codes yields to social practices with highly refined sets of distinctions. The problems encountered by the semiologist who contends with social practices concern their indirect and often unstable modes of production via connotation. We all agree without question that choices in clothing, food, or cars can be motivated by a desire to communicate, even though we may not always be able to specify that communication in detail. Thus the semiologist examines daily life as a process in which an infinite amount of data takes on intelligible form: "The task of the semiologist in dealing with clothing, commercial objects, pastimes, and all other social entities, is to make explicit meanings they seem to bear and to reconstruct the system of connotations on which these meanings are based."[6]

After the social critiques set forth in *Writing Degree Zero* and the *Mythologies*, the *Erté* combines a study of how connotation works in the third-order sign system of fashion design with a more pointed approach to its historicity. Some fifteen years after the *Mythologies*, Barthes's adaptation of Saussure's semiology bends the linguistic model toward questions of ideology and representation: the breaking up or semioclasm he describes as a personal reaction to the breakup of social institutions in the spring and summer of 1968. While it may prove convenient to tie this revised semiology to political events, there is also evidence to support an orientation toward questions of ideology integral to Barthes's practice. For as early as *Système de la mode*—published in 1967 but undertaken some ten years earlier as a *Doctorat d'Etat* thesis Barthes never completed—the reappraisal of Saussure's *Course* inverts the original relationship between linguistics and semiology:

It is therefore necessary to overturn Saussure's definition and affirm that semiology is part of linguistics; the essential function of this work is to suggest that, in a society such as ours where myths and rituals have acquired the form of an explanatory principle and meaning definitively that of an utterance, human language is not merely the model of meaning, but its grounding.[7]

In his preface to the 1970 re-edition of the *Mythologies*, Barthes describes in retrospect the project undertaken some fifteen years earlier as an ideological critique of the *language* of French mass culture and a dismantling of its system: "I had just read Saussure and taken from that reading a conviction that by dealing with 'collective representations' such as sign systems, one might hope to go beyond pious denunciation and account *in detail* for the mystification that transforms lower middle-class culture into a universal nature." By 1970 it was no longer possible for Barthes to separate the linguistic model he had developed from the ideological critique he was compelled to follow through: "What remains, beyond our capital enemy (the middle-class Norm), is the necessary conjunction of the twin gestures: no denunciation without its instrument of fine analysis, no semiology which cannot, in the last analysis, be acknowledged as *semioclasm*" (*M*, 9).

The movement from semiology to semioclasm is evident in the *Erté* in the emphasis on the means and objects of representation. Those who might see Erté's alphabet as an exploitation of the female body ought not to confuse Barthes's choice of a semiological system with his inquiry into what makes that system coherent and intelligible: "The meaningful point of departure, in Erté, is not Woman (she becomes nothing, except her own coiffure; she is simply the cipher of mythic femininity): it is the Letter" (*E*, 40). Barthes is certainly something less (or other) than a feminist; yet his observation that violence to the female body is a necessary condition for the existence of this particular alphabet helps clarify the differences between cultural and biological femininity such as those at work in *S/Z*. Having shown how the alphabet inscribes the female body into a system of social exchange, Barthes wants also to explore it as the separate but related cultural system of alphabetism. Displacing his inquiry momentarily from the feminine problematic, he turns to the status of the (alphabetic) letter in Christian societies which see it traditionally as secondary to the spirit: "For a long time, following a famous aphorism in the gospels, the Letter, which kills, has been opposed to the Spirit, which gives life" (*E*, 40). The reference to the Christian *Logos* as expression of an orthodoxy is suitably ironic, because Barthes wants to argue *para*doxically; that is, against the convention of correct interpretation that raises popular opinion (or *doxa* in the Greek) to the status of truth. As in the *Mythologies*, Barthes wants to expose the illusion of fabricated and historical values at work in the means of representation a society uses to assert a collective identity. But where the *Mythologies* set denunciation within the terms of a linguistic model, the *Erté* furnishes a revised model capable of executing a critique without the illusion of historical or ideological detachment. Unlike the progression from *Writing Degree Zero* to the *Mythologies*, where Barthes is unable to set vision and method into effective combination, the *Erté* executes its stated critique in the very process of deploying its linguistic model in the name of semioclasm.

The felicitous convergence of vision, method, and writing in the *Erté* has a number of possible causes. Coming after the 1966–70 period of transition away from structural analysis and toward another semiotics, the *Erté* illustrates a self-reflexive quality that is keenly present in *S/Z* and *L'Empire des signes* as a corrective to the values of a scientism Barthes could no longer defend. The change in critical practice is not merely a consequence of Barthes's personal evolution. For Gérard Genette and Tzvetan Todorov—both of whom collaborated on the 1966 *Communications* no. 8 for which Barthes wrote the "Introduction to the Structural Analysis of Narratives"—a similar reassessment of the structuralist project led to a necessary split between an all-encompassing science of literature and the analysis of individual texts. In addition, the scope of Barthes's approach to the alphabet and letter in the *Erté* complements what Derrida describes in *Of Grammatology* as the metaphysics of presence peculiar to Western philosophy since Plato. When Barthes argues in the *Erté* for a return to the letter, his concern for the relation between its specific materiality and the cultural phenomenon of the Christian Letter supports the critique set forth by Derrida against the subordination of the written word to utterance. What Barthes finds in the Derridean position of the late 1960s (and what motivates his references to Derrida in the *Erté*) is the impact of the bias against writing on writing and the letter. In this sense, *Of Grammatology* works in conjunction with the *Erté* to correct this bias by affirming the qualities which make the letter a "creature of writing" resplendent in its graphic materiality, "an irreducible ideal element, linked with mankind's most profound experiences" (*E*, 42).

Barthes adapts the Derridean position in *Of Grammatology* to his immediate concern with Erté by showing the inherent contradictions and paradoxes within the alphabet as a cultural phenomenon. Where the letter functions traditionally in Western alphabets both as phonetic and graphic entity, Barthes finds the reemergence in Erté's alphabet of a more primitive state in which the letter is removed from the larger semantic units of word and sentence. Where Barthes's semioclasm breaks apart signs, so he sees Erté's approach to the letter as breaking apart the word: "He dismisses the word: who could feel like writing a word with Erté's letter?" (*E*, 48).

If Erté's letters do not write words, what other functions might they serve? In a review of Massin's *La Lettre et l'image*, Barthes provides an answer to this question that supports the semioclastic approach toward alphabetism in the *Erté*. Massin is art director at the Editions Gallimard in Paris and well known for his design of book covers and calligraphy. His compendium of the written letter in various Western contexts offers Barthes additional evidence of graphic materiality as a sign system removed from phoneticism. Like Barthes, Massin is fascinated by those material qualities of the written letter that promote self-reference and imagery, what Barthes describes as a second (or "shadow") writing at work in the endless profusion of written symbols. As seen by Barthes, this second dimension of writing noted by Massin is part of a symbolic process, product of a metaphoric bond between letter and body similar to that which he had admired in the Erté alphabet:

The second object of meditation (and not the least important) raised by Massin's book is the metaphor. These twenty-six letters of our alphabet, animated, as Massin says, by hundreds of artists from every century, are placed in a metaphoric relationship with something *other* than the letter: animals (birds, fish, snakes, rabbits, some occasionally eating the others in order to form a *D*, *E*, *K*, *I*, etc.), men (silhouettes, numbers, postures), vegetation (flowers, shoots, trunks), instruments (scissors, serpes, sickles, glasses, tripods, etc.), a whole catalogue of natural and human products comes to double the short list of the alphabet; the entire world is incorporated in the letter (is literally incorporated), the letter becomes an image in the carpet of the world.[8]

The lengthy enumeration Barthes allows himself in the preceding passage is justified by the metaphoric and allusive gestures associated by Massin with the symbolic function of the letter. On the basis of this excess of graphic and symbolic profusion, Massin asserts against the Saussurian conception of the sign as interplay between acoustic image and concept a material letter almost wholly independent of phonetic qualities. When, for example, Barthes sees the letter as "an image in the carpet of the world," the expression invokes a primary association to the Henry James narrative of the same title. Furthermore, the role of interpretation in the James text illustrates symbolic representation as a process of writing, supporting Barthes's view that Massin's thesis in *La Lettre et l'image* is to affirm the materiality of the written sign as a meaningful entity irreducible to semantic or phonetic functions.

Barthes's choice of Erté's alphabet supports what I have described as his increased sensitivity to the material and figurative qualities of writing. The choice also reflects the function of alphabetical ordering in Barthes's own writings. For some readers, alphabetical ordering is ornamental, a side effect of his addiction to fragmentary modes of expression evident since *S/Z* and *The Pleasure of the Text*. A closer look at the entire *corpus* shows a predilection for the fragment as early as *Writing Degree Zero* and the early text on Gide's journals, written in 1942 while Barthes was in the sanatorium at Leysin. Because alphabetism gains in complexity through the period marked by *The Pleasure of the Text*, the *Roland Barthes*, and *A Lover's Discourse*, a number of points suggest a more substantive function for the letter and the alphabet.

In "Les Sorties du texte," delivered at the 1972 Artaud/Bataille conference at Cerisy-la-Salle, Barthes characterized alphabetical ordering as simultaneous order and disorder, the zero-degree of order. In view of the semioclastic attitude adopted in the *Erté*, alphabetical ordering works against the claims to truth associated with systematic processes. The artifice of alphabetical ordering detaches representation from its content much along the lines of the *Mythologies*. By 1970, however, the pursuit of ideology within sign systems becomes self-reflexive. It includes a critique of the practices and presuppositions of structural analysis such as those Barthes had supported through the mid-1960s. A more personal factor to be considered is the example of alphabetical ordering in the *Dictionary of Received Ideas*, the posthumous supplement to Gustave Flaubert's *Bouvard et Pécuchet* for which Barthes repeatedly stated his admiration.

In the spirit of the discourse on stupidity (*bêtise*) essential to these two Flaubert texts, the relation of alphabetical ordering to semioclasm would promote a new cultural "language" to be called alphabetese — or, homonymically, *alpha-bêtise* ("prime foolishness"). The *Dictionary of Received Ideas* is a compendium of cliches and platitudes which turns the quest for a reassuring and encyclopedic knowledge into an endless superficiality meant to question the systematic ordering of experience. The trite aphorisms and flippant bits of popular wisdom are a parody of universal knowledge set into alphabetical order. Its internal inconsistencies preclude any serious (unironic) reading of the text. As Barthes states in a 1975 interview on Flaubert, the book's share of *bêtise* is located as much in its alphabetical order as in the vacuousness of its banalized knowledge:

The encyclopedias of the 18th, 19th and even 20th centuries are encyclopedias of knowledge or knowledges. In the midst of this history is Flaubert's moment, the moment of *Bouvard et Pécuchet* which is that of farce. The *Encyclopédie* becomes an object of derision. But this farce is accompanied by something quite serious; the encyclopedias of knowledge are succeeded by encyclopedias of language. What Flaubert records and marks down in *Bouvard et Pécuchet* is languages.[9]

If, as Barthes maintains in the *Erté*, the desire to order and contain knowledge fails because it is predicated on the *spirit* of the letter and a bias against the word and in favor of the concept, one might look at Flaubert's *Dictionary* to free the word from its concept in order to account for its materiality. That is, approach the body of the letter rather than its spirit.

In the gesture of acknowledging the materiality of writing in any account of concept or system, Flaubert's *Dictionary* offers an antecedent illustration of semioclasm as a cultural practice. In order to move from semioclasm to figuration, the inquiry into the materiality of writing returns again to the letter. And here the antecedent is anything but modern. The *Champ Fleury* (1529) by Geoffroy Tory is a Renaissance guide: a definitive treatise on the art and science of calligraphy based on the human body and face as models for the "proper and true" proportions of letters. In the *Champ Fleury*, Tory subjects the letter to the figure of exchange and reversibility known as metalepsis. In short, he suggests by metaphor that the body of the letter is also the letter of the body. In our own culture, the return to the letter from the side of the body has been explored—probed and questioned rather than understood—by Freud and his various interpreters. For Barthes psychoanalysis is incarnated by Lacan, whose views in the following passage complement those of Barthes in the *Erté*:

Of course, as it is said, the letter killeth while the spirit giveth life. We can't help but agree, having had to pay homage elsewhere to a noble victim of the error of seeking the spirit of the letter, but we should like to know, also, how the spirit could live without the letter. Even so, the claims of the spirit would remain unassailable if the letter had not in fact shown us that it can produce the effects of truth in man without involving the spirit at all.[10]

The link between the spirit and the body of the letter is likely to be sought in what Lacan refers to above as the effects of its own truths, what Barthes describes in the texts on Erté and Massin as its symbolic function. Toward the end of the *Erté*, Barthes returns to the alphabetical figure to elucidate the extent of this function in terms that prophesy the final stage in his own writings. Commenting on the letter *T*, he distinguishes between its literal and symbolic functions, neglecting its phonetic potential in order to emphasize the specificity of its graphic materiality: "Where the literal alphabet says: *the arms in a cross*, Erté's symbolic alphabet says: *the arms offered*, in a gesture both modest and inviting" (*E*, 54). The interplay between literal and symbolic functions follows that between woman and letter necessary to the alphabet's coherence as cultural language. As in *S/Z* and *The Pleasure of the Text*, the collapse of the terms of an ostensible binary works against the kind of formalist practice essential to structural analysis derived from Saussure's *Course* and the studies on kinship and social exchange by Lévi-Strauss. By the time he writes the *Erté*, Barthes no longer sees the collapse of the binary structure as a shortcoming to be deleted in a future theory of greater refinement. Instead he seems to have withdrawn from formal analysis in favor of a more dynamic reading in which meaning is produced through alternation and perceived difference. Where semantics can scan a single word with a determinate number of stable meanings, Barthes seeks to set overdetermined meaning into a continual movement to supplement double hearing with double vision: "You perceive, as you choose, the woman or the letter and, secondarily, the composition of the one or the other" (*E*, 54). Where double hearing casts the excess of meaning within the metaphysics of presence and the spoken word, double vision accounts for the materiality of the written letter within the ongoing process of symbolic activity that evolves toward figuration in *A Lover's Discourse* and *Camera Lucida*.

Barthes ends his reading of Erté's alphabet by commenting on the letters *S* and *Z*, the pair whose cleaving—simultaneous contact and distance—also serves as a key to his reading of "Sarrasine." As in the Balzac novella, the end of the narrative projects a symbolism of defeat and death onto the figure of the Roman alphabet's last letter. The term of the alphabet becomes the term of life: "Is *Z* not an inverted, angular *S*, a denied *S*, in short? For Erté, *Z* is the mournful letter, crepuscular, veiled, bluish, in which woman expresses both her submission and her supplication" (*E*, 68). But unlike alphabetical order as we know it, *Z* is not quite the end. What follows it in Barthes's text is the letter *M*, which, since he describes it as the only non-anthropomorphic letter in the Erté alphabet, becomes the inhuman letter of death. The terminal function of *M* in the *Erté* points to a detail taken up by the lover/ narrator in *A Lover's Discourse* in what looks very much to be a belated gesture of framing or enclosure. Alluding to the Hasidic legend of the golem, Barthes suggests that the ultimate truth of life's completion in death can be contained in a simple letter: "The truth is what, being taken away, leaves nothing to be seen but death (as we say: life is no longer worth living). Thus with the name of the Golem: *Emeth* (Truth); take one letter away and he becomes *Meth* (he is dead)" (*FDA*, 230).

The symbolic profusion of death associated in the *Erté* and *A Lover's Discourse* with alphabetical ordering testifies to the fallibility of systematic knowledge. It dramatizes the self-reflexive practice Barthes had undertaken in the wake of his move away from scientism between 1966 and 1970. The force of that move as a rejection of structural analysis as a literary science is active at the level of concept and polemic in the *Erté*. Both subject and method mobilize a linguistic model revised in the name of ideology and a critique of representation. But in retrospect, the *Erté* also marks a distinct progression toward active figuration, a progression whose ultimate form as harbinger of death in *A Lover's Discourse* and *Camera Lucida* suggests a personal recognition scene beyond any kind of theoretical inquiry.

III. Notes on Teaching

Photograph by Arthur W. Wang

What follows depends on the
idea that there is a fundamental tie
between teaching and speech.

Barthes,
"Writers, Intellectuals, Teachers"

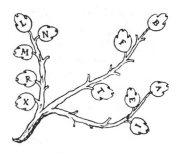

CHAPTER SIX

Classroom Struggles

The current vogue of the term "pluralism" in
critical debate refers to the issue of valid versus
open interpretation that invariably pits the
values of the American New Critics against the
specter of a foreign ("continental") practice. Because of the notoriety surrounding his mid-1960s
polemic in defense of the French *nouvelle critique*,
Barthes tends to be cast in the role of a devil's
advocate who supports modernity in the face of
traditional institutions (*la critique universitaire*)
represented by Raymond Picard. Even though
this outdated portrait is still invoked in some
quarters, Barthes's evolution acquires an exemplary status for American students of French
literature and ideas because of the cultural blind-

ness it exposes. When we read Barthes and evaluate his writings from the perspective of American institutions, the tendency to distort or misunderstand can all too easily become self-serving. In this sense, Barthes has always located his writings within institutional contexts that relate literary activities to the human and social sciences. The *Mythologies* draws from the sociology of Emile Durkheim and Marcel Mauss as well as from the studies of kinship by Lévi-Strauss and Freud.

Barthes's early emphasis on the popular myths of French culture evolves after the *Mythologies* toward the use of a linguistic model for the close reading of literary and social texts. As an extended application of that model, the *Système de la mode* is disappointing, a temporary dead-end whose imbalance between theory and practice obscures its contribution to Barthes's eventual move beyond a primitive semiology. For many readers, that move is not intelligible until 1973 and *The Pleasure of the Text*. The immediate differences are striking: a concise, almost lapidary writing set in fragments that set breaks and blank spaces against the ploys of system and order. What happened? This "new" Barthes displays none of the aridity and little of the contentiousness of the mid-1960s. A retrospective reading of *S/Z*, *L'Empire des signes*, and *Sade, Fourier, Loyola* clarifies the interim and the move away from structural analysis toward what Barthes had referred to in the "Introduction to the Structural Analysis of Narratives" as *une sémiotique autre*. What Barthes writes in the wake of his break with the scientific project is no longer criticism in the traditional sense of description, analysis, evaluation, and interpretation, but something closer to a personal narrative organized as a diffuse account of the reading experience.

The appearance of the "new" Barthes of the early 1970s leads to a number of problems for readers of a pragmatic bias. One could no longer "do things" with his writings as one might have before. In terms of a distinction Barthes first sets forth in 1959, his writings after *S/Z* function less as critical commentaries on primary objects of literature than as primary objects in their own right. Which is to assert that the earlier distinction had become ineffectual to the point where Barthes states outright in *A Lover's Discourse* that he no longer believes in a metalanguage removed from its ostensible object.[1]

With the rules of Barthes's game thus changed—in keeping with Saussure's contention that language as an abstract notion is in constant flux—the prospect of a university seminar *on* Barthes led to very real problems concerning the implications of his evolution for a wider understanding of his *corpus*. My decision as organizer of the seminar was to relate that evolution to the various projects undertaken by structural and formalist critics since 1950 in order to trace how Barthes supports, extends, and ultimately retreats from a science of literature.

In a contribution to a 1971 issue of *Tel Quel* devoted to his writings, Barthes examines the pedagogical dimension of critical thinking by studying the status of the professor who alternates between spoken and written discourses. Those who associate this division with Derrida's argument against logocentrism might be struck that Barthes should be drawn to speech rather than to writing. In this case, however, Barthes is less of an anti-Derrida than a closet existentialist who is still responding to the social role of the intellectual Sartre had sketched in *What Is Literature?*: "Over against the teacher, who is on the side of speech, let us call a *writer* every operator of language on the side of writing; between the two, the intellectual, the person who prints and publishes his speech. Between the language of the teacher and that of the intellectual there is hardly any incompatibility (they often co-exist in a single individual); but the writer stands apart, separate" (*IMT*, 190).

As a writer who is also a teacher, Barthes is aware of the limitations writing and speech impose on utterance. Whoever prepares to speak as a teacher, he notes, confronts inevitably the constraints of physical performance akin to those of a stage actor whose *persona* is none other than that of an actor on stage. (Once again, Barthes draws his comparison from Sartre and the notion of role playing set forth in *Being and Nothingness* as a model for dealing with real-life situations.) For Barthes, the professional risks of the teacher's performance are those that many of us encounter daily: "Speech is irreversible: a word cannot be *retracted*, except precisely by saying that one retracts it. To cross out is here to add: if I want to erase what I have just said, I cannot do it without showing the eraser itself (I must say: '*or rather . . .*' '*I expressed myself badly*'); paradoxically, it is ephemeral speech which is indelible, not monumental writing. All that one can do in the case of a spoken utterance is to tack on another utterance" (*IMT*, 190).

But if the physical performance of the professor entails an inevitable degree of vulnerability—as possible *faux pas, gaffes,* or botched delivery—a number of benefits are also received as part of the implicit relation setting his actions within an institutional guarantee. A professor speaks for the institution of learning and the implied values that support the mutual recognition of "teachers" and "students" in a pedagogical context. The fact that this relationship is relative—Barthes describes it as imaginary—does little to undo the roles and relations which it promotes. Even if the professor tries to subvert his *persona* by adopting a liberal attitude and speaking "badly" or refusing to abide by convention, his or her gesture only reaffirms the stability of an educational institution capable of assimilating the exception as minor and ineffectual. In this case, the liberal exception only confirms the rule by assimilating the individual within a second constraint from which Barthes sees no simple release: "Conscientious functionary or free artist, the teacher escapes neither the theatre of speech nor the Law played out on its stage: the Law appears *not in what is said but in the very fact of speech*" (*IMT*, 192). Between writer, intellectual, and teacher, Barthes is foremost a writer who looks for the hidden links between literary and social institutions he describes in *Writing Degree Zero* as the morality of form known as writing.

Commenting in *Writing Degree Zero* on the limitations imposed on the writer who supports the exercise of political power, he notes the attempt in Marxist writing to achieve a uniform language whose claim to function as a tool of explanation and knowledge does not hide its dependence on a pre-existent system of values outside of language: "In the Stalinist world, in which *definition*, that is to say the separation between Good and Evil, becomes the sole content of all language, there are no more words without values attached to them, so that finally the function of writing is to cut out one stage of a process: there is no more lapse of time between naming and judging, and the closed character of language is perfected, since in the last analysis it is a value which is given as an explanation of another value" (*WDZ*, 24). In reaction to any values that do not allow for deviation from an absolute norm, Barthes argues that the expansion of social institutions since the middle of the nineteenth century has produced a new writer (*scripteur*) whom he situates between the militant who does *not* write and the traditional man of letters (*écrivain*). From the former, the *scripteur* derives an ideal of commitment, from the latter the notion of writing as an art. The predicament of the teacher as Barthes sees it in 1971 extends the earlier definition of writing set forth in the late 1940s: "The writing to which I entrust myself already exists entirely as an institution; it reveals my past and my choice, it gives me history, it blazons forth my situation, it commits me without my having to declare the fact" (*WDZ*, 27).

Neither a man of letters nor a politicized scribe, the intellectual must confront alternatives that point to compromise or oblivion, with

the resulting alienation that stems from resistance turned to frustration: "The intellectual is still only an incompletely transformed writer,
and unless he scuttles himself and becomes forever a militant who no
longer writes (some have done so, and are thereby forgotten), he
cannot but come back to the fascination of former modes of writing,
transmitted through Literature as an instrument intact but obsolete"
(*WDZ*, 27–28). Having remained an intellectual whose prime activities
involve speaking and writing, Barthes sees language and form as
expressions of political values institutionalized as tacit norms (*valeurs
d'usage*). In *Writing Degree Zero*, he analyzes the use of the *passé simple*
tense as a sign of the universality he sees as integral to bourgeois
fiction: "The Novel—and within the Novel, the preterite—are mythological objects in which there is, superimposed upon an immediate
intention, a second-order appeal to a corpus of dogmas, or better, to a
pedagogy, since what is sought is to impart an essence in the guise of
an artefact" (*WDZ*, 33–34).

Barthes's mythological project has entailed both a critical practice
and a revised pedagogy with direct impact on the study of literature as
a social doctrine. That impact can be felt as a series of questions. How
exactly does the writer/critic cope with speech? What is the relationship—either real or ideal—between the negative force of debunking and the pedagogy such debunking makes possible? To restate this
problem more pointedly, we might ask how Barthes's early critique of
popular myths relates to his activities since 1961 at the Ecole Pratique
des Hautes Etudes. Even more pointedly, we might ask how Barthes's
pedagogy affects our reading of his writings. Can we (should we) do
things with Barthes? If so, where do we start?

The common practice of doing things with Barthes occurs as
reading in a pedagogical context. We may, for instance, suggest that a
particular text (let us suppose "The Metaphor of the Eye" from the
Critical Essays) be read in conjunction with Bataille's *Story of the Eye*. The
procedure is so familiar that we may fail to consider exactly what is at
stake. To relate texts by Barthes and Bataille (Barthes *on* Bataille)
presupposes a functional primacy of the critical text over its literary
counterpart, although an ontological primacy of the latter over the
former can also be argued. Ultimately, the relation is variable and both
texts are necessary for there to be any relation at all.[2] I have already
suggested how it becomes increasingly difficult and ineffectual to
attempt direct applications of Barthes's writings since *S/Z*. What remains in place of direct application is an attitude toward reading

increasingly receptive to self-reflexivity and introspection. Extending this attitude to its limit, we might ask whether direct application was ever a prime concern even in the earlier writings. I am not suggesting that the *Critical Essays* are of little or no pragmatic value to promote an understanding of texts by Bataille, Robbe-Grillet, or Brecht. But the unambiguous rejection of the distinction between metalanguage and literary object imposes a rethinking of the presuppositions which support a will to pragmatic application.

Imagining a student about to undertake a structural analysis of a literary text, Barthes advises the student in a 1970 piece to drop the goal of a definitive explanation in order to experience the production of meaning in its full complexity: "It is a matter of entering, by analysis (or what resembles an analysis), into the play of the signifier, into the writing: in a word, to accomplish, by his labor, the text's *plural*" (*NCE*, 79). The above statement also points to a tendency noted by many critics as a retreat into subjectivity and narcissism. A more attentive reading shows Barthes exploring textual effects such as those he admires in Saussure's study of anagrams in classical poetry. The expression he uses to characterize Saussure's study is that of "dramatizing science." It serves also in reference to his own writings after 1970. The emergence of a dramatic metaphor points as well to the growing distance between the "new" Barthes and the earlier ideal of scientism. *A Lover's Discourse* inscribes theory within the practice of writing; it dramatizes critical utterance while rejecting the metalanguage/literary object distinction of the "heroic" period: "The description of the lover's discourse has been replaced by its simulation; and this discourse has recovered its fundamental person, the 'I,' so as to produce or stage [*mettre-en-scène*] an utterance, not an analysis" (*FDA*, 3).

From where the lover/narrator speaks as *dramatis persona*, it is no longer possible to separate him from his utterance according to a stable dissociation between narrator and presumed author. To attempt to do so is to confront the resistance of textual utterance to the standard categories of genre and determinate meaning. To the degree that the *persona* of the *lover/narrator* is made up of *figures* of the body in motion, the reader attempting to interpret these figures would have to rely on the idiosyncrasies of utterance and the wider production of meaning that Barthes refers to as *signifiance*.

In order to show how *A Lover's Discourse* illustrates a change in the practice of reading, it is helpful to turn to an intermediary phase between the mid-1960s and the "new" Barthes of the 1970s. In a perceptive account, Fredric Jameson comments on the revised critical method visible in *S/Z*. What interests Jameson is the passage from a linguistic model toward what Barthes announces in his 1966 "Introduction to the Structural Analysis of Narratives" as another semiotics. Writing as a sociologist of critical method, Jameson traces that passage and situates it within histories of literary and critical writings. At the same time, he wants to insert the phenomenon of passage within wider cultural values in order to see it as something more than a voguish post-modernity. For Jameson, Barthes's evolution is a case in point of how key notions such as "structure" and "text" chart a progression through the 1966–70 period I have described as that of Barthes's break with structural analysis:

Textuality may rapidly be described as a methodological hypothesis whereby the objects of study of the human sciences (but not only of the human ones; witness the genetic "code" of DNA!) are considered to constitute so many texts which we decipher and interpret, as distinguished from older views of those objects as realities or existants or substances which we in one way or another try to know. The advantages of such a model are perhaps most clearly visible in the non-literary disciplines, where it seems to afford a more adequate "solution" to the dilemmas of positivism than the more provisory one of phenomenological bracketing. The latter merely suspended the ontological problem and postpones the ultimate epistemological decision, while in some ways actually reinforcing the old subject/object dichotomy which was at the root of the contradictions of classical epistemology. The notion of textuality, whatever fundamental objections may be made to it, has at least the advantage of a strategy, of cutting across both epistemology and the subject/object antithesis in such a way as to neutralize both, and of focusing the attention of the analyst on his own position as a reader and on his own mental operations as interpretation.[3]

The shift in method has a direct bearing on the Barthes of *S/Z* and after. When he textualizes reading as he does in *S/Z*, the former object of study expands to include the reader/analyst to produce an account of reading in place of what might otherwise pass for interpretation. *S/Z* is thus neither an interpretation nor a close reading in the tradition of the *explication de texte*. It provides an account of how a reader such as Barthes might go about making sense of Balzac's "Sarrasine." As he explains in an interview with Raymond Bellour, Barthes had sought in *S/Z* to focus on the problems of reading and interpretation that his previous critical position had excluded (*GV*, 79). *S/Z* is thus a prime example of the shift in Barthes's post-structuralist practice toward textuality and an account of the reading experience as process. It is, I am convinced, less a preface to a theory or program than an account of textuality based on changes in method that distinguish it from earlier nonreflexive approaches. So much attention has been paid to how the five codes might or might not be applied as tools of analysis and interpretation that they have seldom been seen as a working model which may have no application beyond its immediate implications for method.

In view of the above changes, it becomes increasingly more diffi-cult to read *A Lover's Discourse* (or the *Roland Barthes*) according to the conventions of genre that would classify it as confessional narrative, autobiography, or *roman-à-clef*. While features of autobiography clearly circulate within this book of love, any assumption of identity between the lover/narrator and author is weakened by the text's unstable mix of narrative modes. If we want to locate the "place" of the writer in this particular text, we would probably do better to distinguish among a number of "voices" or registers out of which an authorial presence might be set up. But since Barthes's writings tend to disperse that kind of stability, our reading will follow a more formal approach.

The eighty fragments which compose the main body of the text are preceded by two prefatory statements of method. The first, a kind of *apologie personnelle*, justifies the choice of topic and posits discursive identities for the writer and the public of readers addressed:

The necessity for this book is to be found in the following consideration: that the lover's discourse is today *of an extreme solitude.* This discourse is spoken, perhaps, by thousands of subjects (who knows?), but warranted by no one. . . . Once a discourse is thus driven by its own momentum into the backwater of the "unreal," exiled from all gregarity, it has no recourse but to become the site, however exiguous, of an *affirmation.* This affirmation is, in short, the subject of the book which begins here. (*FDA,* epigraph) n.p.

Even if we persist in wanting to read *A Lover's Discourse* as a personal statement by Barthes, its status as a book of literary criticism needs to be clarified. How might it relate to the analyses and discus-sions of two decades ago? Can Barthes continue to write parafictions and still claim to be a critic? Despite the prevalence of fictional elements throughout the text of the book, the project undertaken strikes me as consistent with the revisionary nature of Barthes's work after 1970.

One key to understanding this shift involves the function of fictional elements in the context of a critical writing. Following views on language expressed by Nietzsche and Hans Vaihinger, Barthes expands the sense of the term "fiction" to refer to the conventional and thus relative nature of verbal systems which fabricate a false sense of fixity. In the *Mythologies*, Barthes adopts a similar strategy to analyze popular myths of French middle-class. More recently, Barthes's change of attitude toward a science of language attenuates the earlier references and explains his invocation of the Nietzsche who ultimately came to see languages as grounded in rhetorical and persuasive functions.

A Lover's Discourse condenses description and analysis in a simulation which supports Barthes's refusal of a metalanguage as objective or masterful explanation. In its place, Barthes illustrates the specificity of an utterance irreducible to analysis along the lines of conventional formalist and semiological practices: "Recent theory, in the area which is mine, has focused on the problem of utterance [*énonciation*]: a central problem within which converge linguistics, semiology, logic, psychoanalysis and ideological criticism."[4]

A second statement of method describes how *A Lover's Discourse* is generated via reference to Raymond Roussel's "Comment j'ai écrit certains de mes livres":

Everything follows from this principle: that the lover is not to be reduced to a simple symptomal subject, but rather that we hear in his voice what is "unreal," i.e., intractable. Whence the choice of a "Dramatic" method which renounces examples and rests on the single action of a primary language (no metalanguage). The description of the lover's discourse has been replaced by its simulation, and to that discourse has been restored its fundamental person, the *I*, in order to stage an utterance, not an analysis. (*FDA*, 3)

Between this statement of method and the eighty fragments, a single phrase—"C'est donc un amoureux qui parle et qui dit" ("So it is a lover who speaks and who says")—qualifies the specific context of what follows as utterances to be read *as though* spoken by a lover.

From where the lover/narrator speaks as *dramatis persona*, it is no longer possible to decode his utterances by referring to a stable or self-present subject. To the degree that this *persona* is nothing other than a chain of figures, an appropriate critical response on the part of the reader would be to trace their sequence. But to do so along the lines of speech act theory would disclose multiple speakers and a straining of the model. As found in *A Lover's Discourse*, the specificity of utterance confounds application and resists assimilation to the limits placed on utterance described by Barthes in "Writers, Intellectuals, Teachers." The impact of *A Lover's Discourse* is keenly felt in its irreducibility to modes of reading centered on an originating or consistent subject. For many readers, that impact is likely to promote confusion and hostility, particularly on the part of those who may no longer find that Barthes's writing "serves" as it may have in the past. As a result, its resistance to pragmatic discourse promotes a reassessment of the presuppositions which make criticism possible. Ultimately, that may be the best way to do (or not do) things with Barthes.

In order to situate the changes in Barthes's pedagogy within wider contexts of French cultural institutions, it is helpful to contrast it with the activities of the Groupe de Recherches sur l'Enseignement Philosophique, known as GREPH. Formed in 1975 as a collective response to changes proposed by the Ministry of Education, GREPH seized on the topical issue in order to expose the convergence of politics and pedagogy in the teaching of philosophy in the secondary (high-school) system. The so-called Haby proposals allowed the group to recast debate around the traditional question of upholding or denying a general philosophy into a more delicate approach to the philosophy of teaching implied in the teaching of philosophy:

For those who observe our work without participating in it, and especially for many teachers, an image of GREPH has slowly taken shape as that of a highly politicized movement attached to the idea that there is no natural age for philosophy, from which all implied consequences should be drawn. The image is partial, but not false. It is true that GREPH accepts and promotes its thoroughly political nature. It has never denied this under an alleged neutrality, nor has it ever yielded to politicism or political dogmatism. It has also never wanted to be an association of specialists. And although it aims initially at a teaching intelligible within the present system of disciplines, it seeks to question that system, along with the allegedly apolitical corporation generally associated with it.[5]

For Sarah Kofman, the Haby proposals update the traditional question of the suitable age at which philosophical study should be undertaken. Supporting her position with references to Plato, Descartes, and Nietzsche, she maintains that the debate surrounding the government proposals is inseparable from the study of doctrines of truth, knowledge, and value traditionally associated with philosophical inquiry. Describing an interaction similar to that characterized by Barthes in "Writers, Intellectuals, Teachers," Bernard Pautrat approaches the teaching of philosophy as a process of indoctrination in which students' bodies are constrained in the name of tradition to endure the lessons of their master:

> The only course is magisterial, one which dangerously exploits the discipline of the student, the discipline of his body. It is based, without scruples, on what is most suspect in the student's behavior: his absence of body, of a body which is nevertheless present, but present for what unavowed, unavowable pleasure? None of this would be a problem if the master were not also expected to uphold, for instance, that it is necessary to do away with the revocation of the body for the benefit of the pure mind, that philosophical thought is caught like any other thought in the grasp of an unconscious which is of the body as much as it is of the psyche, that thought is sexualized as well as social, and all other propositions inseparable from our situation of belatedness; after Freud, Marx, Lacan, or any such one.[6]

Central to Pautrat's account of teaching is a staging of the philosophical inquiry in an encounter where the teacher's embodiment of mastery assumes a forceful (almost physical) control over the revelation of truth, knowledge, and pleasure. What passes in most cases for the acquisition of knowledge and skills in institutions of learning masks a more fundamental exercise of authority and power. The student who chooses to study philosophy does not do so merely in the hopes of obtaining a marketable skill, but also out of a conviction that such knowledge as might be acquired would also allow him or her to arrive at some kind of truth. Because the latter concern tends to be neglected and even dismissed by institutions geared to producing technical competence, the status of philosophical inquiry is subverted. In the hope of rectifying this situation, Pautrat calls for a paradoxical teaching opposed to the doctrine of technical competence as the primary objective of philosophical study. To this end, he invokes dramatic models in order to point to a physicality of teaching he finds repressed by a process of transference and a myth of eternal knowledge transmitted from master to disciple.

A similar subversion of this transference process animates "Pas de deux," a sketch for a Nietzschean pedagogy by Martine Meskel and Michael Ryan. Taking their cue from Nietzsche's project of transvaluation, they draft a strategy for the overthrow of paternalism and idolatry in the classroom. To do so, they expand the scope of their gesture to the Nietzsche reference itself. For where Nietzsche ultimately resigned his professorship at the University of Basel to pursue his work outside a formal institution, Meskel and Ryan align their activity fully within the educational system. For what they do to Nietzsche—reduce the status of invoking him from example or doctrine to individual biography—is what they would hope to achieve in their teaching: "If the professor wants to provoke an imitation which would have the student seek his or her own law rather than assimilate that of the master in a narcissistic specularity of transference, he must undertake autobiography, he must find his own law—for example."[7] As an antidote to realism and the mimesis it entails, biography as critical self-reflexion replaces the authority of the received written text with the presence of a voice speaking to and for itself.[8]

Despite differences of context, a common focus shared by the GREPH collective and Barthes is that of pedagogy as the staging of physical and ideological forces. Unable to shake the authority afforded by the social roles of writer and teacher, Barthes forgoes an institutional critique in favor of a more personalized ethic in the form of self-reflexion. Seldom, if ever, does he enter into direct political confrontation in anything other than a personal capacity. Far from refusing power and the privileges of authority, Barthes's pedagogy is predicated on a belief in the ubiquity of institutions. Similar in this respect to Foucault, Barthes has learned from Sartre's experience that the intellectual cannot and should not speak *for* others. So that the challenge for those who are relatively unoppressed is to speak only for themselves.

In relation to Barthes, two closing examples demonstrate the implications of this attitude with respect to teaching and power. Jacques Leenhardt, author of a political reading of Robbe-Grillet's *La Jalousie*, relates in a 1977 interview how Barthes's teaching led him to explore the formalization of myths into "hard elements of ideology," which he was later to study under the tutelage of Lucien Goldmann's sociocritical approach: "Here, rather than speak of an actual influence, as I may in the case of Goldmann, I would say that for me Barthes played the role of an awakening, a kind of incentive to complete, to open up the work of analysis of texts carried out in the tradition of Lukács and Goldmann, not so much to open it to the formal dimension of the texts, but rather to find a discourse in which to speak of writing itself from a sociological perspective."[9]

A final example is in the form of a testimonial by Barthes in praise

of the film theoretician Christian Metz. Refusing to distinguish between the knowledge to be communicated and the process of communication embodied as voice, Barthes is struck by the free and
generous tone Metz is able to maintain in his teaching: "He not only
communicates, he *gives*, in the full sense of the term; there is a true
gift—of knowledge and language; a gift of the subject in so far as he
takes to heart to speak (does he not say in his own way, he whose work
comes so explicitly from linguistics, that the error of this science is to
make us believe that messages 'are exchanged'—forever the ideology
of exchange—when the *reality* of the word is precisely to give itself or
to take back, in other words to *demand?*)."[10] After "Writers, Intellectuals, Teachers" and subsequent texts on body, self, and utterance, the
physicality of teaching reappears in these final two examples to posit a
persona or figure of the teacher as an operator of language.

Imagine that I am a teacher: I speak, endlessly, in front of and for someone who remains silent. I am the person who says I (the detours of *one, we,* or impersonal sentence make no difference), I am the person who, under cover of *setting out* a body of knowledge, *puts out* a discourse, *never knowing how that discourse is being received* and thus forever forbidden the reassurance of a definitive image—even if offensive—which would constitute *me.*

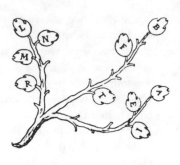

CHAPTER SEVEN

Barthes,
"Writers, Intellectuals, Teachers"

The Professor of Desire

Readers of the *Roland Barthes* may well recall a photograph of Barthes *professeur* surrounded by a dozen or so young men and women. As every picture tells a story, so this informal group portrait commemorates a seminar given by Barthes at the Ecole Pratique des Hautes Etudes. But the documentary function of this image is, as the saying goes, only part of the story so long as it fails to account for the singular place of the seminar in Barthes's pedagogy: "The space of the seminar is phalansteric, i.e., in a sense, fictive, novelistic. It is only the space of the circulation of subtle desires, mobile desires; it is within the artifice of a sociality whose consistency is miraculously extenuated, according to a phrase of

Nietzsche's: 'the tangle of amorous relations'" (*RB*, 171). As an interplay of word and image, the passage asserts the irreducible difference of the seminar space as a privileged site where eros and knowledge converge. All of which might lend itself to a Platonic discussion of souls and truth, were it not for the troublesome presence of "subtle desires, mobile desires" to remind us, as if we did not already know, that teaching can become utterly personal because of the intimacy it is capable of producing: "Teaching is not only very personal, it is also very physical. That teacher there, walking from the library to his office, dispensing smiles and warm greetings to fresh-faced students, is me. I talk a lot about souls—perhaps too much—but no soul have I ever seen that did not come in a body and when I teach somebody I teach some body."[1]

Barthes's comments on teaching temper traditional notions of how knowledge is transmitted with an attitude that borders on the confessional. A teacher who confesses or professes desire is no longer scandalous except to those who still believe that the so-called life of the mind has nothing to do with the rest of the body. The comments also point to the pedagogical dimension of what had become the thrust of Barthes's critical practice after *S/Z*—namely, that a personal motivation needs to be recognized in the face of what is otherwise mistaken for an objective or indifferent project of critical understanding. As his writing moved away from straightforward structural analysis, the role of Barthes's annual seminar as a testing -ground for theory evolved to the point where *S/Z*, *The Pleasure of the Text*, and the *Roland Barthes* are quite openly the products of collective elaboration. On its own, this relationship would have been the exception in an educational system built on the *cours magistral* and an absolute minimum of verbal exchange, for what American students take for granted as an institutional or legal right to participate in the classroom is only sparingly tolerated in France after the educational reforms enacted in the 1960s.[2] When this freedom of exchange is understood beyond its institutional context, the pursuit of knowledge can, in turn, be approached as part of a more personal affirmation of values. No longer a simple laboratory for theory, the seminar space becomes for Barthes a prime site of discovery around which any subsequent formulation as theory is but a trace. To relate this pedagogy back to Barthes's revised critical practice, we might ask exactly what kind of knowledge might be gained from professing desire *in the classroom*. From letters to life, what kind of knowledge does the lover of knowledge seek?

A traditional answer to this question can be organized around the differences between *philias* and *eros*, Greek terms commonly translated as "friendly feeling" and "love." As they appear in the Socratic dialogues, the terms overlap, with the latter distinguished as a desire more intense than affection and more closely tied to the sexual drive than the former.[3] Etymology suggests that the love of knowledge and concomitant knowledge of love are not what we had believed them to be, but rather (always already) internally divided into a play of difference along the lines of those between *plaisir* and *jouissance* set forth in *The Pleasure of the Text*. From letters to life, the concepts of *plaisir* and *jouissance* reappear in the seminar as *philias* and *eros*, less in order to resolve or deconstruct the question of knowledge and pleasure than to give it a living and dramatic expression.

From letters to life, the professor of desire teaches the text of difference and plurality: sex and love, two master *topoi* and two versions of classical and modern knowledge. From the first volume of Michel Foucault's projected history of sexuality, this passage on the author of an underground Victorian classic:

The solitary author of *My Secret Life* often says, in order to justify his describing them, that his stranger practices were shared by thousands of men on the surface of the earth. But the guiding principle, for the strangest of these practices, which was the fact of recounting them all, and in detail, from day to day, had been lodged in the heart of modern man for over two centuries.[4]

From *A Lover's Discourse*, this prefatory remark addressed directly to the reader:

The necessity for this book is to be found in the following consideration: that the lover's discourse is today *of an extreme solitude*. This discourse is spoken, perhaps, by thousands of subjects (who knows?), but warranted by no one; it is completely forsaken by the surrounding languages; ignored, disparaged, or derided by them, severed not only from authority (science, techniques, arts). Once a discourse is driven by its own momentum into the backwater of the "unreal," exiled from all gregarity, it has no recourse but to become the site, however exiguous, of an *affirmation*. That affirmation is, in short, the subject of the book which begins here. (*FDA*, 1)

Against Foucault's claim that sexuality has replaced eros with a compulsion to say everything that can be said in the name of an institutional will to truth, Barthes revels in the untimeliness of his reflections. Because both writers treat love and sex as discursive objects—as things written or spoken—their inquiries focus on questions of method and interpretation pointing to the convergence of doctrine, meaning, and authority. In French and American cultures presently saturated with manuals, studies, and gossip dealing with sex and love, there is something scandalous—either willfully naive or openly backward—in attempting to rethink the ways we think and talk about what is all too evidently present. For Foucault, the questions of method are not merely those of how to talk about sex without hypocrisy, but how to resist a prevailing view of sexuality as the product of a sustained rule of clinical thinking, and thus a privileged secret shared by Western societies since the seventeenth century.

In contrast to Foucault, Barthes concentrates on what he finds repressed by the practices Foucault cites as having led to a middle-class sexuality. As a result, Barthes explores how to write about love at a moment when, from all indications, it is a labor of lust, nothing more than sex. This makes for a willful attempt at untimeliness, an ostensibly unpopular attitude which might be dismissed as quaint or precious except for its unsentimental basis in the critical view of the repressed as that which comes back.

In order for love to return as that which a practice of clinical sexuality represses, it must first do so at the level of discourse from which it has been displaced. Thus, in keeping with the spatial metaphor Foucault uses to talk about the place of discourse, Barthes states that *A Lover's Discourse* is constructed less as an analysis than as the staging of an utterance:

Whence the choice of a "dramatic" method which renounces examples and rests on the single action of a primary language (no metalanguage). The description of the lover's discourse has been replaced by its simulation, and to that discourse has been restored its fundamental person, the *I*, in order to stage an utterance, not an analysis. What is proposed, then, is a portrait—but not a psychological portrait; instead a structural one which offers the reader a discursive site: the site of someone speaking within himself, *amorously*, confronting the other, who does not speak. (*FDA*, 3)

While both Foucault and Barthes consciously write about and within discourse, the above passage illustrates a positionality of address much more bound to interpersonal communication than the anonymous and institutional phenomenon studied by Foucault. And although I intend to return to Foucault's comments on the various connections between knowledge, power, and pleasure, the concrete discursivity of dramatic address takes priority in *A Lover's Discourse* as part of the pedagogy tied to Barthes's practice of semiology after the 1966–70 break with straightforward structuralist practice.

The amorous discourse—not a discourse *on* love but *in* or *of* love—relates that semiotic practice to a dramatic formulation which derives alternately from the most intimate of pleasure principles and insights into the most institutionalized of social relations. At first glance, a political reading would seem to be incongruous with the artifice of confessional fragments which composes the *Discourse*. But only if we fail to link theory and criticism with the rule of the written or spoken word. Because of the evident physical and cultural differences, American students of French culture and ideas are in a singular position to observe the impact of foreign discourse on native institutions. We may read Proust, Colette, Genette, or Cixous as "French," but we do so within cultural institutions which heighten our awareness of the social factors affecting the distribution of French ideas as something other than duty-free imports. If we agree with Foucault that discourse is predicated on exclusion and inclusion, the reception of French ideas by American readers needs to be accounted for as something more than the abstract translation from one language or culture to another.

Any general statement about the evolution of Barthes's critical practice during the so-called post-structuralist period after 1968 should address the relations between criticism and teaching. Whenever intellectuals are accused of an unwillingness or an inability to move from word to act, the presence of a pedagogical imperative ought to remind us, via a Kantian resonance, of the moral rule known to every fully formed human being. Whatever attitudes we claim to hold about literature and criticism carry with them an implied pedagogy which we experience firsthand in the classroom, seminar, or lecture hall as a lived relation of power and knowledge. Adjusted with varying degrees of discretion and subtlety under the guise of authority and doctrine, the Great Books teach a personal experience of institutional power. No one who has been criticized (or reprimanded) as a student for holding ideas or attitudes unacceptable—that is, antagonistic—to those of the teacher or professor will believe in the autonomy of critical exchange from an educational process of indoctrination. When, for example, we cite Althusser's notion of ideology and ramble on about practical relations between the "real" and the "imaginary," we need also to recognize that our will to distinguish between the "real" and the "imaginary" expresses in cultural terms and as needs what we already know in more personal terms to be closer to desires. Because Barthes's revised practice of reading responds to the interplay between need and desire and because he uses the seminar space to stage critical inquiry as a personal act, the evolution of his critical practice is also a case in point for the issues of pedagogy it confronts.

For issue no. 8 of the Parisian journal *Communications,* which appeared in 1966, Barthes wrote an "Introduction to the Structural Analysis of Narratives" that is still considered a basic text of literary semiotics. Toward the end of the article, in a passage devoted to narrative situation, he writes the following on the principle of immanence which maintains the narrational codes as the final level or limit of analysis:

> Narration can only receive its meaning from the world which makes use of it; beyond the narrational level begins the world, other systems (social, economic, ideological) whose terms are no longer simply narratives but elements of a different substance (historical facts, determinations, behaviors, etc.). Just as linguistics stops at the sentence, so narrative analysis stops at discourse—from there it is necessary to shift to another semiotics. (*IMT,* 115–16)

I have felt somewhat uncomfortable with the article because I am unwilling to believe that the operation of reading can be adequately conceptualized as processes of switching, distributing, and integrating, actions evoking the image of a vast computer terminal with an unlimited potential for assimilating, processing, and storing data.

The period from the "Introduction to the Structural Analysis of Narratives" through *Camera Lucida* forms a historical space within which the shift toward another semiotics has entailed not merely the expansion of the Parisian structuralism of the 1950s and early 1960s practiced by Lévi-Strauss, Barthes himself, and other contributors to the *Communications* issue, but what I see as a distinct and substantive break in both the theory and practice of criticism. For Barthes, the shift appears to be acute and irreversible: less a gradual progression than an emphatic break. And while it is possible and perhaps even felicitous to insist on the constant elements in Barthes's career, to do so is to neglect why later texts such as

A Lover's Discourse and *Camera Lucida* are less the products of a fully articulated semiotics ("Une autre sémiotique") than a paradoxical or antithetical response to the earlier practice in view of something completely different ("une sémiotique autre") in which the distinction between theory and practice is no longer applicable. *A Lover's Discourse* addresses problems of analysis and interpretation intelligible as the traditional concerns of literary critics. At the same time, Barthes's manner of addressing those problems needs to be confronted in view of what is no longer a mere revision of the mid-1960s practice. Specifically, his choice of *topoi* as well as the refusal to apply a metalanguage devolve from theoretical considerations which, although pertinent to any reading of the *Discourse*, are secondary to the textual presence of the amorous discourse and the narrative function of the fragments. Thus, Barthes writes that we should resist our desire to locate a fixed origin out of which the sequence of fragments might acquire a necessary order, describing that will to order as monstrous. Instead, he adds, we should look for "no more than affirmation" (*FDA*, 8).

Saying yes, to systematic discourse or to love, as the case may be, is neither a simple affirmation nor the handle of some pop sentimentality. For even if I persist in taking Barthes at his word, his statement needs to be (re)situated in the context of a discourse which is no longer simply critical, as in a hypothetical discourse *on* love. To affirm love in the name of . . . love? In the name of literary criticism? What is it that can be said today — critically and otherwise — about love without falling into untimeliness or repetition? Whom can Barthes be addressing? And finally, who is (and also, *what* is) the subject of love encountered in this book? To look for no more than the affirmation of love is then not at all a simple task when that affirmation calls for an attention whose rigor and sensitivity are none other than those of critical reading. To affirm love is thus to consider that its subject — overdetermined as both discursive voice and humanist *topos* — is perhaps nothing other than its polymorphous affirmation.

All of which is not at all to suggest that *A Lover's Discourse* formulates an idealist theory of love. For what counts in the amorous discourse — what gives it a textual or differential effect — is its repositioning of critical utterance as dramatic address. The lover's monologue is staged (simultaneously set on stage and simulated), addressed to the loved one whose silence appears only to feed the anxieties of the lover/narrator in search of signs of response. For despite the disclaimers set forth in the preface, the *Discourse* is a kind of psychological portrait—a playful one at that—of the semiotician in love. The amorous discourse extends a semiotics whose uncanniness derives from the fact that the *world* of the lover is indistinguishable from the *word* of the lover and thus from the processes of symbolization speech. In this sense, the word/world of the lover is one of universal signification where even silence (and especially silence) simulates an illusion of system bordering on the paranoid. Faced with a number of possible meanings, the lover's predicament is that of choosing between a number of conflicting interpretations: "*Everything signifies:* by this proposition, I entrap myself, I bind myself in calculations, I keep myself from enjoyment" (*FDA*, 63: the French version ends, "Je m'empêche de jouir").

The lover on the lookout for signs of loves engages in a semiotics in which ambiguity heightens the central function of value. Writing on or about love in order to semiotize it is thus always to locate it on the side of the *plaisir* described in *The Pleasure of the Text* as a cultural and verbal phenomenon in contrast to the ineffable *jouissance*, commonly translated as "bliss" but more directly rendered by Heath as orgasm. The bind of the semiotician-in-love is the body, which a conventional semiotics cannot contain without equating *jouissance* and *plaisir*. The excess of signs produces discomfort and arousal, so that the lover turns into a semiotician whose desire to locate and interpret leaves him invariably unsatisfied. Between his desire to find signs of love and his reluctance to accept the uncertainty of signs in general, the lover/narrator derives a fearful pleasure in the compression or reduction of feeling to concepts. In addition, the very same excess allows the verbal discourse to continue. As in the French expression, *ça laisse à désirer* ("it leaves something to be desired").

The best way to approach that excess via a revised semiotics comes from the critiques of idealist love found in current psychoanalysis and feminist writing. As characterized by two Frenchmen in a passage that echoes the prefatory remarks in *A Lover's Discourse*, sexual liberation and feminist movements have all but destroyed traditional notions of love in terms of both personal experience and cultural discourse:

If there is a romanticism today, it is libidinal and no longer sentimental. In place of passion, there is desire; in place of the heart, the genitals. The former construct of body and soul has been gotten at by the various ideologies of pleasure, and in order to say the following: (that) there are not two loves, the first spiritual and the other material, one noble, the other vulgar, low—because emotions have but a single fatherland: the body.[5]

Barthes's book of love is then very much also a book of the body. That is, a book which inscribes elements of classical rhetoric around a primary concern with the gestures of the body (*figures*) and the rhetorical term *actio*, equated by Barthes with drama, gymnastics, and choreography. Priority of the body does not, however, exclude the word, body and word interacting in what Lacan describes as the convergence of the Imaginary, the Symbolic, and the Real: "Underneath the figure, there is something of the verbal hallucination (Freud, Lacan)" (*FDA*, 6).

In the *Roland Barthes*, the reader is offered a twenty-page section of annotated photographs of Barthes's youth. In one shot, the young Roland sits on his mother's lap as she points toward the camera. The caption reads: "The mirror stage, that's you," which both acknowledges and retorts to Lacan's theory of the development of identity in the preverbal child. In the *Discourse*, Freud and Lacan continue to be reinvoked in order to relate various corporeal figures to contacts with the Symbolic, Lacan's term for the process toward mastery of language. In *Beyond the Pleasure Principle* (1920), Freud relates the story of the little boy who compensated for his mother's frequent absences by inventing a game in which he could—symbolically—make her return at will. In *A Lover's Discourse*, the lover/narrator states: "Absence: any episode of language which stages the absence of the loved object—whatever its cause and its duration—and which tends to transform this absence into an ordeal of banishment" (*FDA*, 13). The lover/ narrator invokes the insecurities of the child who stages the events of everyday existence within a highly developed mental life surrounding the interplay between presence and absence: "As a child, I didn't forget: interminable days, abandoned days, when the Mother was working far away; I would go, evenings, to wait for her at the U^{bis} bus stop, Sèvres-Babylone; the buses would pass one after the other, she wasn't in any of them" (*FDA*, 14–15). The insecure lover revives the figure of the child who waits, not yet completely severed (*sevré* is the past participle of the French verb *sevrer*, "to wean"); that is, not yet detached from the Mother and thus ever a lonely baby at Babylone.[6] From the child's play emerges a model of the symbolic activity later expanded by the adult to cope with feelings of dependency and infrequent abandonment: "There is a scenography of waiting: I organize it, manipulate it, cut out a portion of time in which I shall mime the loss of the loved object and provoke all the effects of a minor mourning. This is then acted out as a play" (*FDA*, 37).

Following little Hans in *Beyond the Pleasure Principle*, the lover / narrator produces a symbolic fiction, a story to compensate for the absence of the loved one, transforming anxiety into a business (*affaire-ment*) where the oscillation of verbal activity—analogous to throwing and retrieving the spool—stages utterance as a fiction with multiple roles (impatience, jealousy, infatuation, enamoration) and figures (doubts, reproaches, desires, depressions).

As much as the lover / narrator might value the ineffable pleasures of *jouissance* over its cultural counterpart, the amorous discourse also affirms the specific pleasures of narration and speech. And despite Barthes's stated desire to rethink the logic of binary distinctions formulated and applied in the mid-1960s period, the bulk of the discourse illustrates verbal pleasures which only approach *jouissance* by insisting on corporeal figuration. In *Critique et vérité*, Barthes had attacked the naive conception which, in his view, the "old" criticism (in the person of Raymond Picard) had held of psychoanalysis and its perception of the human body: "The man of the old criticism [*l'ancienne critique*] is, in fact, made up of two anatomical regions. The first is, so to speak, superior-external: the head, artistic creation, noble appearance, that which can be shown, which can be seen; the second is inferior-internal: the genitals (which must not be named), instincts, 'summary drives,' the dark world of anarchical tensions" (*CV*, 25). Barthes may know better than to believe in such clearcut distinctions. But the lover / narrator does not, and continues to hold at least a residual fondness for other binaries which point to the ambiguities of his predicament: "I can do everything with my language, *but not with my body*. What I hide by my language, my body utters. I can deliberately mold my message, not my voice. By my voice, whatever it says, the other will recognize 'that something is wrong with me.' I am a liar (by preterition), not an actor. My body is a stubborn child, my language is a very civilized adult" (*FDA*, 45).

For the lover / narrator, the binary is a willed construct, a useful fiction by means of which he hopes to maintain the break between his narration—pleasurable on its own account—and the excess of sensations and signs he wants to interpret only up to a point. Caught within the bind of wanting both to semiotize and leave an excess or surplus of signs, the semiotician-in-love adopts an ironic attitude toward his narration, an attitude which makes the *Discourse* something more (and something "other") than an essay of straight critical writing.

The frequency of corporeal figures needs to be seen in relation to the wider project of undermining the stable and consistent subject. Since 1970 and the appearance of *S/Z*, that project had been elucidated in two ways: first, by studying the discourses which resist conventions of "classical" and "modern" narration, and subsequently by clarifying the presuppositions at work in those conventions as what allows literary critics to operate as such. All of which had led Barthes away from the applied practice of the mid-1960s period toward an extended reflection on the attitudes toward language seldom acknowledged by critics of a pragmatic orientation. Hence Barthes's disillusion with the "scientific" Saussure and his later allegiance to the "dramatic" views on language set forth by Nietzsche, Freud, and the Saussure of the anagrams. But where the notion of figuration visible in the *Roland Barthes* derives in large part from Nietzsche's lectures and writings on language as rhetoric, the *Discourse* reveals an active practice of figuration closer to the orientation toward *signifiance* encountered in the writings of Freud, Lacan, Benveniste, and Kristeva. More pointedly, the elaboration of the amorous discourse within a wider practice of critical activity locates figuration as the gesture that affirms personal value. As a result, the amorous discourse counteracts illusions of indifferent inquiry while mixing textual effects of essay, confession, and fictional narrative. As an intertext composed of a number of materials, the *Discourse* also has a direct effect on interpretation. Because of its hybrid composition, it does not lend itself to the common modes of reading. In this sense, the condition of uncertainty experienced by the lover/narrator is projected onto the reader, whose desire to interpret the *Discourse* must account for the singular writing and figuration encountered in the text.

The frustrations of the lover/narrator are a result of his attempts to semiotize personal involvement in the face of his admitted desire to keep the loved one beyond classification. To this end, he produces as well as interprets signs. When, for example, he describes the loved one as unclassifiable, he nonetheless preserves a discursive relationship whose formality (the "I-to-you" in words and power) implies a number of positions. Invoking a passage from Goethe's *Sorrows of Young Werther*, the lover/narrator identifies with the fictional hero who wants to occupy the singular "place" already taken by Carlotta's fiancé,

Albert. To dramatize his isolation, the lover/narrator compares his situation to that of a player in a parlor game: "There are as many chairs as children, minus one; while the children march around, a lady pounded on a piano; when she stopped, everyone dashed for a chair and sat down, except the clumsiest, the least brutal, the unluckiest, who remained standing, stupid, *de trop:* the lover" (*FDA*, 45). The parlor game, yet another evocation of childhood anxiety projected by the civilized adult, prefigures the obscenity or exposure of the lover's physical desire characterized in the sexual arousal evident in the adjectives: standing, stupid, *de trop*. In French, the parlor game is known as *le jeu du mouchoir*. In English, it is musical chairs, which inadvertently combines the game name with the written form of the French word for flesh and a verbal link between childhood and adult desires.

At a later point in the *Discourse*, the flesh figure returns as that of love's obscenity, which, in a disarming gesture of modesty, the lover/ narrator tries to veil by deforming the word "love" into something more affectionate and corny such as "luv" (in the French text, the transformation is from *amour* to *amur*). After comparing himself to the incompetent tenor in his imagined version of "A Night at the Opera," the lover/narrator adds another image in which the figure of the tenor becomes that of the teacher giving a course on love in the guise of Paul Géraldy, the minor poet whose syrupy *Toi et moi* (1923) has remained a perennial bestseller.

The use of language like a lover . . .
not the language of love, but the love
of language, not matter, but meaning,
not what the tongue touches, but what
it forms, not lips and nipples, but
nouns and verbs.

William H. Gass, *On Being Blue*

The figure of the sentimental lover who reveals desire on stage or in the classroom dramatizes almost to the point of caricature a personal vulnerability so disarming that we might easily forget the critical function of the amorous discourse. The lesson of love cannot merely be

its confession or profession unless we maintain the illusory split between public and private acts. My comments have tried to integrate the
amorous discourse within the evolution of Barthes's practice of semiotics. In view of the dramatization of that practice, I want to trace some
of the pedagogical implications of the space of the seminar as part of
the shift toward "another semiotics" referred to in the "Introduction to
the Structural Analysis of Narratives."

At a 1969 colloquium on the teaching of literature, Barthes speaks
on the presentation of literary history found in standard French manuals. Elucidating the position taken in *Critique et vérité* against Lansonian
scholarship, Barthes calls for a rethinking of literary periods similar to
what Michel Foucault provides in *The Order of Things*. Characterizing
literary history as a series of institutional exclusions, Barthes foresees a
set of counter-histories of the censures against class differences, sexuality, and the concept of literature itself. At first glance, it appears that
Barthes has found in Foucault the methodology he might have needed
some twenty years earlier to elaborate the project set forth in *Writing
Degree Zero*. But where Foucault goes on to trace the disappearance of the
individual within discourse, Barthes seeks to reassert the possibility of
individual utterance as an act of resistance against such disappearance.
In view of the function and value Barthes ascribes to the seminar space, it
is not surprising that literary study is seen in this earlier text as felicitous
for that reassertion. Barthes writes initially of an irreducible difference in
literature between writing and teaching: "This antinomy is serious because it is linked to what is perhaps the most serious of today's problems:
the transmission of knowledge and the problem of alienation. For if the
larger structures of economic alienation have been brought to light, those
of the alienation of knowledge have not. I believe that, on this scale, a
political conceptualization is insufficient and that a psychoanalytic conceptualization is necessary."[7]

A version of that revised teaching appears in the long memorandum (*aide-mémoire*) prepared by Barthes for a 1964–65 seminar on
classical rhetoric. Reprinted with a brief preface six years later in
Communications, the memorandum spans the 1966–70 period I have
characterized as that of Barthes's break with structural analysis. In
addition, it shows clearly to what extent the shift in theoretical position
bears upon the transmission of knowledge referred to in the 1969 paper
cited above. He begins by commenting after the fact on his choice of
topic. The terms he uses reinscribe the history of writings announced
as early as *Writing Degree Zero* within newer concerns he is to elaborate

more fully in *S/Z* and *The Pleasure of the Text:* "At the origin (or horizon) of this seminar, as always, was the modern text; in other words, the text which does not yet exist."[8] Of particular interest in Barthes's exposition is his listing of the domains or functions of rhetorical activity. For in 1964–65, Barthes still conceives of rhetoric as a metalanguage, a "discourse on discourse" distinct from what it projects as a language object. As far as critical method is concerned, we are still "before" the break with the scientific project; that is, not yet at the more reflexive practice inaugurated in *S/Z.* At the same time, however, the actual description of functions reveals pedagogical and institutional questions more in tune with Barthes's critical practice "after" the break.

Of the six functions listed, four subscribe to traditional views dividing rhetoric in classical antiquity into disciplines of art, science, teaching, and ethics. As in the Socratic dialogues, rhetoric blends with philosophy and serves as the center of all education dealing with language. First and foremost a technique or art of persuasion, the term designates sets of rules as well as the acquisition of skills to be conducted under the guidance of a master. In addition, since the art of persuasion can conceivably serve truth as well as untruth or illusion, rhetoric also touches on a body of ethical prescriptions for its proper use.

Two final practices or functions take rhetoric out of the classroom, so to speak, and into the wider public places of the market, the temple, and the law court. As a social practice, rhetoric also serves to maintain class distinctions by which those able to pay for acquiring the skills of persuasion assure themselves this property of the spoken word: "Language being a power, laws of access to it were set forth in order to establish it as a pseudo-science, closed to those unable to speak and dependent on a costly initiation. Born 2,500 years ago, classical rhetoric is worn down and dies in the 'rhetoric class,' initiatory consecration of bourgeois culture."[9] The privileges of access to power are also those which close off and exclude access, leading to a subversive practice fully contained within the institution of rhetoric described above: "As all these practices constitute a formidable institutional system ('repressive,' as one says nowadays), a kind of 'black' rhetoric, a certain derision of rhetoric (suspicions, contempt, ironies), was to be expected: games, parodies, erotic or obscene references, adolescent jokes."[10]

Once he associates the social practice of rhetoric with privilege and preserving class differences, Barthes faces the same problem as teacher he faced in *Writing Degree Zero* as writer and critic. On its own, denunciation of privilege can only go so far before it, like *la rhétorique noire*, becomes formalized and ineffective, easily contained within the institution it seeks to subvert. Barthes's response some fifteen years after *Writing Degree Zero* is twofold. At the so-called level of content (or curriculum), he extends the earlier historical project by proposing to trace the evolution of rhetoric as a metalanguage with specific functions and values in different periods and cultures: "Yes, a history of Rhetoric (as research, as book, as teaching) is necessary today, made wider by a new way of thinking (linguistics, semiology, historical science, psychoanalysis, Marxism)."

In a second approach focused on pedagogy itself, the very practice of "revolutionary science" imposes a change in the roles traditionally taken by master and disciple. As Barthes sees it, this change would have the activity of teaching serve the functions of *exemplum* and *argumentum* generally set on the side of content as figures to be emulated: "The object of this synoptical knowledge is the correspondence or interaction linking types of souls with types of discourse. Platonic rhetoric displaces writing to focus on personal interlocution, the *adhominatio;* the fundamental mode of discourse is the dialogue between master and student, united by inspired love. *Thinking in common;* such mght be the motto of the dialectic. Rhetoric is a dialogue of love."[12] The goal of this change in teaching is admittedly utopian. It recalls the liberatory values of the late 1960s counterculture and those who directed those values toward more political uses. It also invokes a generalized knowledge beyond the model instituted by the sophists, coming closer to a love of knowledge (and knowledge of love) illustrated throughout the Socratic dialogues. Whether or not such a practice of teaching is possible in the classroom, its image reappears in the figures of the lover/narrator in *A Lover's Discourse.*

Here are some facts of experience: it is at
the moment when a man of genius enters
an academy that he seems to become
ordinary. I see no other reason
for this except that genius in the arts and
sciences tolerates only those tasks it sets
for itself. It does badly whatever it undertakes
as a duty.

Diderot, "Des Académies et surtout
d'une académie de langue"

Some seven years later, Barthes returns to the interplay between
teaching and desire in his inaugural lecture at the Collège de France.
Acknowledging the status afforded by this honorary appointment, he
tries to set it within the conflict he sees exerted by society and tech-
nocracy on one side and the revolutionary desires of its youth and
students on the other. A longtime foe of university critics, Barthes is
also a maverick who bucked the system by teaching at one of the elite
Grandes Ecoles. without ever completing the *Doctorat d'Etat* required for
a permanent professorship (the *Système de la mode,* undertaken to fulfill
the thesis requirement, was published without any formal defense).
As a result, Barthes's elevation to the Collège de France sets him in a
somewhat delicate position. While his election to the first Chair in
Literary Semiology carries academic recognition, his acceptance also
acquiesces to personal and professional vanity. Sartre, for one, refused
the Nobel Prize awarded him in 1964.

Barthes attempts to confront the question of vanity when, in his
opening remarks, he describes his elevation as culminating his earliest
aspirations to a vocation as writer. In the tradition of the inaugural
address, the new member of the Collège de France evokes the memory
of the predecessor whose passing is the pretext for the new appointment. When, as in this case, a new chair precludes the homage to a
direct predecessor, the inaugural lesson serves to set off the area of
inquiry to be pursued from those already occupied within the institution. In this sense, Barthes's appointment to the Collège needs to be
seen in conjunction with those of Lévi-Strauss and Foucault; that is,
within the appropriation of the "human sciences" and structuralism
by French cultural institutions. So after setting the ritual into motion
with nods to Michelet, Valéry, Benveniste, Merleau-Ponty and

Foucault, he states that this honor will make it that much easier for him to enlarge the scope of his pedagogy: "To teach or even to speak outside the limits of institutional sanction is certainly not to be rightfully and totally uncorrupted by power: power (the *libido dominandi*) is there, hidden in any discourse, even when uttered in a place outside the bounds of power. Therefore, the freer such teaching, the further we must inquire into the conditions and processes by which discourse can be disengaged from all will-to-possess" (*L*, 4).

Sensitive to the pressures which define teaching as a social activity entailing power and a will-to-possess, Barthes seeks their impact on what the individual is left able to say and do. He finds power so diffused within daily life that one is loath to admit its presence in the social mechanism of the language we speak and write. If, as Barthes implies, there is no escape from institutions of power, then what lesson can the professor of desire teach? To offer a lapidary answer to an equally lapidary question: the lesson is that of resistance and its means are those of literature as Barthes defines it in the following passage: "I mean by *literature* neither a body nor a series of works, nor even a branch of commerce or of teaching, but the complex graph of the traces of a practice, the practice of writing. Hence, it is essentially the text with which I am concerned—the fabric of signifiers which constitute the work. For the text is the very outcropping of speech, and it is within speech that speech must be fought, led astray—not by the message of which it is the instrument, but by the play of words of which it is the theater" (*L*, 6).

Because it stages language as the production of meaning and affirmation of value, literature promotes a reflexivity in which each of us can recognize the discourses of power as we experience them, so to speak, "outside the text." When that staging reveals the censure or distortion of individual utterances in the name of institutions of power and authority, the act of utterance reasserts a subversive potential Barthes sees as unique. Because utterance also asserts the materiality of language, literature can temper the lofty abstractions of scientism with the irreducible corporality of a speaking subject: "The act of stating, by exposing the subject's place and energy, even his deficiency (which is not his absence), focuses on the very reality of language, acknowledging that language is an immense halo of implications, of effects, of turns, returns, and degrees. It assumes the burden of making understood a subject both insistent and ineffable, unknown and yet recognized by a disturbing familiarity. Words are no longer mistaken for simple instruments; they are cast as projections, explosions, vibrations, devices, flavors. Writing makes knowledge festive" (*L*, 7).

As they are characterized above, the teaching and study of literature are less concerned with ill-fated attempts to pursue a science than with leading the individual to recognize what happens between the signs emitted by a text and those it elicits via reading in a process of what Barthes, following Lacan, terms "the Real." To this end, literature and semiology correct each other in a continuous process reminiscent of what Heraclitus saw as mutual adjustment. Today one might more readily refer to intertextuality and a vision of the reading experience as a turn toward other writings as antidote to myths of pure creativity. For Barthes, the knowledge made possible by literary semiology remains limited as it is equated with pragmatic science. In direct antithesis to the interpretive model set forth in the *Michelet*, Barthes rejects pragmatic interpretation as a prime focus of the reading process: "In other words, semiology is not a grid; it does not permit a direct apprehension of the real through the imposition of a general transparency which would render it intelligible" (*L*, 13). Semiology is a language about other languages. Because it is no longer a metalanguage, it allows for focus on the historical determinants affecting the production and interpretation of texts as a process of signification. Where straightforward political or scientific readings would, respectively, demystify or formalize sign production, Barthes once again asserts a utopian function for a literature attuned to the inevitability of power: "Utopia, of course, does not save us from power. The utopia of language is salvaged as the language of utopia—a genre like the rest. We can say that no writer who began in a rather lonely struggle against the power of language could or can avoid being co-opted by it, either in the posthumous form of an inscription within official culture, or in the present form of a mode which imposes its image and forces him to conform to expectation. No way out for this author than to shift ground—or to persist—or both at once" (*L*, 9).

In 1957, the *Mythologies* provides a first semiology by reading popular culture as a form of mythic writing worked over by capitalist institutions. By 1970, the militancy spawned in France by the events surrounding May 1968 leads to a more violent semioclasm where the study of signs imposes their destruction. By 1977, the impasse of militancy as an ill-fated attempt to break out from the inevitability of power imposes a third version as abjuration and change. Continuing the Greek paradigm, Barthes terms this final version semiotropy, or "turning-toward-signs." The third version is an attempt to accept the immediacy of signs while accounting for qualities rejected by earlier approaches via science and politics. Barthes notes first of all how the play of signification relates to its apophatic nature; that is, its dependence on verisimilitude and the uncertainty such verisimilitude implies. After the earlier versions derived from scientific and political projects, the final version of semiology as semiotropy is an attempt to adjust theory and practice to account for the ongoing semiotic process within history. In the terms of Saussurian linguistics, Barthes appears to support the notion that *langue* needs to be understood as a methodological convenience, an illusion of fixity opposed to the plurality of utterances. Only a semiology which affirms the uncertainty of signs can trace within history the differences on which later scientific or political projects are formulated.

In what amounts to a final testament or statement of faith to his generation and those of his students, Barthes defends semiotropy as a direct result of historical change and its impact on his practice as literary critic:

The pleasure of the imaginary sign is conceivable now due to certain recent mutations, which affect culture more than society itself: the use we can make of the forces of literature I have mentioned is modified by a new situation. On one hand and first of all, the myth of the great French writer, the sacred depositary of all higher values, has crumbled since the Liberation; it has dwindled and died gradually with each of the last survivors of the *entre-deux-guerres;* a new *type* has appeared, and we no longer know—or do not yet know?—what to call him: writer? intellectual? scribe? In any case, literary mastery is vanishing; the writer is no longer center stage. On the other hand and subsequently, May '68 has revealed the crisis in our teaching. The old values are no longer transmitted, no longer circulate, no longer impress; literature is desacralized, institutions are impotent to defend and impose it as the model of the human. It is not, if you like, that literature is destroyed; rather it is no longer *protected,* so that this is the moment to deal with it. Literary semiology is, as it were, that journey which lands us in a country free by default; angels and dragons are no longer there to defend it. Our gaze can fall, not without perversity, upon certain old and lovely things, whose signified is abstract, out of date. It is a moment at once decadent and prophetic, a moment of gentle apocalypse, a historical moment of the greatest possible pleasure. (*L,* 14)

Having recognized the decline of traditional values and the illusions of mastery, Barthes seems to have projected into his teaching the lessons of his own evolution. As a professor of desire, he has demonstrated that while it is unrealistic to compete against institutions of power and authority, teaching can loosen their discourses by revealing their tendentiousness and artifice. For each of us, the study of signs and meaning needs to be recognized as dependent on value and primal scenes of recognition relating knowledge and pleasure. By dramatizing discourse, Barthes can lighten its impact and demonstrate its ties to symbolic processes, a loosening by means of fragment, digression, and excursus described in the very terms of the primal scene recounted in *A Lover's Discourse:* "I should therefore like the speaking and the listening that will be interwoven here to resemble the comings and goings of a child playing beside his mother, leaving her to bring a pebble, a piece of string, and thereby tracing around a calm center a whole locus of play within which the pebble, the string come to matter less than the enthusiastic giving of them" (*L,* 15).

When, in the *Symposium,* Socrates states that love is the one thing in the world he understands, he is immediately desired by those who believe mistakenly that to possess the Master physically would be somehow to possess the knowledge to which he claims. What Alcibiades takes to be a jilting by Socrates is also the only way to assure that he might eventually proceed toward self-knowledge. Only by refusing Alcibiades can Socrates prevent him from accepting a subservient role in a social hierarchy of marked class differences. The final entry in *A Lover's Discourse* invokes a similar act of refusal which, following Socrates, is less a simple refusal than an apophasis: "So desire still irrigates the non-will-to-possess by this perilous movement: *I love you* in my head, but I imprison it behind my lips. I do not divulge. I say silently to who is no longer or is not yet the other: *I keep myself from loving you*" (*FDA,* 234). Only by acknowledging desire in the very moment of denying it can the professor of desire teach the knowledge of love and love of knowledge, thus fulfilling the nurturing function essential to the learning process as a continuous affirmation of joyful wisdom.

IV. The Triumph of Writing

The novel is always the critic's horizon:
the critic is the man who is going to write
and who, like the Proustian narrator, satisfies
this expectation with a supplementary work,
who creates himself by seeking himself and
whose function is to accomplish his
project of writing even while eluding it.

Barthes, *Critical Essays*

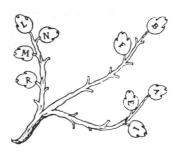

CHAPTER EIGHT

Circular Memories: Via Proust

In a review of George Painter's biography of
Proust, Barthes questions the relation between a
writer's life and his or her work. In particular, he
questions the assumed identity between author
and narrator that posits parallels between biography and fiction: "Taken in their extension (and
not in their substance), the parallel lives of Proust
and his narrator come together only in rare instances; what they share in common is a fundamental series of events or articulations."[1] Questioning the priority of the life over the work does
not, however, suggest a neat reversal; instead, it
collapses the distinction into a more general
activity of writing. As if, Barthes adds, Proust
had written the same work twice: once in his

book and once in his life. Who is Proust for Barthes? Neither a model nor an origin; as Montesquiou is not merely the model for Charlus, although some of him resonates in the fictional character and thereby refracts the historical referent much in the same way that some of Agostinelli is refracted in Albertine and Cabourg in Balbec. The status of these links between the life and the work needs to be clarified, since its understanding points to what remains incomplete in Barthes's projection, what has come to be known as the intertext: "Proust is what comes to me, not what I summon up; not an 'authority,' simply a *circular memory*. Which is what the inter-text is: the impossibility of living outside the infinite text—whether this text be Proust or the daily newspaper or the television screen: the book creates the meaning, the meaning creates life" (*PT*, 36). Neither Barthes read via Proust nor Proust read within Barthes, but an ongoing movement between the two.

The "Projets de préface" at the start of *Contre Sainte-Beuve* sketch the principles of a future program of reading to correct what Proust sees as the blind spots of Sainte-Beuve's critical method. Sketch or suggest, rather than formulate, because the reader is left to assemble into coherence a set of what are more properly statements of difference. Proust's literary vision remains incomplete, to be supplemented in the writing of *A la Recherche du temps perdu*. But even at this stage in his development, Proust is already at work elucidating the place of critical thinking within literary invention in order to write the *Recherche* as a fictional narrative on a fully formed critical position: "Thus it seems to me that about Sainte-Beuve, and presently much more in respect of Sainte-Beuve than about him, I might have things to say which perhaps are not without their importance; whilst in pointing out where, in my opinion, he sinned as a writer and as a critic, I might perhaps manage to say some things, things I have long had in mind about what criticism should do and what art is."[2]

Because he sought to apply to literary thinking a methodology borrowed from the natural sciences, Sainte-Beuve tended to equate the work and writer, invoking the author's life to explain the literary work. In so doing, he remains blind to what Proust describes as the specific value of literary invention for critical understanding and self-knowledge: "This method ignores what a very slight degree of self-knowledge teaches us: that a book is the product of a different *self* from the self we manifest in our habits, in our social life, in our vices. If we would try to understand that particular self, it is by searching our own

bosoms, and trying to reconstruct it there, that we may arrive at it."[3]
Where Proust questions the sovereignty of intelligence in the cause of
what he sees as the true matter of art, Barthes inscribes critical writing
within a more personal discourse of reminiscence and introspection.
Despite a playful mixing of genres since *S*/*Z*, he appears never to have
completely rejected a critical orientation even in his experiments with
narrative forms such as the *journal intime*, the fragment, and autobiography. The same point could be made concerning Proust's evolution
from *Contre Sainte-Beuve* to the *Recherche*. For despite the antecedent of
Jean Santeuil, the movement toward the novel extends a prerequisite
critical project.

Between the appearance of *A Lover's Discourse* in April 1977 and
the death of his mother later the same year, Barthes began to take notes
for an extended narrative which he hoped to turn into his first novel.
Readers of the *Discourse* and the 1975 *Roland Barthes* might well have
foreseen the project, for the prevalence of fictional elements in these
texts—"du romanesque sans le roman"—pointed increasingly toward conventional *belles-lettres* and a retreat from the rear-guard of the
avant-garde Barthes had occupied during the 1960s. Like Proust before
him, the progression toward a culminating work of fiction—Barthes
termed it a "true" novel—devolved from personal experience and the
urgency of a vision elucidated in the face of sickness and death. When
his mother died in the fall of 1977, Barthes overcame his grief, noted
the biographic parallel with Proust, and set to work in earnest. With
full respect to both parties concerned, Barthes was never a match for
Proust. And by the winter of 1979–80—some months before his own
death in March 1980—Barthes admitted as much in his lectures at the
Collège de France.

In *The Pleasure of the Text,* Barthes invokes Freud's claim that the
new is not merely a fashion and much less a fad, but the value by which
life becomes an ongoing (if discontinuous) assertion of difference. In
retrospect, the scope of that assertion is intelligible in the encompas-
sing movement identified by Freud in *Beyond the Pleasure Principle* as
the death drive. An orientation toward death—noted in his mother
and later in himself—is not, however, a mere symptom, not simply a
clinical concept by which we might classify and dismiss Barthes as a
case in point. If Barthes is ultimately unequal to Proust, he also admits
it. Rather than insist on Barthes's failed repetition of a Proustian
itinerary, it is more instructive to trace the limits of that repetition in
view of what he has left as the unwitting legacy of his final texts:

notably, the book published under the title, *Camera Lucida: Reflections on Photography*.

Toward the end of *The Pleasure of the Text*, Barthes writes that explorations of text form the literary dimension of what he refers to as the theory of the materialist subject. That is, a corrective to emphasis on the objects of critical thinking via a revised attitude toward the critical consciousness or subject. Two or three points need to be clarified. First of all, the pendulum swing away from the object of critical activity toward its subject is itself a remainder of sorts, a holdover from the subject/object binary associated with structures of intentionality and a phenomenological tradition Barthes acknowledges by dedicating *Camera Lucida* to Sartre's 1940 study on imagination. For a critic commonly seen as a co-traveler of the *Tel Quel* group and their free-wheeling mixture of literature, philosophy, and politics, the revived ties to phenomenology signal that Barthes was already aware in 1973 of his residual debts to the values of a recent past. After structuralism and post-structuralism, with their intimations of post-modern sensibilities, could it be that what was new was neither the modern nor post-modern, but the past of a retrograde vision animated by introspection and self-analysis?

In addition, the status of the materialist subject had somehow to mediate as a construct of theory between Barthes's growing nostalgia for literary values embodied by Gide, Proust, and Brecht and a revised critical attitude which was the consequence of his own intellectual evolution with its debts to Nietzsche, Freud, and Lacan. If, like the author of *Contre Sainte-Beuve*, Barthes was finding that intelligence alone could not supply him with the vision he wanted to achieve in his writing, he was unwilling to allow temperament alone to refute completely what intelligence had allowed him to see. All of which produced a most personal critical quandary, one Barthes never resolved to his satisfaction.

Instead of resolving this quandary, Barthes appears to have curtailed his writing in the hopes of descending from high generalities to something more personal and earth(l)y. As a result, his descent has all the trappings of an identity crisis at the age of sixty. A trace of Montaigne's "Of Experience" creeps into *The Pleasure of the Text* as Barthes notes the dependence of any theory of the self on the more mundane truths of anatomy and physiology. Consequently, Barthes's approach to materialist theory—materialist in the sense of language—returns invariably to the frailties of the human body and the ways we deal with those frailties as a life (and death) work: "Then perhaps the subject returns, not as illusion but as *fiction*. A certain pleasure is derived from a way of imagining oneself as *individual*, of inventing a final, rare fiction: the fictive identity. The fiction is no longer the illusion of a unity; on the contrary, it is the theater of society in which we stage our plural: our pleasure is individual—but not personal" (*PT*, 62).

But even in the very terms of introspection, the fiction of the subject—especially that of the "open" subject aware of its inherent loss as *sujet aperte (à perte)*—remains very much a cultural entity formed in terms of biography, history, sociology, and neurosis. Thus, what Sartre describes in *Being and Nothingness* as the elements of facticity becomes for Barthes the systems of classification used to keep the fiction of the subject in some kind of coherence. And within the interplay between temperament and critical position, the Proustian intertext appears as a recurrent figure or leitmotif, less a privileged presence or authority than a ghost which cannot be shaken: "I recognize that Proust's work, for myself, at least, is *the* reference work, the general *mathesis*, the *mandala* of the entire literary cosmogony—as Mme de Sévigné's letters were for the narrator's grandmother, tales of chivalry for Don Quixote, etc." (*PT*, 36). Unwilling even to assimilate the Proustian *souvenir circulaire* totally into his literary concerns— "Cela ne veut pas dire du tout que je sois un 'spécialiste' de Proust"— Barthes opts for the more personal category of *amateur* and inscribes literary questions within the introspection of his recent texts.

Camera Lucida is very much of a *note* on photography; that is, less a treatise or systematic analysis than a sequence of fragments divided into two sections or movements. As with Barthes's other writings since the early 1970s, a loose formal structure soon reveals a discontinuous pattern and a textual movement closer to narrative progression than to systematic reflection. As in *The Pleasure of the Text* and *A Lover's Discourse*, a critical project set forth at the start of the text is replaced by a narrower inquiry pointing to the affective dimension of writing. Since 1973 the orientation of Barthes's final writings no longer extends the structural analysis of narratives of the mid-1960s, but moves instead toward self-analysis with debts on one side to Gide and Proust and on the other to Freud and Lacan. As a result, those who like their criticism "neat, a secondary and clearly separated activity in style and function" (the words are those of Geoffrey Hartman in *Criticism in the Wilderness*), are likely to be put off by the stylistic peculiarities of *Camera Lucida*. Unlike the musical structure Lévi-Strauss uses to write *The Raw and the*

Cooked as theme and variation, the fragmentary writing in *Camera Lucida* supports an essential break in whose terms ode is set against palinode in order to assert difference.

Part one—the ode—begins as a theoretical meditation on the specificity of photography—the photograph opposed to the cinema—and a search for the suitable criteria to account for that specificity. *Camera Lucida* extends an inquiry begun in 1961 with "The Photographic Message" with a notable intervention of pleasure as value in the latest text.[4] In marked contrast to his earlier approaches, Barthes sets the essential immobility of the photograph against the fluidity of cinematic images. The effect of that immobility leads Barthes to an initial formulation of the *punctum* or striking detail which traverses the cultural codes of knowledge (the *studium*). The *punctum*, in turn, sets off a momentary shock and leads to a revised approach to the image based on the temporal jump it provokes in the viewer. As with the interplay between *plaisir* and *jouissance* in *The Pleasure of the Text*, the *punctum* breaks the *studium*, as a displaced detail that reanimates the image in terms of the personal value Barthes had found lacking in classical phenomenology. This displacement does not, however, suggest the functional priority of the *punctum* over its counterpart. Instead, Barthes collapses any simple distinction between the two by inscribing the *punctum* as an integral factor of the perceived image—"a stilled center, an erotic or lacerating value buried in myself" (*CL*, 16). It is thus part of an expanded *studium* which, at this point in Barthes's text, remains without complete formulation and open to the more personal interpretation Barthes provides in the second half of his text.

A second attempt to develop and revise the *studium/punctum* binary emphasizes temporality and a documentary function for the photograph, which reproduces mechanically and chemically what can never recur existentially. By giving objective form to a single moment and removing it from the passage of time, the photograph forever repeats the same tautology: "A pipe, here, is always and intractably a pipe. It is as if the Photograph always carries its referent with itself, both affected by the same amorous or funereal immobility, at the very heart of the moving world" (*CL*, 6–7).

At first glance, the above passage is essentially playful. The offhand reference to René Magritte's painting *Ceci n'est pas une pipe* adds levity to the more serious reflection on the status of the photographic image. The passage also suggests a critical position which sacrifices conceptual consistency to personal value. In fact, once the opening meditation on photography is seen as incomplete without its palinode, the entire first part of the text is undermined. To restate this point in the idiom of phenomenology invoked throughout part one, Barthes's inquiry is incomplete as long as he fails to specify the intentional links which allow him to compose its critical object. Rather than question what photography is *for him*. And what it comes to be *for him* through *Camera Lucida* reformulates the original inquiry in a personal thematics of love, death, and mourning. When Barthes contrasts the existential singularity of the moment with its unlimited photographic reproduction, he also recasts it as action or dramatic event. Commenting on a photograph of Lewis Payne, convicted of attempting to murder U.S. Secretary of State W. H. Seward in 1865, Barthes notes the documentary *studium* before adding: "But the *punctum* is: *he is going to die. I read at the same time: This will be* and *this has been*" (*CL*, 96). Beyond the photo's invocation of an historical event with fixed referents in time and space, Barthes seeks an additional function to reinscribe the *studium* within a more intimate and fateful drama of death in the future.

As the dramatic force of the *punctum* pierces the *studium* by a detail, Barthes notes a momentary collapse of past and future he terms a catastrophe of love and death. The critical position implied by these concepts is open to a number of challenges. Where Barthes upholds the irreducibility of the moment to its representation, he does not follow through to question the ideological implications of that representation as he did in the *Mythologies*. Nor does he question ongoing attitudes in light of critiques found in Husserl's *Phenomenology of Inner Time Consciousness* (1908) and Proust's *Recherche*. Barthes seems to have revised his claim in "The Photographic Message" that the photograph functions as a message without a code.

The early sections of *Camera Lucida* do not always make for conceptual clarity, nor do they strive for internal consistency. In full recognition of these shortcomings, the *studium / punctum* binary is necessary, despite its flaws, as an integral moment in the process of self-analysis at the core of Barthes's project. Since the fragmentary nature of *Camera Lucida* works against any kind of synthesis or finality, the only way for Barthes to proceed as a materialist subject divided between critical and expressive languages is to assert a discontinuous movement between the two. This is, in fact, yet another binary, but one located fully within the text as a corrective against the illusion that a note *on* photography is possible without a more personal grounding. No single statement can be set apart from the others; as in *A Lover's Discourse*, there is no metalanguage.

But even in view of such qualifications, a number of questions persist. Why does Barthes invoke terms and modes of analysis he immediately questions and later rejects? Why would he go through such elaborate motions when he might just as easily drop the preliminaries and enter directly into the pertinent context of the palinode? Two answers to these questions are immediate. First of all, the palinode can only operate as such in conjunction with an ode: in response to it, after it, *against* it. Difference is asserted within repetition, even when (especially when) the initial assertion serves only as point of departure.

Secondly, the entire sequence of fragments composed by the ode and its palinode points to self-analysis and the process of surfacing or bringing to utterance of feelings, values, and personal truths within the critical subject. Barthes is aware of the resistance he brings to his self-analysis as false moves or opening statements. The sequence of fragments functions on the order of what Freud describes as a screen memory whose transformation is necessary to the process of articulation. At the same time, Barthes ascribes to the articulation process an expressive or surfacing function referred to by Husserl and other phenomenologists as desedimentation. Unlike Derrida in *Speech and Phenomena*, Barthes upholds the priority of the expressive function over any reference or indication. Where Derrida insists on the indicative function as a necessary supplement without which expression remains incomplete, Barthes's position in *Camera Lucida* is ambivalent and uncertain.

The ambivalence of the critical subject torn between two languages can be charted schematically as a convergence of axes at the points where the values of verticality associated with deep structures converge with the horizontal movement of indication. When, in turn, we note that *Camera Lucida* is itself a syntagm animated by a fascination with the immobile and silent paradigm of the photographic image, the status of the critical subject as internally divided and ambivalent should become clearer. To return to the opening terms of this digression, the recurrent pattern of invoking and subverting binary constructs allows Barthes—or, more specifically, the critical subject who narrates *Camera Lucida*—as free a rein as possible to set forth what might otherwise be repressed in a more conventional note *on* photography. In the opening section of *Camera Lucida*, the object of that attempt to revive or reanimate critical writing via introspection is the phenomenology seemingly at odds with what has come in its wake.

Is a return to phenomenology possible after Foucault, Lacan, and Derrida? Can such a return be at all in line with a theory of the materialist subject? Both as critic and person, Barthes has always been too contentious to accept without question the limitations imposed by conventions, be they social or literary. And so it is not too surprising that Barthes would flout convention by invoking a phenomenological idiom when, for all practical purposes, it is no longer fashionable to do so. In this respect, the dedication to Sartre's *Psychology of the Imagination* and references to phenomenology should not be misconstrued as refuting more recent critical positions. Unrepentant phenomenologists need not rejoice. Barthes's untimeliness is less an instance of compromise or backsliding than a reassessment of phenomenology within the differences represented by psychoanalytic and linguistic models of perception. When Barthes invokes Sartre or refers to Lyotard's 1954 monograph, he does so beyond the position these references suggest in themselves and within a more intimate scope of introspection and self-knowledge: "Classical phenomenology, the kind I had known in my adolescence (and there has not been any other since), had never, so far as I could remember, spoken of desire or of mourning" (*CL*, 21).[5]

As the *studium/punctum* construct is subsumed within a more intimate thematic of love and mourning, the temporal jolt which certain photos provoke is reexamined beyond its initial formulation and within what looks increasingly like the dramatic staging (or *"mise-en-scène"*) of a recognition scene. The palinode repeats the ode, but asymmetrically and with added intensity. The palinode repeats the thematics of the first part, rewriting it more compulsively along the lines of critical introspection which further solidify the Proustian connections. Barthes writes: "Now, one November evening shortly after my mother's death, I was going through some photographs. I had no hope of 'finding' her, I expected nothing from these 'photographs' of a being before which one recalls less of that being than by merely thinking of him or her (Proust)" (*CL*, 63). This opening statement of part two tempers the conceptual inconsistencies of part one by situating the ostensible note on photography within a narrower meditation on certain photos, and within this reduced scope of inquiry, a single image whose *découverte*—once again in the phenomenological sense of surfacing—might account for the entire sequence of writing.

The opening statement also recasts the force of the *punctum* measured in the simple criterion of pleasure throughout part one toward the death drive referred to by Freud in *Beyond the Pleasure Principle*. Where Barthes had previously seen the appeal of certain photos in the breaks or loss of continuity they elicit by drawing him momentarily into the future anterior, he now recognizes this break as a *découverte*. Which is to suggest that it functions both as a willed masterful discovery and as a more elusive uncovering within which will and mastery reveal their own inability to offset the movement of time. As grief comes to displace pleasure, Barthes can no longer ignore his predilection for certain photos related to his personal vision of catastrophe. In keeping with the strategy of the screen confession, Barthes casts the source of his identity crisis in cultural terms. In order to introduce the direct cause—the death of the mother—he notes that the Greeks used to say they entered death backwards: "what they had before them was their past" (*CL*, 71).

As Barthes recalls leafing through the collection of photos, the personal and cultural associations proliferate. A number of references to Proust and Valéry focus on an intellectual context which also evokes the historical period of his childhood. Thus Barthes notes that he follows the Proustian narrator in wanting to respect the integrity of grief expressed in the *Recherche* after the death of the narrator's grandmother. At the same time, he adds, several pages later, the old photos do not simply evoke—"ne remémore[nt] pas"—the past within the present: "Nothing Proustian in a photograph" (*CL*, 82). Instead of the synoptic vision Proust's narrator eventually sees as a sign of his future vocation, the double reading of the photo pursued by means of the *studium/punctum* binary occurs fully within the present by tempering the force of nostalgia and melancholy released by certain photographs with an understanding of how this process works on the materialist subject. The reduced scope of inquiry—from the general toward the particular—is intelligible over and above the discontinuity of the fragments as a narrative movement of confession. A photograph of the mother reprinted in *Roland Barthes* becomes a screen image which simultaneously reveals and covers. What it reveals, what Barthes "finds" (*découvre*) in it is an image of the body. What it fails to reveal—and what Barthes comes to identify as the detail he seeks through the photos and the entire note on photography—is the face of the mother, a face later encountered in an earlier photo:

The photograph was very old. The corners were blunted from having been pasted into an album, the sepia print had faded, and the picture just managed to show two children standing together at the end of a little wooden bridge in a glassed-in conservatory, what was called a Winter Garden in those days. My mother was five at the time (1898), her brother seven. He was leaning against the bridge railing, along which he had extended one arm; she, shorter than he, was standing a little back, facing the camera; you could tell that the photographer had said, "Step forward a little so we can see you"; she was holding one finger in the other hand, as children often do, in an awkward gesture. The brother and sister, united, as I knew, by the discord of their parents, who were soon to divorce, had posed side by side, alone, under the palms of the Winter Garden (it was the house where my mother was born, in Chennevières-sur-Marne). (*CL*, 67–69)

After the theoretical discourse *on* photography in the first part of *Camera Lucida*, Barthes stages the *découverte* of the photograph of the Winter Garden as the primal scene or encounter around which the fragments are organized. From all appearances, the photograph described above is at the center of the note. But of all the qualities which establish its value and function within the fragments, the most surprising is Barthes's refusal to reproduce the photo in the text. As a result, what ought to have been the thematic center becomes instead an absent and withheld origin. Fully consistent with the confessional strategy used to articulate the note in fragmentary form, the unrevealed truth of the photo also functions dynamically to prolong the narration by the very kind of unresolved question Barthes describes in *S/Z* as the hermeneutic code. As Barthes leads the reader toward and beyond his ostensible object of inquiry, misapprehension points to the illusion of direct and definitive interpretation. The disappointed expectations reveal the priority of the process of articulation over any kind of end result. As in Lacanian discourse, Barthes always speaks the truth, even if he does not always speak all of it. The absence of the photo affects interpretation of the fragments in that it asserts their openness beyond the convenience of immediate understanding. It does not prevent or deconstruct interpretation as much as relativize it by deferring a definitive reading where a more precipitous one might be seen as preferable.

The photo portrait is an appropriate format to stage this primal scene in Barthes's personal catastrophe. For what he discovers in the photo is the little girl who plays at being an adult. The illusion of the image which is staged or posed corresponds to the illusion of a family on the verge of dissolution. Sarte writes in *Being and Nothingness* that we move toward authentic identities by first acting them out fully aware of our imitation. Likewise, Barthes locates in the pose of the five-year-old the features of the future adult. The immediate meaning of the photo—its *studium*—is felt as a quaint nostalgia and comforting illusion of continuity between past and present. But where the *studium* 'is reassuring, the supplement of the *punctum*—the more intimate sting or jolt that really attracts Barthes to the photo—imposes a further reading which is something other than comforting.

Where the *studium* authenticates the reality of the mother before Barthes, the *punctum* provoked by the photo of the mother as child is less a collapse or convergence of past and present than an assertion of their difference. Where a less forthright critic might characterize his or her inquiry in terms of belief, doctrine, or dogma—and surely Barthes does just this throughout his polemics against Raymond Picard in the mid-1960s—the Barthes of *Camera Lucida* recasts that inquiry as a relation to belief and value.

On the basis of *Camera Lucida,* the progression from the earlier structuralist stance to something more intimate is neither clean nor irreversible. Residual projects and terms resurface in later writings that resonate with the opening lines of *Contre Sainte-Beuve*—"Each day I attach less and less importance to intelligence." To this parallel which Barthes does *not* invoke can be set another from the *Recherche* cited in a passage where Proust's narrator bends down to remove his boots and suddenly sees the face of his dead grandmother, whose living reality he was experiencing for the first time, in an involuntary and complete memory. Returning several fragments later to the same section of *Sodom and Gomorrha,* Barthes again compares himself to the Proustian narrator who not only admits the extent of his grief, but wants also to have it reflect the singularity of its object. Which is the way Barthes tries to account for the loss of his mother as the real and irreversible difference between past and present beyond art or symbolic resolution. Barthes may be smitten with the illusory stasis of the photographic image, but his infatuation has discernible limits, serving only to assert temporal difference and a *punctum* of loss located fully in the present.

The last reference to the *Recherche* is perhaps the most poignant in

its refusal of nostalgia. Unlike the Proustian narrator, Barthes rejects
an artistic resolution as a potential response to his incomplete vision.
But since Barthes goes to great lengths to comment on this particular
episode in the *Recherche*, it is strange that he fails to mention the central
role played in the same section of the novel by a photographic image.
The photograph in question is one which the narrator's grandmother
had taken of herself, after she realized the seriousness of her illness.
Unable to see at the time that the photo portrait is meant to soothe a
future grief whose imminence only the grandmother recognizes, the
narrator does not hide from her his aversion at what he mistakes for a
gesture of tasteless vanity.

Long after her death, the truth of her absence is felt by the narrator
involuntarily as he bends to remove a boot and is overcome by the
recognition that his grandmother used to help him in this minor ritual
and would never again do so. Subsequently the initial jolt is elaborated
by the narrator's embarrassment at his former insensitivity, as if the
painful memory of his inadvertent cruelty somehow tied its object to a
present from which it was irresolvably absent.

I did not seek to mitigate my suffering, to set if off, to pretend that my
grandmother was only somewhere else and momentarily invisible, by addressing to her photograph (the one taken by Saint-Loup, which I had beside me)
words and prayers as to a person who is separated from us but, retaining his
personality, knows us and remains bound to us by an indissoluble harmony.
Never did I do this, for I was determined not merely to suffer, but to respect the
original form of my suffering, as it had suddenly come upon me unawares, and
I wished to continue to feel it, according to its laws, whenever those strange
contradictory impressions of survival and obliteration crossed one another
again in my mind.[6]

When Proust's narrator refuses to give in to the illusion of presence embodied in the photographic image, his act also allows him to
explore further the relationship between absence and presence which,
in turn, he resolves in the final sections of *Time Recaptured*. The narrators of *Camera Lucida* and *Sodom and Gomorrha* both affirm the force of
the photographic image in the very gesture of refusal. Barthes does not
reproduce the photo of his mother in the Winter Garden and Marcel
does not console himself with the photograph of his grandmother. For
the Barthes who traces this particular stage on Proust's way, the truth

of the photo is located less in the image itself than in the revelation of time it allows to occur. From the initial meditation on photography to a slower exploration of specific photos, the meanderings of *Camera Lucida* are best summarized by an image of the labyrinth drawn from Greek mythology and a claim via Nietzsche that movement within the labyrinth reveals only the figure of Ariadne rather than any definitive truth: "The Winter Garden Photograph was my Ariadne, not because it would help me discover a secret thing (monster or treasure), but because it would tell me what constituted that thread which drew me toward photography" (*CL*, 73).

Once the criterion of pleasure is recast in the palinode as a more complex mixture of love and mourning, the intensity of feeling grows with each additional movement along the (metaphoric) length of Ariadne's thread. As noted earlier, a schematic form of that movement projects the horizontal axis or syntagm formed by the process of reading. The image of movement along Ariadne's thread modifies this schema; it implies that the movement of the reading process might instead be closer to an alternation between progressive and regressive visions. Where the initial schema suggests a one-way direction, the addition of a return movement sketches a circular figure of reading Paul de Man notes in "the intricacy of every sentence as well as the narrative network as a whole."[7] What de Man suggests about reading and rereading in Proust also holds true for *Camera Lucida*—with the essential difference that the fragmentary note on photography leads to no final synthesis or resolving vision. The narrator of *Camera Lucida* neither finds nor recaptures time as does Proust's Marcel.

The instability of the fragmentary writing in this last book is supplemented poignantly and pointedly—*punctum* and other forms of the Latin *pungere* recur frequently—by Barthes's unexpected death. In view of this biographic supplement to his discourse on mourning, a final section in this final text provides a commentary on the impact of repetition on the materialist subject. *Camera Lucida* ends by restating the initial question—"What is the essence of photography? What is photography 'in itself?' "—in cultural terms linking the photograph to a generalized Imaginary such as that of Jacques Lacan. In the wake of the intervening meditation on the *punctum* and its role in staging time as a primal drama of love and death, the impossibility of the initial note *on* photography stems from what Barthes comes to describe as the taming or banalizing of the *punctum*. At this final point in his text,

Barthes appears to be moving toward a social critique which would explore this banalizing as a consequence of external values bearing on mythic activity. Among other possible supports, Walter Benjamin's "Work of Art in the Age of Mechanical Reproduction" would extend the analyses of the *Mythologies* and *Critical Essays*. For what Benjamin terms the "aura" of the work of art is precisely what is absent in the "tame" photographic images seemingly produced as objects of commercial exploitation.[8] By 1979, however, the replacement of a pointed social critique by a more contemplative attitude stifles that project, for better or worse, in a more personal meditation.

Barthes concludes that photography is not a discrete object: neither this nor that in a formal or logical sense. It cannot be approached "in itself" without recognizing that the values inherent in such an approach are a matter of choice. Depending on a decision Barthes sees as actively made on a personal basis, photography becomes an art "tamed" by habit or convenience. *Or* it becomes something else closer to madness and the excess of figuration of the *punctum*. The very last set of fragments ends with a choice between these attitudes directed as a challenge to the reader: "Such are the two ways of the photograph. The choice is mine: to subject its spectacle to the civilized code of perfect illusions, or to confront in it the wakening of intractable reality" (*CL*, 119).

The Sartrian ring of this concluding passage reinvokes the vocabulary and ethos of Barthes's first writings. Along with the dedication to Sartre, the act of rereading neatly frames the entire note on photography. Frames it too neatly, because the "two ways" of photography also invoke the "two ways" in Proust's *Recherche* and the circular memories invoked in *The Pleasure of the Text*.

A final return to Proust. In 1971, shortly after his break with structural analysis, Barthes turns to Proust's novel in order to formulate how his change in critical vision relates to the reading process as "an idea of quest." At first, the term *recherche* designates a reading from which Barthes wants to delete any trace of scientism:

Thus can we set forth an "idea of quest" without yielding to the slightest positivist ambition: the *Recherche* is one of the great cosmogonies the 19th century, principally, has been able to produce (Balzac, Wagner, Dickens, Zola), whose character, both monumental and historical, is precisely that of being spaces (galaxies) open to infinite exploration. Which removes critical work far from any illusion of "results" toward the simple production of a supplementary writing whose tutor text (the Proustian novel), if we were to write out our quest, would be only a pretext.[9]

Reading as a *recherche* entails a continually changing vision and the continuous possibility of rereading beyond what is perceived at any single moment. This process of flux is not, however, necessarily cast as correction or progression. It is closer to an inversion such as Barthes finds throughout Proust's (own) *Recherche*. For example, Barthes notes how the odd and vaguely repulsive woman the narrator sees reading *La Revue des Deux Mondes* on the little Balbec train is later identified as Princess Sherbatoff, "pearl of the Verdurin salon." Inversion does not invalidate the initial portrait as much as demonstrate how the passage of time recasts almost all claims to knowledge as precipitous. Inversion of this kind is not totally open-ended. Not, at least, in the *Recherche*, where the narrator arrives at a vision in which, according to Barthes, inversion ceases:

There is, however, a moment in the *Recherche* when the great structure of inversion no longer functions. What blocks it? Nothing less than Death. It is well known that all of Proust's characters reappear in the final volume of the novel (*Time Recaptured*). But in what state? Not at all inverted (as might have been expected in view of the great lapse of time at the end of which they find each other brought together at the party given by the Princesse de Guermantes). But, on the contrary, *prolonged*, even more than aged, *preserved* and one would want to be able to add "persevered." In a life of reprieve, inversion no longer takes hold; the story has only to finish—the book has only to begin.[10]

The last words on the subject are those of Barthes, completing the passage from his 1963 preface to the *Critical Essays*, and bringing us, so to speak, full circle: "The critic is a writer, but a writer reprieved; like the writer, he wants to be believed less because of what he writes than because of his decision to write it, but unlike the writer, he cannot *sign* that desire; he remains condemned to error—to truth" (*CE*, xxi).

Faithful—almost by default—to the inversions of reading as *recherche*, Barthes seems to have had the vision of temporal movement he describes first in *Roland Barthes* and later in *Camera Lucida*. The vision, perhaps, but not the supplement of writing. In this sense, he is less the projected counterpart of the narrator of the *Recherche* than an offshoot of

Bergotte, the writer and early tutor figure of the narrator's literary vocation, who dies unable to write the vision he attains—too late—of what his writing ought to have been. It is admittedly unwise to equate Barthes with any character in the *Recherche*, much less with Proust himself. But within the Proustian novel and the *idée de recherche* rewritten by Barthes as critical reading is a vision which, in time, may disclose whether Barthes attains in his own writings what he saw in Proust's evolution and sought to retrace in the form of circular memories.

Who could avoid being
touched by a text whose
declared "subject" is death?

Barthes, "Textual Analysis
of Poe's 'Valdemar'"

CHAPTER NINE

Last Words and Primal Scenes

Barthes's progression from a critical discourse on
writing toward active figuration revises his practice according to the materialist program first set
forth in *The Pleasure of the Text*. In theoretical
terms, that revised practice is visible as an expansion of the symbolic functions of writing. But
while Barthes uses such expansion to full textual
effect, his revised practice is not without its own
complications, what Christian Metz refers to in
The Imaginary Signifier as "the problem of the
word."[1] The problem arises from a confusion
since for all practical purposes we equate the
notion of figure with the figure of speech and a
classical tradition in which the figure is an object
of study to be described and classified. When

Barthes writes in *A Lover's Discourse* of the strategic function of anacoluthon, tmesis, and asyndeton, he revives the traditions of persuasion and elocution that lead to a new exploration of tropes within systems of discourse open to the materialist revision. All the same, the supplement of rhetorical models does not yet fully account for figuration, not so long as it isolates the figure from discourse much in the way Saussure tries to extract speech (*parole*) from the wider social phenomenon of language (*langue*).

Commenting on this isolation of the figure, Metz argues that the special attention paid to word-based figures occurs at the expense of both the sentence and the live moment of utterance. Because he wants to clarify the possible links between the study of film and the techniques of psychoanalysis, Metz sees the emphasis on the word-based figure as limited in view of film processes where the word is continually set against visual perception. Recognizing the potential value of condensation and displacement, Metz explores these prime features of the dreamwork to approach film as a point of convergence where multiple processes assert the added factor of the body in movement beyond the tradition of word-based rhetoric associated with classical antiquity and the Renaissance. Not surprisingly, the revised rhetoric of corporeal representation set forth by Metz for film study recalls the gymnastic and choreographic movements invoked by Barthes in the preface to *A Lover's Discourse:*

These fragments of discourse can be called *figures.* The word is to be understood, not in its rhetorical sense, but rather in its gymnastic or choreographic acceptation; in short, in the Greek meaning: is not the "schema," but, in a much livelier way, the body's gestures caught in action and not contemplated in repose: the body of athletes, orators, statues: what in the straining body can be immobilized. (*FDA*, 3–4)

This attempt to grasp or immobilize the body in action as a figure has two direct consequences for the processes of figuration described conceptually by Metz and textually by Barthes. First, the isolation of the figure is an artifice or fiction at odds with the ongoing movement of the body. When such isolation occurs as a verbal effect, it shows how figuration brings together qualities of verbal and visual modes of perception. For Metz, psychoanalysis and film are both capable of providing a vocabulary that adjusts the linguistic model to account for the symbolic processes that inscribe language within the wider processes of corporeal representation Barthes terms *signifiance*. Second, the isolation of the figure within a word-based approach neglects those aspects of figuration that allow for a determination of the materialist subject via body image. Because this positionality of the subject is developed via a number of spatial and visual associations, it provides a more dynamic account of symbolic activity than is possible by approaching the figure as a discrete and seemingly autonomous entity.

A final consequence of approaching the figure via figuration involves the application of psychoanalytic models of reading, in static and dynamic practices that warrant closer examination. On the side of the static reading based on a fixed relation of one sign to another, Barthes's use of the fragment in *Camera Lucida* disperses the notes or reflections on photography within a system of writing that undermines definitive interpretation. As a result, each fragment works against the cumulative series in what amounts to a strategy of interruption. Beyond this economy of the fragment, an alternative approach to figuration examines the activity of writing as the staging of a confessional discourse that defers disclosure as long as possible. Instead of the fixed association characteristic of static interpretation, this second approach looks to the phenomenon of repetition much along the lines of Lacan's commentary on the *Fort/Da* passage in *Beyond the Pleasure Principle*. Viewed as part of an ongoing process of figuration, *Camera Lucida* extends the confessional strategy at work since *S/Z* and *The Pleasure of the Text*, playing out the gesture of confession beyond the more immediate concerns of critical discourse.

But that is not yet, so to speak, the whole picture, because it turns out that *Camera Lucida* is the last text published while Barthes was alive. As a result, it functions inadvertently as a last word that carries the burden of completion. For better or worse, those who read the reflections on photography today can hardly avoid seeking the signs of personal prophecy in the account of his mother's death. When Barthes describes the drama of future catastrophe in the photograph of the Winter Garden he finds after his mother has died, the verbal account of that discovery prefigures a similar discovery or recognition on the part of the reader. By emphasizing the account of the mother's death as a verbal form, it is possible to see it as an instance of metonymy, the figure of substitution *par excellence*. Thus the inadvertent immediacy of Barthes's own repetition of the movement toward death recounted in *Camera Lucida* provides the suitable conditions for an interpretation that would fill in what the final account leaves unsaid.

At the same time, however, the movement toward interpretation needs to be justified by something more than circumstantial coincidence. In order to provide a more substantive basis for interpretation, the metonymic account in *Camera Lucida* must not be cut off from the symbolic activity of figuration it completes. This is another way of stating that the impulse to interpret the final figure of detour or substitution cannot be based solely on its specific content. Instead, a more inclusive approach to figuration must animate the prime figure of metonymy as part of an ongoing activity discernible in earlier texts such as *S/Z* and *The Pleasure of the Text*. In terms of the *Roland Barthes*, the figure is not simply an apparatus, not just part of a system beyond the mastery of the materialist subject. Instead, it is closer to the process of writing Barthes expands into the more generalized symbolic activity of figuration. The implied split between apparatus and writing— "Dismiss the system as an apparatus, accept the systematic as writing"—is hasty, particularly in the case of *Camera Lucida*, where the comments on photographic representation gain thematic intensity as the narrative of repetition and recognition uncovers a supplementary commentary on writing that goes beyond the figure of metonymy toward figuration itself. Between apparatus and writing, how do reflections on the photographic image operate in the movement of Barthes's final writings? Even more directly, one might ask, why the *camera lucida* rather than the *camera obscura*?

The original French title used by Barthes—*La Chambre claire: Note sur la photographie*—evokes the values of light and brilliance associated with the photograph of the Winter Garden that serves as thematic center of the entire narrative. As the antithesis of *la chambre obscure*, the title supports the movement toward consciousness and verbal disclosure recounted by Barthes and centered on the discovery of the image of the mother as child. Integral to this scene of recognition, the leitmotif of the *camera lucida* also allows the reader to project onto the account of the mother's death the image of future catastrophe whose central figure is the narrator.

A second function of the *camera lucida* and *camera obscura* refers to the history of photography and two primitive means of reproduction. The *camera obscura* ("dark room") was one of the earliest mechanical means used by craftsmen and painters to create a lasting image. A second apparatus was the *camera lucida*, invented in 1807 by William Hyde Wollaston. Here is Beaumont Newhall's account of how it was used: "Drawing paper was laid flat. Over it a glass prism was suspended at eye level by a brass rod. Looking through a peephole centered over the edge of the prism, the operator saw at the same time both the subject and the drawing paper; his pencil was guided by the virtual image."[2] The drawing of a *camera lucida* in use that appears in Newhall's *History of Photography* is the same one used by Barthes on the cover of the French edition of *La Chambre claire*. That in itself may be nothing more than coincidence, or possibly a sign that Barthes had used Susan Sontag's *On Photography* for a number of secondary references. Be that as it may, the reproduction in question shows an apparatus that lends itself to the very process of figuration at work in Barthes's last texts. As in the use of the *camera lucida*, the virtual image that guides the pencil (or stylus of inscription) superimposes writing over the specular image reflected through the prism. At the very least, the apparatus in question fulfills Lacan's account of the ongoing interplay between the Symbolic and the Imaginary. In such terms, the force that drives the pencil and propels the process of writing is a combination of artful mastery and something close to compulsion. The movement of writing as a progression toward figuration is thus a process in which the force of intentional meaning becomes dispersed into a more generalized and heterogenous symbolic activity that tempers intentional meaning with its opposite. As early as the *Mythologies*, Barthes had seen that opposition in the binary of denotative and connotative functions. In *S/Z*, however, he comes closer to the figuration at work in *Camera Lucida* when he notes the special place of connotation in the dynamics of interpretation. To be sure, the elusive quality of connotation as a secondary or substratum to denotation lends itself to the movement of metonymy noted by Metz. It thus turns each successive term of denotation into an index. As a result, the process of interpretation moves along the various denotative meanings toward their respective objects (or signifieds), toward a truth Barthes describes in *S/Z* in the very terms of liberation and catastrophe he demonstrates via figuration in *Camera Lucida:*

The connotative signified is literally an *index:* it points but does not tell; what it points to is the name, the truth as name; it is both the temptation to name and the impotence to name. . . . Thus, with its designating, silent movement, a pointing finger always accompanies the classic text: the truth is thereby long desired and avoided, kept in a kind of pregnancy for its full term, a pregnancy whose end, both liberating and catastrophic, will bring about the utter end of discourse. (*S/Z*, 62)

In place of a final word undercut by the immediacy of a sudden and unexpected death, I want to suggest a number of endings—three, to be exact—as alternative interpretations. No last words, then, without the supplement of corresponding primal scenes. The first scene is staged as an inversion of *Camera Lucida*. The photo by Nadar provided by Barthes in place of the photo of the mother as child has its own *punctum*, its own striking detail in the title commonly given to it, *Portrait of the Artist's Wife or Mother*. Coincidence or inadvertent supplement? Perhaps, although it is hard not to see the reflections on photography as a barely disguised address of love to the mother. Written in the wake of *A Lover's Discourse*, the discourse on the image of the absent mother is a variant on what the earlier text had staged as an extended apostrophe addressed to the absent other. To be sure, what counts here is less a matter of a fixed or definitive meaning (*le sens*) than the possibility of the modern produced (*du sens*) as a condition of personal value. Thus, to suggest the address of love to the absent (m)other is to impose a loose model of primal scenes in keeping with the dramatic force of writing that Barthes develops in the writings since *The Pleasure of the Text*.[3] Where the theory of that force goes by the name of *signifiance*, its active demonstration—from *Roland Barthes* to *Camera Lucida*—is what I have called figuration. In both instances, the production of meaning occurs with a fullness and an intensity for which the linguistic model cannot account. After the formal systems of the mid-1960s period, Barthes thus arrives at the excess of meaning in which the absence of system carries with it a loss of mastery that he asserts as the primacy of writing over its systematic analysis. And so this first primal scene takes us back—full circle, in a sense—to *Writing Degree Zero* and the isolation of the modern writer beyond any sense of historical identity Barthes might have sought in Sartre's model of committed literature.

The second primal scene is that staged as a tribute to André Gide, who, along with Proust and Sartre, served as an early tutor-figure of the writer. Like Gide, Barthes sought self-knowledge through numerous acts of writing whose variety was belied by a program of perpetual self-correction. The result in both cases was a protean identity based on the possibility of asserting change in the wake of discoveries such as those Barthes had noted in Proust's *Recherche* as inversions. Derived from an image of the older Gide, who had passed the peak of his career when Barthes first read his writings in the 1930s, the tutor-figure of the writer as Proteus supplies what Susan Sontag describes aptly as a patrician model: "supple, multiple; never strident or vulgarly indignant; generous but also properly egotistical; incapable of being deeply influenced."[4] Beyond the personal affinities, there is additional coincidence at the level of writing or text. For the impact of the tutor-figure on the act of writing is clearest in Barthes's first text, his 1942 essay on Gide's "Journal." From this apparent point of departure to the inadvertent last word, it is again the question of the journal—what Gide termed his "work of egoism"—that frames Barthes's career of writing within a project of introspection and discovery.

From the first text on Gide's "Journal," Barthes sets forth the following portrait of the work, a portrait that lends itself, in retrospect, as much to his own work as to that of Gide:

Gide's work is a web whose every link must be held taut. I find it completely useless to cut it up into chronological or methodological slices. It would almost have to be read like certain Bibles, with a synoptic table of references; or perhaps like those pages of the *Encyclopédie* whose marginal notes give the text its explosive power. Gide is often his own commentator. This was necessary in order to preserve for the work of art its gratuity, its freedom. Gide's work of art is willfully fleeting; it escapes—thank God—from every seizure attempted by politics or dogma, even revolutionary. Were it otherwise, it would not be a work of art. But to infer from this that Gide's work is fleeting is an error. Gide allows himself to be taken and defined in his critical works as well as his Journal. When that particular Gide is known, his poetic work releases new resonances and a courageously systematic view of the man.[5]

From the first text on the journal to the last (published in a 1979 issue of *Tel Quel*), Barthes moves from asserting the singularity of the literary work to something more or less removed from literary concerns—something similar to what he describes elsewhere as his peculiar disease of "*seeing* language" where others only hear it (*RB*, 161). Barthes confronts his desire to keep a journal as a *diary disease* that is faint, intermittent, and without seriousness: "an insoluble doubt as to the value of what one writes in it."[6] What he seeks in the journal is less a matter of literary justification than a more intimate record of day-to-day observation that might allow him a degree of self-knowledge. Intended basically to be read only by himself—especially when its individual entries are crossed out one after another—Barthes's journal fulfills a function of writing whose irregularity stops it from ever achieving the status of a complete book or literary work. Instead it is closer to what Mallarmé describes as an Album: "a collection of leaflets not only interchangeable . . . but above all infinitely suppressible."[7]

Barthes's meditation on the journal is inseparable from a more personal confrontation with sickness and death. The question of whether or not to write the journal carries with it the wider issue of the value of writing in the face of what Barthes had come to accept during the period surrounding his mother's death. As in *Camera Lucida,* the access to this recognition scene is facilitated by the literary figures of Kafka, Proust, and Blanchot, in whom Barthes finds a common association between the journal form and an acceptance of death. As he records the death of a loved one, he notes his own panic at the inevitability of other deaths to follow. (as this entry is dated July 13, 1977, the loved one referred to is not Barthes's mother, who was to die several months later.) Similarly, when he observes that Gide's old age and death were surrounded by witnesses of record such as Madame de Rysselberghe, Barthes wonders what, in turn, will occur when the witnesses themselves will have died without their own witnesses: "Death, real death, is when the witness himself dies."[8]

Cast in terms of a projected catastrophe that is the fantasy of his own death to come, Barthes's journal becomes an exercise in self-discipline on a par with the *Spiritual Exercises* he had studied in *Sade, Fourier, Loyola.*[9] In fact, Barthes's attempts at an ascetic approach to writing seem doomed to failure by their very desperation. His desire to keep a daily record fails because the urgency of its true purpose—to help him cope with his own future death—is too great: "At bottom, all these failures and weaknesses designate quite clearly a certain defect of the subject. The defect is existential."[10] The work of the journal is thus a doomed project because its origins in a personal vision of catastrophe make for a paradox—a condition of "Play and Despair," Barthes writes as he quotes Kafka—where the only way to redeem the journal is by working it *to death.* Only by writing the journal for himself can Barthes hope to attain the insight of the essential defect that makes the act of writing a mania. Once he locates the defect in himself, the writing of the journal becomes a matter of trying to write out the drama of his own death to come. But where this drama already exists in *Camera Lucida,* what Barthes sets forth in "Deliberation" is the possibility of viewing his own death from the perspective of a witness. It is, of course, an impossible drama to stage, although its model would likely be Poe's "Valdemar," which Barthes had analyzed in 1973.

In this sense, the tutor-figure of Gide frames Barthes's career to incarnate the changing relations between writing and self-knowledge. What Barthes saw in 1942 in the journal as a text of egotism, he comes to see in "Deliberation" as a defect he locates in the subject. As described in this later text, the defect is both vital and fatal. It is vital because its recognition inspires an act of writing that Barthes hopes will defer the last word as long as possible. Like the narrators in Beckett's trilogy, he continues to write in the hope that he will have time to say everything that he feels he might want to say.[11] But since he is incapable of the asceticism necessary to maintain his diary as anything more than an intermittent writing, the gap between desire and performance situates the potential for prolonging life through writing into a decline toward death. As Barthes writes in a text left all but complete at the time of his death, one inevitably fails at trying to talk about what one loves.[12]

If writing is thus caught up with an inevitable decline Barthes attributes to the subject who writes, then the obvious question—why write the journal?—is a variation of the more direct question: why write at all? If Barthes takes the defect of the materialist subject with any seriousness, then the obvious question becomes: what makes Roland write? Love . . . of writing? . . . of others? Perhaps, but his evolution over the last ten years of his career suggests another motivating force. *The Pleasure of the Text* begins with an epigraph from Hobbes that translates roughly as "Fear has been the sole passion of my life." At Cerisy-la-Salle in 1977, Barthes offered a fuller formulation closer in tone and substance to the recognition scene he plays out in *Camera Lucida* and "Deliberation":

At the origin of everything, Fear. (Of what? of blows? of humiliations?) Parody of the *Cogito*, as a fictional instant when everything having been levelled, this *tabula rasa* is going to be reoccupied: "I fear, therefore I am." A remark: according to current custom (an ethology of intellectuals would be needed), fear is never spoken of: it is foreclosed from discourse and even from writing (could there be a writing of fear?). Set at the origin, it has a value of *method* from which departs a way toward initiation.[13]

What Barthes fears as he deliberates on whether or not to keep a journal is a feeling of inessentiality that he cannot dismiss as a literary consideration. Consequently, the question of whether or not to write the journal is alternately laughable and catastrophic: "What the Jour-

nal posits is not the tragic question, the Madman's question: 'Who am
I?', but the comic question, the Bewildered Man's question; 'Am I?' A
comic—a comedian, that's what the Journal-keeper is."[14]

The last scene is actually one of the very first: a pastiche of the *Crito*
written by Barthes in 1933 while he was still a *lycéen*. As a portrait of
Socrates, the pastiche offers a peculiar twist on what is the more
standard account of the subversive teacher described by Plato. In the
original dialogue, Socrates's execution is delayed until the return of a
state galley from a sacred annual mission. The interval between his
trial and his execution allows his friends to approach him about the
possibility of bribing his jailers and fleeing to safety outside Athens.
His devoted friend Crito makes a most eloquent plea for this solution,
which Socrates rejects out of respect for the laws, his country, his
friends, and himself. Barthes starts his account after Crito leaves
without having convinced Socrates to accept his offer. In fact, Barthes's
Socrates is more of a sensualist and less resolute in his refusal than his
Platonic predecessor. He allows Glaucon, Apollodorus, and Alcibiades to persuade him to reconsider. Thus Glaucon argues that it is
both just and natural for Socrates' friends to want to spare him an
untimely death: "The way we see it, our duty would be to make you
leave prison even without your consent, because we think it preferable
that the majority continue to benefit from your teaching, rather than
have it perish because of worthy but inhuman laws."[15] As he listens to
these arguments, Socrates is struck by the sight of a jailer eating from a
plate of fresh figs. Reaching out toward the plate, Socrates holds back
when he realizes that he will probably be dead before the figs are
digested.

While he is slowly yielding to the possibility of remaining among
his faithful friends, he begins to justify a change of heart that is closer to
a physical reaction, as if the plate of figs before him is a last test of his
virtue and self-restraint. As he ponders whether or not to accept what
his friends propose to him, a window is opened. Barthes writes:

A ray of sunlight came to caress the figs, and revealed along their golden lengths
dark openings from which was flowing a sugary warmth that intoxicated the
senses. Socrates closed his eyes; it was in order to see the little house near
Thebes with its fig tree, bench and terrace; and he thought he could sense the
taste of the figs mixed with the saltier smell of the sea wind, the living symbol of
freedom. Then, quite simply, he reached out and ate a fig.[16]

Giving in to the sensual force of life, Barthes's Socrates forestalls death and rejects the law in order to live among his friends. Ever the professor of desire, Barthes prefigures in this first primal scene the very evolution that takes him through a career in and of writing whose singularity will nurture its own offspring as those who assert desire through reading will move toward asserting it through writing. As Barthes maintains in *The Pleasure of the Text*, the text must prove that it desires its readers, prove it in writing. Because it stages the elements of pleasure and knowledge that Barthes came to assert both as teacher and writer, his pastiche of the Socratic tutor-figure incarnates the joyful wisdom he asserts in a practice of writing that urges his readers to write their own desire.

The evolution of Barthes's later work toward figuration is likely to disappoint those who prefer to view Barthes as the semioclast of the *Mythologies* or the advocate of modernity in the *Critical Essays* and *Critique et vérité*. In the same way, Barthes's reversal of the biblical myth of Babel into a blissful cohabitation of languages is sure to frustrate those who prefer the pleasures of ideology to the ideologies of pleasure. As semiology yields progressively to semioclasm and ultimately to semiotropy, the transition from politics through science toward writing is open to the various critiques set forth in the name of political change against aestheticism. When the point of reference for such change is found in the semioclasm of the *Mythologies* and the "liberatory" reading set forth in *S/Z*, the switch from direct critique of the existing social values points to an attitude that is clearly utopian. Once the traditional notion of the literary work is dropped for the wider notion of the text as general site where meaning is produced, the practice of reading functions in a scope of personal value seemingly at odds with collective change. By the time *Camera Lucida* appears in 1980, its inversion of the *camera obscura* notion linked by Marx with the phenomenon of ideology begs the question of Barthes's apparent turn away from earlier positions that had been described variously as committed, revolutionary, and emancipatory.

But is this necessarily the case? Why must Barthes's assertion of the aesthetic reflex in the *Roland Barthes* cast him definitively as a political misfit? David Silverman and Brian Torode see a way out of the apparent bind:

We must not assume at the outset that an aesthetic project is self-evidently apolitical. Is this not the very teaching of the bourgeois order? The real argument begins when we consider whether revolutionary practice can establish itself through a rejection of a given social order as entirely reactionary and the consequent attempt to generate a (moral? political?) community who share that rejection.[17]

The questions surrounding the relationship between the moral and the political nature of the community described above point clearly to the change in orientation that has frustrated many a potential disciple from emulating what might be called a Barthesian practice. For once *S/Z*, *The Pleasure of the Text*, and the *Roland Barthes* set critical practice within a more intimate problematic of personal value, the subversion of the political by the ethical all but rules out militancy. Like the tutor-figure of Socrates he adapts to his own vision in the 1933 pastiche, Barthes rejects the doctrines of literature, science, and criticism in favor of a pedagogy that forces the student as potential disciple to be responsible for the ethical values at the core of his or her practice.

It is too soon to discern with accuracy what impact Barthes's career will have on literary and critical thinking. At this point, however, its trajectory is toward a pedagogy of assertion and personal value that, prefigured in the Socrates of his first text, dramatizes writing and reading as close to utopian activities. For those who continue to read Barthes, that dramatization holds the promise—tentative, idealist, and disarming—that social change begins when individual value is shared within a collectivity such as the community of friends Barthes had portrayed in his version of the Socratic myth.

And afterward?
    —What to write now? Can you
still write anything?
    —One writes with one's desire
and I am not through desiring.

    Barthes, *Roland Barthes*

Notes

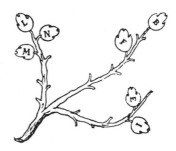

Introduction: Double Figure

1. Graham Hough, "The Importation of Roland Barthes," *Times Literary Supplement*, 9 December 1977, p. 1443. For comparison, see Annette Lavers, "A Mode of Knowledge," *Times Literary Supplement*, 1 August 1975.

2. Hough, "Importation," p. 1443.

3. Philip Thody, *Roland Barthes: A Conservative Estimate* (Atlantic Highlands, N.J.: Humanities Press, 1977), p. 157. I have written at greater length on Thody's study in *Sub-Stance*, no. 22 (1979).

4. Rosalind Coward and John Ellis, *Language and Materialism: Developments in Semiology and the Theory of the Subject* (Boston: Routledge and Kegan Paul, 1977), pp. 45–46.

5. In a 1977 interview with Bernard-Henri Lévy, Barthes states that he has never been a Marxist: "To be a 'Marxist'—what does the verb 'to be' mean in this expression? I have said it before: I 'came' to Marxism relatively late, thanks to a friend who has since died and who was a Trotskyite. So that I came to it without ever having militated and by a distant connection which had nothing to do with what was then called Stalinism. Let's say that I have read Marx, Lenin, Trotsky. Not everything, of course, but I have read some. And, for quite a while, I have reread nothing, except a text of Marx here and there" (*GV*, 252).

Chapter One: Writing in History

1. See, for example, the opening remarks of Charles F. Altman in "Psychoanalysis and Cinema: The Imaginary Discourse," *Quarterly Review of Film Studies* 2 (1977): 257–72.

2. Iris Murdoch, *Sartre: Romantic Rationalist* (New Haven: Yale University Press, 1952), p. 7.

3. Barthes, "Deliberation," *Partisan Review* 47 (1980): 539.

4. Jonathan Culler, *Ferdinand de Saussure* (New York: Penguin, 1977), p. xvii.

5. The Gide piece was reprinted as "Sur André Gide et son journal" in *Magazine Littéraire*, no. 97 (1975): 24–27. A 1954 text on Camus, "*L'Etranger*, roman solaire*," is reprinted in *Les Critiques de notre temps et Camus*, ed. Jacqueline Lévi-Vareuse (Paris: Garnier, 1970), pp. 60–64.

6. Barthes, "Réponses," *Tel Quel*, no. 47 (1971): 92.

7. John Sturrock, "Roland Barthes," *Structuralism and Since: From Lévi-Strauss to Derrida* (New York: Oxford University Press, 1979), p. 53.

8. Thody, *Barthes: A Conservative Estimate*, p. 157. Similar remarks are to be found in Hough's "The Importation of Roland Barthes" as well as in Donald G. Marshall's "Interpretation without Representation," *Partisan Review* 42 (1975): 469–73.

9. In *S/Z*, Barthes invokes a similar difference around the terms *écriture* and *écrivance*. On the latter term, he comments elsewhere on an instrumental practice of writing seemingly removed from any self-reflexive dimension: "In other words [this practice] remains imprisoned within the Imaginary of the scientist who wants—or even worse, who believes himself—removed from his object of study and who claims with full assurance and naivete to set his own language in a position of extraterritoriality" ("Jeunes Chercheurs," *Communications*, no. 19 [1972]: p. 2).

10. Oswald Ducrot and Tzvetan Todorov, *Encyclopedic Dictionary of the Sciences of Language*, trans. Catherine Porter (Baltimore: The Johns Hopkins University Press, 1979), p. 150.

11. Barthes, "Aujourd'hui, Michelet," *L'Arc*, no. 52 (1973): 19.

12. Ibid., p. 22.

13. Ibid., p. 20.

14. Barthes, "Historical Discourse," trans. Peter Wexler, in *Structuralism: A Reader*, ed. Michael Lane, (New York: Harper and Row, 1972), pp. 153–54.

15. The statement is not quite exact. Despite the disclaimer, a number of later texts qualify as supplements to the 1954–56 mythologies, notably "Change the Object Itself: Mythology Today," *Image-Music-Text*, pp. 165–69. See also "Pour une psycho-sociologie de l'alimentation contemporaine," *Annales* 5 (September–October 1961); "Mythologie de l'automobile," *Réalités*, no. 213 (October 1963); and "Un Cas de critique culturelle," *Communications*, no. 14 (1969).

16. In the *Mythologies*, see the two texts devoted to Pierre Poujade, a baker from the Paris suburbs whose demagoguery fanned discontent within the lower middle-class during the 1950s. During the 1981 presidential elections, the

same political sector was exploited—in a mode of parody all too close to its model—by Coluche, a thirty-five-year-old professional comedian who staged a raucous campaign for the presidency before bowing out at the last moment. In fact, Coluche is mentioned a number of times in the middle sections of *A Lover's Discourse*.

17. For more on the anagrams, see Jean Starobinski, *Words Upon Words: The Anagrams of Saussure*, trans. Olivia Emmet (New Haven: Yale University Press, 1979); two special issues of the journal *Semiotext(e)*—vol. 1, no. 2 (Fall 1974), and vol. 2, no. 1 (Spring 1975); and Louis-Jean Calvet's *Pour et contre Saussure: vers une linguistique sociale* (Paris: Payot, 1976).

18. Published under the name of V. N. Vološinov as *Marxism and the Philosophy of Language* (New York: Academic Press, 1971).

Chapter Two: Linguistics and the Dream of a Science of Literature

1. Robert Scholes and Robert Kellogg, *The Nature of Narrative* (New York: Oxford University Press, 1967), p. 4.

2. Scholes, *Structuralism in Literature* (New Haven: Yale University Press, 1974), p. 148.

3. For an overview of the polemic as seen from this side of the Atlantic, see Germaine Brée, "French Criticism: A Battle of Books?" *Emory University Quarterly* 22 (1967): 25–35, and David Paul Funt, "Roland Barthes and the *Nouvelle Critique*," *Journal of Aesthetics and Art Criticism* 26 (1968): 329–40. A more personal account is provided by Jean-François Revel in an interview with Lucette Finas entitled "J'ai cherché à ouvrir une discussion," *Quinzaine Littéraire*, no. 3 (15–30 April 1966): 14–15.

4. Barthes, "The Structuralist Activity," in *The Structuralists: From Marx to Lévi-Strauss*, ed. Richard DeGeorge and Fernande DeGeorge (Garden City, N.Y.: Anchor, 1972), p. 149.

5. Ibid., p. 149.

6. Ibid., p. 153.

7. Ibid., p. 154.

8. See Serge Doubrovsky, *The New Criticism in France*, trans. Derek Coltman (Chicago: University of Chicago Press, 1973), for what has come to be accepted as the standard account of the Barthes vs. Picard debate.

9. Barthes, "The Two Criticisms," *Critical Essays*, trans. Richard Howard (Evanston: Northwestern University Press, 1972), pp. 250–51.

10. Ibid., p. 252.

11. Barthes, "What is Criticism?" *Critical Essays*, p. 258.

12. *Elements of Semiology*, trans. Annette Lavers and Colin Smith (Boston: Beacon Press, 1970), p. 11. Both the *Elements* and the "Introduction" appeared first in *Communications*, in issues 4 (1964) and 8 (1966), respectively.

13. "Textual Analysis of Poe's 'Valdemar,'" trans. Geoff Bennington, in *Untying the Text: A Post-Structuralist Reader*, ed. Robert Young (Boston: Routledge and Kegan Paul, 1981), p. 135.

14. Thomas A. Sebeok, "The Semiotic Web: A Chronicle of Prejudices," *Bulletin of Literary Semiotics*, no. 2 (1975): 16.

15. See also Barthes's contribution to the 1966 Johns Hopkins seminars on literary criticism, published as "To Write: An Intransitive Verb?" in *The Languages of Criticism and the Sciences of Man: The Structuralist Controversy*, ed. Richard Macksey and Eugenio Donato (Baltimore: The Johns Hopkins University Press, 1970), pp. 134–45.

Chapter Three: On the Subject of Loss

1. See "Pierre Loti: Aziyadé," in *New Critical Essays*, trans. Richard Howard (New York: Hill and Wang, 1980), pp. 105–21, and "On échoue toujours à parler de ce qu'on aime," *Tel Quel*, no. 85 (1980): 32–38.

2. Lynn A. Higgins, "Barthes's Imaginary Voyages," *Studies in Twentieth Century Literature* 5 (1981): p. 166; see also her discussion of Barthes's *Alors la Chine?* on pp. 162–63.

3. Barthes, "Barthes puissance trois," *Quinzaine Littéraire*, no. 205 (1–15 March 1975): 3.

4. Barthes, "Les Sorties du texte," in *Bataille* (Paris: Union Générale d' Editions, 1973), p. 49.

5. Ibid., p. 59.

6. Ibid., p. 54.

7. See the texts on Nietzsche collected in Georges Bataille, *Oeuvres complètes*, vol. 6 (Paris: Gallimard, 1973), and Maurice Blanchot, "Du Côté de Nietzsche," *La Part du feu* (Paris: Gallimard, 1949), pp. 278–90, and "Réflexions sur le nihilisme," *L'Entretien infini* (Paris: Gallimard, 1969), pp. 201–55.

8. Sarah Kofman, *Nietzsche et la métaphore* (Paris: Payot, 1972); Paul de Man, "Nietzsche's Theory of Rhetoric," *Symposium* 28 (1974): 40. For additional commentaries on rhetoric, value, and truth in Nietzsche, see Jean Granier, *Le Problème de la vérité dans la philosophie de Nietzsche* (Paris: Seuil, 1966); Bernard Pautrat, *Versions du soleil* (Paris: Seuil, 1971); Jean-Michel Rey, *L'Enjeu des signes* (Paris: Seuil, 1971); and Jacques Derrida, "La Mythologie blanche," *Marges de la philosophie* (Paris: Minuit, 1972). In English, see John T. Wilcox, *Truth and Value*

in *Nietzsche* (Ann Arbor: University of Michigan Press, 1974), and Patrick J. Keane, "On Truth and Lie in Nietzsche," *Salmagundi*, no. 29 (Spring 1975): 67–94.

9. Georges Mounin, *Introduction à la sémiologie* (Paris: Minuit, 1970), p. 194.

10. Wilcox, *Truth and Value*, p. 170.

Chapter Four: Figuration, Musicality, and Discourse

1. Erich Auerbach, "Figura," *Scenes from the Drama of European Literature*, trans. Ralph Manheim (New York: Meridian, 1959), p. 16.

2. Roland Barthes and Maurice Nadeau, *Sur la littérature* (Grenoble: Presses Universitaires de Grenoble, 1980), p. 23.

3. Barthes, "Rasch," in *Langue, discours, société: Hommage à Emile Benveniste*, ed. Julia Kristeva, Jacques-Alain Miller, Nicolas Ruwet (Paris: Seuil, 1975), p. 223. The notation *quasi parlando* makes for a curious comparison with attempts by the Canadian pianist Glenn Gould to achieve a dry and detached sound in his playing, a sound seemingly removed from the corporeal quality referred to by Barthes. That Gould is known to hum or sing while he plays only adds to the complexity of the comparison.

4. Barthes, "Le Chant romantique," *Gramma*, no. 5 (1976): 165.

5. Ibid., p. 167.

6. Ibid., p. 168.

7. Ibid.

8. Choderlos de Laclos, *Les Liaisons dangereuses*, trans. Richard Aldington (New York: New American Library, 1962), p. 73.

9. Emile Benveniste, "Relationships of Persons in the Verb," *Problems in General Linguistics*, trans. Mary Elizabeth Meek (Coral Gables: University of Miami Press, 1971), p. 195.

10. Gregory L. Ulmer, "The Discourse of the Imaginary," *Diacritics* 10, no. 1 (Spring 1980): 66. On the relation of the amorous discourse to Lacan's Imaginary, Barthes states the following in 1977: "The subject is developed principally in a register known since Lacan as the Imaginary—and I acknowledge that I am a subject of the Imaginary. I have a living relation to past literature exactly because this literature supplies me with images, with a good relation to the image" (*GV*, 265).

11. Sherry Turkle, *Psychoanalytic Politics: Freud's French Revolution* (New York: Basic Books, 1978), p. 147.

12. Jacques Lacan, *Le Séminaire I: Les Ecrits techniques de Freud* (Paris: Seuil, 1975), p. 9.

13. Lacan, p. 242.

14. Benveniste, *Problems in General Linguistics*, p. 225.

Chapter Five: Alphabetese

1. See the catalogue and selected essays published under the title *Roland Barthes: Carte Segni* (Milan: Electa, 1981).

2. Lucette Finas, "Entre les mots et les choses," *Quinzaine Littéraire*, no. 35 (16–31 May 1967): 3.

3. I. J. Gelb, *Grammatology: A Study of Writing*, rev. ed. (Chicago: University of Chicago Press, 1963), pp. 6–7.

4. Ferdinand de Saussure, *Course in General Linguistics*, trans. Wade Baskin (New York: Philosophical Library, 1959), p. 16.

5. Ibid., p. 17.

6. Culler, *Saussure*, p. 110.

7. Barthes, *Système de la mode* (Paris: Seuil, 1967), p. 7.

8. Barthes, "L'Esprit de la lettre," *Quinzaine Littéraire*, no. 96 (1–15 June 1970): 3. See also Barthes's comments on the composed heads by the Renaissance painter Giuseppe Archimboldo, published as "Rhetor and Magician," trans. John Shepley, in *Archimboldo* (Milan: Ricci, 1980).

9. Barthes, "La Crise de la vérité," *Magazine Littéraire*, no. 108 (January 1976); 28.

10. Lacan, "The Insistence of the Letter in the Unconscious," *Yale French Studies*, no. 36–37 (1966): 127.

Chapter Six: Classroom Struggles

1. Arriving at a similar conclusion, Gregory L. Ulmer writes that Barthes has tried to move beyond conflicts within positions of power, toward a consideration of what prefigures analysis: "Because traditional literary criticism is acratic [out of or without power], Barthes, seeking a utopian alternative to the war of rhetoric, refuses to 'do' criticism and turns to a writing that precedes the sociolect" ("Fetichism in Roland Barthes's Nietzschean Phase," *Papers on Language and Literature* 14 [1978]: 335).

2. My example is less than arbitrary since the status of Bataille's writings forms part of what Barthes refers to as the passage from work (*oeuvre*) to text: "In the same way, the Text does not stop at (good) Literature; it cannot be contained in a hierarchy, even in a simple division of genres. What constitutes the Text is,

on the contrary (or precisely), its subversive force in respect of the old classifications. How do you classify a writer like Georges Bataille? Novelist, poet, essayist, economist, philosopher, mystic? The answer is so difficult that the literary manuals generally prefer to forget about Bataille who, in fact, wrote texts, perhaps one continuous text" (*IMT*, 157).

3. Fredric Jameson, "The Ideology of the Text," *Salmagundi*, no. 29–30 (1975–76): 205.

4. Claude Bonnefoy, "Barthes en bouffées de langage," *Nouvelles Littéraires*, 21 April 1977, p. 9.

5. GREPH, "Avant-Projet," *Qui a peur de la philosophie?* (Paris: Flammarion, "Champs," 1977), p. 8.

6. Ibid., p. 266.

7. Ibid., p. 357.

8. For a dissenting view of GREPH's activities, see Jacques Bouveresse, "Pourquoi pas des philosophes?" *Critique*, no. 369 (February 1978): 97–122. Bouveresse sees GREPH as an offshoot of Jacques Derrida's activities within the French educational system and a position that, in my reading of his text, he is unwilling to support. For a third approach to GREPH, see Christopher I. Fynsk, "A Decelebration of Philosophy," *Diacritics* 8, no. 2 (Summer 1978): 80–90.

9. "Jacques Leenhardt: Interview," *Diacritics* 7, no. 3 (Fall 1977): 66.

10. Barthes, "Apprendre et enseigner," *Ça/Cinéma*, no. 7–8 (1975): 5.

Chapter Seven: The Professor of Desire

1. Werner J. Dannhauser, "On Teaching Politics Today," *Commentary* 59, no. 3 (March 1975): 74.

2. For a brief history of the French university system, see the highly informative chapter in the second volume in Theodore Zeldin's *France 1848–1945* (Oxford: Clarendon Press, 1977). On the pact between teacher and student as perceived by two Americans, see Susan Warren and Lori Woodruff, "The Contract: A Stele for Roland Barthes," *Visible Language* 15 (1981): 320–27.

3. Gregory Vlastos, "The Individual as Object of Love in Plato," *Platonic Studies* (Princeton: Princeton University Press, 1973), p. 4. For additional views of Socratic theories of love and knowledge, see Paul Friedlander, *Plato: An Introduction*, trans. Hans Meyerhoff (Princeton: Princeton University Press, 1973), 1:32–58; W. K. C. Guthrie, *Socrates* (New York: Cambridge University Press, 1971), pp. 70–77; and Léon Robin, *La Théorie platonicienne de l'amour*, nouvelle édition (Paris: Presses Universitaires de France, 1964). For a materialist reading of *The Symposium*, see John Brenkman, "The Other and the One:

Psychoanalysis, Reading, *The Symposium*," *Yale French Studies*, no. 55–56 (1978): 396–456.

4. Michel Foucault, *The History of Sexuality: An Introduction*, trans. Robert Hurley (New York: Pantheon, 1978), p. 12. See also Stephen Heath, "Le corps victorien, anthologiquement," *Critique*, no. 405–6 (February–March 1981): 152–65

5. Pascal Bruckner and Alain Finkielkraut, *Le Nouveau Désordre amoureux* (Paris: Seuil, "Fiction et Cie," 1977), p. 121.

6. Randolph Runyon, "Canon in U^{bis}," *Visible Language* 11 (1977): 407.

7. Barthes, "Réflexions sur un manuel," in *L'Enseignement de la littérature*, ed. Serge Doubrovsky and Tzvetan Todorov (Paris: Plon, 1971), p. 176. See also Barbara Johnson, "The Critical Difference," in *The Critical Difference* (Baltimore: The Johns Hopkins University Press, 1981).

8. Barthes, "L'Ancienne Rhétorique: aide-mémoire," *Communications*, no. 16 (1970): 172.

9. Ibid., p. 173.

10. Ibid., p. 174.

11. Ibid., p. 223. The synthesis of multiple methodologies leads also to redefining "new" objects as well as ways of approaching older ones. Interdisciplinary study, as an orientation toward such renewals, "consists in creating a *new* object belonging to no one. The text is, I believe, one of these objects" ("Jeunes Chercheurs," *Communications*, no. 19 [1972]: 3).

12. Barthes, "L'Ancienne Rhétorique," p. 177. In a 1975 interview, Barthes sets forth a clear notion of how an "amorous" pedagogy functions within an academy: "The teaching of language and literature is most often preoccupied with content. But the task does not fall solely onto content; it is also a matter of the relation, the cohabitation between bodies; a cohabitation overseen to a great extent, and largely falsified, by institutional space. The real problem is knowing how one can place in the content, in the temporality of the so-called class in 'letters,' values or desires that the institution does not foresee, when it fails to repress them" (*GV*, 223). For a more personal variant of this attitude, see Jean-François Lyotard, "The Endurance of the Profession," *Yale French Studies*, no. 63 (1982): 71–77.

Chapter Eight: Circular Memories: Via Proust

1. "Les Vies parallèles," *Quinzaine Littéraire*, no. 1 (1–15 March 1966): 11.
2. Marcel Proust, "The Method of Sainte-Beuve," *Marcel Proust on Litera-*

ture and Art: 1896–1919, trans. Sylvia Townsend Warner (New York: Meridian, 1958), p. 94.

3. Ibid., p. 99–100.

4. Reprinted in *Image-Music-Text*. The same collection contains translations of "Rhetoric of the Image" and "The Third Meaning." A more personal account of the film experience appears in Barthes's "En sortant du cinéma," *Communications*, no. 24 (1975).

5. See Jean-François Lyotard, *La Phénoménologie* (Paris: Presses Universitaires de France, 1954). As demonstrated in the *Michelet*, Barthes owes a debt to the phenomenological critics of the postwar era, adding to his understanding of Sartre's existential psychoanalysis the ego-centric orientation of Georges Poulet rather than the inventories of sensations set forth in the writings of Gaston Bachelard and Jean-Pierre Richard.

6. Proust, *Remembrance of Things Past*. trans. C. K. Scott Moncrieff (New York: Random House, 1932), 2:116.

7. Paul de Man, "Reading (Proust)," in *Allegories of Reading: Figural Language in Rousseau, Nietzsche, Rilke, and Proust* (New Haven: Yale University Press, 1979), p. 57.

8. Walter Benjamin, "The Work of Art in the Age of Mechanical Reproduction," in *Illuminations*, trans. Harry Zohn (New York: Schocken, 1969), pp. 217–51.

9. Barthes, "Une Idée de Recherche," in *Recherche de Proust*, ed. Gérard Genette and Tzvetan Todorov (Paris: Seuil, "Points," 1980), p. 35. The article first appeared in the October 1971 issue of the Italian journal *Paragone*. Throughout this text, Barthes uses the term *recherche* to designate both the title of Proust's novel and the concept translated into English as "search" or "quest." Beyond the numerous references to Proust in *Camera Lucida* and *The Pleasure of the Text*, see also Barthes's "Proust and Names" (in the *New Critical Essays*), as well as Jean-François Chévrier, "Proust par Roland Barthes," in *Prétexte: Roland Barthes*, ed. Antoine Compagnon (Paris: Union Générale d'Editions, 1978), and Jacques Derrida, "Les Morts de Roland Barthes," *Poétique*, no. 47 (1981).

10. Barthes, "Recherche," p. 39.

Chapter Nine: Last Words and Primal Scenes

1. Christian Metz, *The Imaginary Signifier*, trans. Celia Britton, Annwyl Williams, Ben Brewster, and Alfred Guzzetti (Bloomington: Indiana University Press, 1982), pp. 227–28.

2. Beaumont Newhall, *The History of Photography* (New York: Museum of Modern Art, 1964), p. 7.

3. Is it a coincidence that the letter *m* appears in Erté's alphabet as the only inhuman figure and thus as the letter of death?

4. Susan Sontag, "Writing Itself: On Roland Barthes," *New Yorker*, 26 April 1982, p. 129.

5. Barthes, "Sur André Gide et son journal," *Magazine Littéraire*, no. 97 (February 1975): 26–27.

6. Barthes, "Deliberation," *Partisan Review* 47 (1980): 532.

7. Ibid., p. 541.

8. Ibid., p. 535.

9. Gérard Genette, "Le Journal, l'antijournal," *Poétique*, no. 47 (1981): 320.

10. Barthes, "Deliberation," p. 543.

11. Here is one way Beckett's Molloy describes his situation with characteristic prolixity: "Not to want to say, not to know what you want to say, not to be able to say what you think you want to say, and never to stop saying, or hardly ever, that is the thing to keep in mind, even in the heat of composition" (Samuel Beckett, *Three Novels* [New York: Grove Press, 1965], p. 28).

12. Barthes, "On échoue toujours à parler de ce qu'on aime," *Tel Quel*, no. 85 (1980): 32–38. Here is the prefatory note supplied by the journal editors: "Destined for the Stendhal colloquium in Milan, this is by all appearances the last text written by Roland Barthes. Its first page was typed. On February 25th, the second page was in the typewriter. Statement to be considered as completed? Yes, in the sense that the manuscript is quite complete. No, to the degree that when he used to transcribe on his typewriter, Roland Barthes always made modifications in his text. This is what he had done to the first page, here."

13. Barthes, "L'Image," in Antoine Compagnon, ed., *Prétexte: Roland Barthes* (Paris: Union Générale d'Editions, 1978), p. 298.

14. Barthes, "Deliberation," p. 543.

15. Barthes, "Premier Texte: En marge du Criton," *L'Arc*, no. 56 (1974): 5. In French the verb I have translated as "benefit" appears as a form of the more intense and sexual term, "jouir," which Barthes uses pointedly in *The Pleasure of the Text*.

16. Ibid., p. 7.

17. David Silverman and Brian Torode, *The Material Word* (Boston: Routledge and Kegan Paul), p. 270.

Bibliography

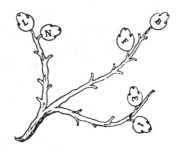

The following lists are meant to serve as a selective guide to Barthes's writings. As in all cases, they constitute a critical statement reflecting the texts and critical sources used in this study. The appearance of posthumous collections and texts will undoubtedly add to Barthes's textual corpus in the years to come. For the benefit of American and British readers, I have supplied English translations wherever possible for texts originally published in French. Additional references are to be found in the books by Stephen Heath and Annette Lavers listed in section III.

I. Books by Roland Barthes

Le Degré zéro de l'écriture. Paris: Seuil, "Pierres Vives," 1953. Reprinted with *Nouveaux Essais critiques*, Paris: Seuil, "Points," 1972. Translated by Annette Lavers and Colin Smith as *Writing Degree Zero*, Boston; Beacon Press, 1970. Translated by Richard Howard as *New Critical Essays*, New York: Hill and Wang, 1980.

Michelet par lui-même. Paris: Seuil, "Ecrivains de toujours," 1954.

Mythologies. Paris: Seuil, "Pierres Vives," 1957. Reprinted, Paris: Seuil, "Points," 1970. Translated by A. Lavers as *Mythologies*, New York: Hill and Wang, 1972. Translated by Richard Howard as *The Eiffel Tower and Other Mythologies*, New York: Hill and Wang, 1979.

Sur Racine. Paris: Seuil, "Pierres Vives," 1963. Reprinted, Paris: Seuil, "Points," 1980. Translated by Richard Howard as *On Racine*, New York: Hill and Wang, 1964.

Essais critiques. Paris: Seuil, "Tel Quel," 1964. Reprinted, Paris: Seuil "Points," 1981. Translated by Richard Howard as *Critical Essays*, Evanston: Northwestern University Press, 1972.

La Tour Eiffel. Paris: Delpire, 1964. Translated by Richard Howard as *The Eiffel*

Tower and Other Mythologies, New York: Hill and Wang, 1979.

Eléments de sémiologie. Paris: Gonthier, "Médiations," 1965. Published as a double volume with *Le Degré zéro de l'écriture.* Translated by A. Lavers and C. Smith as *Writing Degree Zero and Elements of Semiology,* Boston: Beacon Press, 1970.

Critique et vérité. Paris: Seuil, "Tel Quel," 1966.

Système de la mode. Paris: Seuil, 1967. Translated by Matthew Ward and Richard Howard as *The Fashion System,* New York: Hill and Wang, 1983.

S/Z. Paris: Seuil, "Tel Quel," 1970. Reprinted, Paris: Seuil, "Points," 1976. Translated by Richard Miller, New York: Hill and Wang, 1974.

L'Empire des signes. Geneva: Skira. "Les Sentiers de la création," 1970. Reprinted, Paris: Flammarion, "Champs," 1980. Translated by Richard Howard as *The Empire of Signs,* New York: Hill and Wang, 1982.

Sade, Fourier, Loyola. Paris: Seuil, "Tel Quel," 1971. Translated by Richard Miller, New York: Hill and Wang, 1976.

Erté. Translated by William Weaver. Parma: Ricci, 1973. (00)

Le Plaisir du texte. Paris: Seuil, "Tel Quel," 1973. Reprinted, Paris: Seuil, "Points," 1981. Translated by Richard Miller as *The Pleasure of the Text,* New York: Hill and Wang, 1975.

Roland Barthes par Roland Barthes. Paris: Seuil, "Ecrivains de Toujours," 1975. Translated by Richard Howard as *Roland Barthes by Roland Barthes,* New York: Hill and Wang, 1977.

Alors la Chine? Paris: Christian Bourgois, 1975.

Fragments d'un discours amoureux. Paris: Seuil, "Tel Quel," 1977. Translated by Richard Howard as *A Lover's Discourse: Fragments,* New York: Hill and Wang, 1978.

Image-Music-Text. Essays selected and translated by Stephen Heath. New York: Hill and Wang, 1977.

Leçon. Paris: Seuil, 1978. Translated by Richard Howard as "In Inauguration of the Chair of Literary Semiology, Collège de France, January 7, 1977." *October,* no. 8 (1980): 2–15.

Sollers écrivain. Paris: Seuil, 1979.

and Nadeau, Maurice. *Sur la littérature.* Grenoble: Presses Universitaires de Genoble, 1980.

La Chambre claire: Note sur la photographie. Paris: Seuil/Gallimard, "Cahiers du cinéma," 1980. Translated by Richard Howard as *Camera Lucida: Reflections on Photography,* New York: Hill and Wang, 1981.

Le Grain de la voix: Entretiens, 1962–1980. Paris: Seuil, 1981.

A Roland Barthes Reader. Edited by Susan Sontag. New York: Hill and Wang, 1982.

L'Obvie et l'obtus: Essais critiques III. Paris: Seuil, 1982.

II. Articles, Prefaces, and Shorter Texts by Roland Barthes

1933 "En Marge du Criton." Reprinted as "Premier Texte." *L'Arc*, no. 56 (1974).

1942 "Culture et tragédie." *Existences.*

"Notes sur Andre Gide et son journal." *Existences.* Reprinted in *Magazine Littéraire*, no. 97 (1975).

1943 "A propos du numéro spécial de *Confluences* sur les problèmes du roman." *Existences.* "Les Anges du péché." *Existences.*

1944 "Plaisir aux classiques." *Existences.*

"Réflexions sur le style de *l'Etranger*." *Existences.*

"En Grèce." *Existences.*

1947 "Gromaire, Lurçat et Calder." *France-Asie* (15 January).

"Le Degré zéro de l'écriture." *Combat* (1 August). (WDZ)

"Faut-il tuer la grammaire?" *Combat* (26 September). (WDZ)

1950 "Bakounine et le panslavisme." *Combat* (10 August).

"Un Prolongement à la littérature de l'absurde." *Combat* (21 September).

"Triomphe et rupture de l'écriture bourgeoise." *Combat* (9 November). (WDZ)

"L'artisanat du style." *Combat* (16 November). (WDZ)

"L'écriture et le silence." *Combat* (23 November). (WDZ)

"L'écriture et la parole." *Combat* (7 December). (WDZ)

"Le Sentiment tragique de l'écriture." *Combat.* (16 December). (WDZ)

1951 "Michelet, l'Histoire et la mort." *Esprit* (April).

"'Scandale' du marxisme?" *Combat* (21 June).

"Le Temps du récit." *Combat* (16 August).

"Humanisme sans paroles." *Combat* (30 August).

"La Troisième Personne du roman." *Combat* (13 September).

"Phénoménologie et matérialisme dialectique." *Combat* (11 October).

"La Querelle des égyptologues." *Combat* (25 October).

"A propos d'une métaphore." *Esprit* (November).

1952 "Jean Cayrol et ses romans." *Esprit* (March).

"Le Monde où l'on catche." *Esprit* (October). (M)

"Ecrivains de gauche ou littérature de gauche." *L'Observateur* (27 November).

1953 "Compte rendu d'une enquête sur la littérature et la gauche." *L'Observateur* (15 January).

"Folies-Bergères." *Esprit* (February).

"Le Prince de Hambourg au T.N.P." *Lettres Nouvelles* (March).

"Maitres et escalves." *Lettres Nouvelles* (March).

"Les Mots sont aussi des demeures." *Lettres Nouvelles* (May).

"Le Libertin." *Théâtre Populaire* (May–June).

"Le Monde-objet." *Lettres Nouvelles* (June). (*CE*)

"Visages et figures." *Esprit* (July). (*M*)

"Le Théâtre de Baudelaire." *Théâtre Populaire* (July–August). (*CE*)

"Hamlet." *27, rue Jacob* (Autumn).

"Pouvoirs de la tragédie antique." *Théâtre Populaire* (September).

"L'Arlésienne du catholicisme." *Lettres Nouvelles* (November).

"Féminaire de Michelet." *Lettres Nouvelles* (November).

1954 "Jules César au cinéma." *Lettres Nouvelles* (January). (*M*)

"Théâtre et collectivité." *Théâtre Populaire* (January–February).

"*Don Juan.*" *Théâtre Populaire* (January–February).

"Editorial." *Théâtre Populaire* (January–February).

"Au cinémascope." *Lettres Nouvelles* (February).

"Le Silence de Don Juan." *Lettres Nouvelles* (February).

"Fin de Richard II." *Lettres Nouvelles* (March).

"*Ruy Blas.*" *Théâtre Populaire* (March–April 1954).

"*L'Étranger*, roman solaire." *Bulletin du Club Français du Livre* (April).

"Avignon, l'hiver." *France-Observateur* (15 April).

"Je ne crois pas aux influences." *France-Observateur* (16 April).

"Monsieur Perrichon à Moscou." *France-Observateur* (29 April).

"Versailles et ses comptes." *Lettres Nouvelles* (May).

"*Egmont.*" *Théâtre Populaire* (May–June).

"Un bon petit théâtre." *France-Observateur* (13 May).

"Une Tragédienne sans public." *France-Observateur* (27 May).

"Godot adulte." *France-Observateur* (10 June).

"Pré-romans." *France-Observateur* (24 June). (*M*)

"Pour une définition du théâtre populaire." *Publi 54* (July).

"Jean Cayrol: *L'espace d'une nuit.*" *Esprit* (1954).

"*Mutter Courage* au Festival International de Paris." *Théâtre Populaire* (July–August).

"Littérature objective." *Critique*, no. 86–87 (July–August). (*CE*)

"Théâtre capital." *France-Observateur* (8 July).

"Le Comédien sans paradoxe." *France-Observateur* (22 July).

"Editorial." *Théâtre Populaire* (September).

"L'écrivain en vacances." *France-Observateur* (9 September). (*M*)

"Le Grand Robert." *Lettres Nouvelles* (October).

"Comment s'en passer." *France-Observateur* (7 October).

"Littérature inhumaine." *Lettres Nouvelles* (November).

"Propos sur La Cerisaie." *Théâtre Populaire* (November).

"Petites Mythologies du mois": "Martiens," "La Croisière du Sang bleu," Critique muette et critique aveugle," "Saponides et détergents," "Le

pauvre et le proletaire," *Lettres Nouvelles* (November). (all reprinted in *M*)
"Petites Mythologies du mois": "Mythologie perpétuelle," "Les Martiens et la presse," "Les Martiens et l'Eglise," "Nouvelles Mystifications," "L'opération Astra," "Conjugales," "Phénomène de mythe?" *Lettres Nouvelles* (December). (all reprinted in *M*)
"Le Théâtre populaire d'aujourd'hui." *Théâtre de France* (December).

1955 *"La Peste,* annales d'une épidémie ou roman de la solitude?" *Club* (Bulletin du Meilleur Livre) (January).
"Petites Mythologies du mois": "Dominici ou le triomphe de la litérature," "Iconographie de l'Abbé Pierre," "Romans et enfants," "Matisse et le bonheur de vivre," *Lettres Nouvelles* (January). (all reprinted in *M*)
"Rencontre en Forêt-Noire." *France-Observateur* (27 January).
"Editorial." *Théâtre Populaire* (January–February).
"Propos sur Claudel." *Théâtre Populaire* (January–February).
"Macbeth." Théâtre Populaire (January–February).
"Petite Sociologie du roman français contemporain." *Documents* (February).
"Petites Mythologies du mois": "Pour une histoire de l'enfance," "Enfants-vedettes," "Enfants-copies," "Jouets." *Lettres Nouvelles* (February). (all reprinted in *M*)
"Trésor ouvert, trésor retrouvé." *Bulletin de la Guilde du Livre* (February).
"Petites Mythologies du mois": "Paris n'a pas été inondé," "Bichon chez les Nègres," "La Vaccine de l'avant-garde," "Comment démystifier," "Un Ouvrier sympathique." *Lettres Nouvelles* (March). (all reprinted in *M*)
"Editorial." *Théâtre Populaire* (April).
"Les Maladies du costume de théâtre. *"Théâtre Populaire* (March–April). (*CE*)
"Dialogue." *Théâtre Populaire* (March–April).
"Homme pour Homme de Brecht, au Théâtre de l'Oeuvre." Théâtre Populaire (March–April).
"Pourquoi Brecht?" *Tribune Etudiante* (6 April).
"Réponse à Albert Camus." *Club* (April).
"Petites Mythologies du mois": "Le Visage de Garbo," "Puissance et désinvolture," "Le Vin et le lait," "Le Biftek et les frites." *Lettres Nouvelles* (April). (all reprinted in *M*)
"Petites Mythologies du mois": "Nautilus et le Bateau ivre," "Publicité et profondeur," "Quelques paroles de M. Poujade," "Adamov et le langage." *Lettres Nouvelles* (May). (all reprinted in *M*)
"Editorial." *Théâtre Populaire* (May–June).
"Oedipe-Roi." Théâtre Populaire (May–June).
"La Mangeuse d'hommes." *Bulletin de la Guilde du Livre* (June).

"Petites Mythologies du mois": "Le Cerveau d'Einstein," "L'homme-jet," "Le Group Captain Townsend," "Racine est Racine." *Lettres Nouvelles* (June). (all reprinted in *M*)

"Editorial." *Théâtre Populaire* (July–August).

"*Nekrassov* juge de sa critique." *Théâtre Populaire* (July–August).

"Petites Mythologies du mois": "Billy Graham au Vel'd'Hiv," "Le Procès Dupriez," "Photo-chocs," "Deux Mythes du jeune théâtre," "Suis-je marxiste?" *Lettres Nouvelles* (July–August).

"IIe Festival de Nîmes." *Théâtre Populaire* (July–August).

"Oedipe-Roi." *Théâtre Populaire* (July–August).

"Dialogue." *Théâtre Populaire* (July–August).

"Le Cercle de craie caucasien." *Europe* (September).

"Petite Mythologie du mois": "Le Tour de France comme Epopée." *Lettres Nouvelles* (September). (*M*)

"Littérature littérale." *Critique*, no. 100–101 (September–October). (*CE*)

"*L'Orestie* au théâtre Marigny." *Théâtre Populaire* (September–October). (*CE*)

"Ubu Roi." *Théâtre Populaire* (September–October).

"Petites Mythologies du mois": "Le Guide Bleu," "Celle qui voit clair," "Cuisine ornamentale," "La Croisière du *Batory*." *Lettres Nouvelles* (October). (*M*) "Préface" au *Théâtre de Baudelaire*. In *Oeuvres complètes*. Paris: Club du Meilleur Livre, vol. 1. (*CE*)

"Du Nouveau en critique." *Esprit* (November).

"La Querelle du rideau." *France-Observateur* (3 November).

"Petites Mythologies du mois": "L'usager et la grève," "Lexique marocain," "Grammaire marocaine." *Lettres Nouvelles* (November). (*M*)

"*L'Etourdi* ou le nouveau contretemps." *France-Observateur* (2 December).

"Petites Mythologies du mois": "Strip-Tease," "La Critique ni–ni," "La Nouvelle Citroën." *Lettres Nouvelles* (December).

1956 "Maupassant et la physique du malheur." *Bulletin de la Guilde du Livre* (January).

"Petite Mythologie du mois": "La Littérature selon Minou Drouet." *Lettres Nouvelles* (January). (*M*)

"Espoirs du théâtre populaire." *France-Observateur* (5 January).

"Petites Mythologies du mois": "Photogénie électorale," "Continent perdu," "Astrologie," "L'art vocal bourgeois." *Lettres Nouvelles* (February). (*M*)

"Marivaux au T.N.P." *France-Observateur* (2 February).

"Petites Mythologies du mois": "Le Plastique," "La Grande Famille des hommes," "Au Music-hall." *Lettres Nouvelles* (March). (*M*)

"Sur *Marée Basse*." *Théâtre Populaire* (March).

"Petite Mythologie du mois": "Poujade et les intellectuels." *Lettres Nouvelles* (April).

"Cinq peintres de théâtre." *Bref* (April).

"Le théâtre est toujours engagé." *Arts* (18–24 April).

"Petite Mythologie du mois": "La Dame aux camélias." *Lettres Nouvelles* (May). (*M*)

"A l'avant-garde de quel théâtre?" *Théâtre Populaire* (May). (*CE*)

"Brecht à Lyon." *France-Observateur* (10 May).

"Nouveaux Problèmes du réalisme." *Documents* (July).

"*Le Plus Heureux des Trois*." *Theatre Populaire* (July).

"*La Locandiera*." *Théâtre Populaire* (September).

"*Aujourd'hui ou les Coréens*." *France-Observateur* (1 November).

"Le Tâches de la critique brechtienne." *Arguments*, no. 1 (December–January) (*CE*)

1957 "Préface." Stendhal. *Quelques Promenades dans Rome*, suivi de *Les Cenci*. Lausanne: Guilde du Livre.

"Vouloir nous brûle et pouvoir nous détruit." *Bref* (February). (*CE*)

"La Cathédrale des romans." *Bulletin de la Guilde du Livre* (March).

(with Bernard Dort) "Brecht 'traduit.'" *Théâtre Populaire* (March).

"*Le Mariage de Figaro*." *Théâtre Populaire* (March).

"A propos des *Coréens* de Vinaver." *Théâtre Populaire* (March).

"Pourquoi Conrad a-t-il choisi l'anglais?" *Arts* (20 March).

"La rencontre est aussi un débat." *Rendez-vous des théâtres des Nations* (April).

"Le Faiseur." *Théâtre Populaire* (May).

"Histoire et sociologie du vêtement." *Annales* (July–September).

"Brecht, Marx et l'Histoire." *Cahiers Renaud-Barrault*, no. 23 (December).

1958 "Préface." *Iphigénie*. In *Théâtre de Racine*. Paris: Club des Libraires de France, vol. 2. (*R*)

"Voltaire, le dernier des écrivains heureux?" *Actualité Littéraire*. (*CE*)

"Il n'y a pas d'école Robbe-Grillet." *Arguments* (February). (*CE*)

"Situation de Roger Planchon." *Spectacles*, no. 1 (March).

"Brecht et notre temps." *L'Action Laïque* (March). (*CE*)

"Dire Racine." *Théâtre Populaire* (March). (*R*)

"Table Ronde sur Paolo Paoli." *Nouvelle Critique*, no. 94 (March).

"Le Mythe de l'acteur possédé." *Théâtre d'aujourd'hui* (March–April).

1959 "Préface." Michelet, *La Sorcière*. Paris: Club Français du Livre. (*CE*)
"Le Soulier de Satin." *Théâtre Populaire* (Winter).
"Littérature et metalangage." *Phantomas* (January). (*CE*)
"New York vu par Bernard Buffet." *Arts* (11–17 February).
"Tacite et le baroque funèbre." *L'Arc*, no. 6 (Spring). (*CE*)
"Où en est la critique littéraire en France?" *Politika* (Belgrade) (Spring).
"Langage et vêtement." *Critique*, no. 142 (March).
"Petite Mythologie: 'Qu'est-ce qu'un scandale?'" *Lettres Nouvelles* (4 March).
"Petite Mythologie: 'Cinéma, droite et gauche.'" *Lettres Nouvelles* (11 March).
"Petite Mythologie: 'Au Wagon-restaurant.'" *Lettres Nouvelles* (18 March).
"Petite Mythologie: 'Tables Rondes.'" *Lettres Nouvelles* (25 March).
"La Fête du cordonnier." *Théâtre Populaire* (Spring).
"Petite Mythologie: 'Tricots à domicile.'" *Lettres Nouvelles* (1 April).
"Petite Mythologie: 'Le Choix d'un métier.'" *Lettres Nouvelles* (8 April).
"Petite Mythologie: 'Sur un emploi du verbe être.'" *Lettres Nouvelles* (15 April).
"Petite Mythologie: 'Tragédie et hauteur.'" *Lettres Nouvelles* (22 April).
"La Relation d'autorité chez Racine." *Lettres Nouvelles* (10 June). (*R*)
"Reponse à une enquête sur le régime du Général de Gaulle." *Le 14 juillet* (18 June).
"Sept photo-modèles de *Mère Courage*." *Théâtre Populaire* (Summer).
"Zazie et la littérature." *Critique*, no. 147–48 (August–September). (*CE*)
"Les Trois Mousquetaires." *Théâtre Populaire* (Fall).
"L'Eros racinien." *Esprit* (November). (*R*)
"Petite Mythologie: 'Les Deux Salons.'" *Lettres Nouvelles* (4 November).
"De Gaulle, les Français et la littérature." *France-Observateur* (12 November).
1960 "Préface." Racine, *Théâtre*. Club Français du Livre, vol. 11 and 12. (*R*) "Le Problème de la signification au cinéma." *Revue Internationale de Filmologie* (January). (*IMT*)
"Préface." Brecht, *Mère Courage*. L'Arche.
"Je n'est pas un autre." *Critique*, no. 153 (February).
"La Réponse de Kafka." *France-Observateur* (24 March). (*CE*)
"Pour une sociologie du vêtement." *Annales* (March–April).
"*Le Balcon*." *Théâtre Populaire* (Spring).
"La Mode est au bleu cette année." *Revue Française de Sociologie* (April).
"Histoire et littérature: à propos de Racine." *Annales* (May–June). (*R*)

"Sur *La Mère* de Brecht." *Théâtre Populaire* (Summer).

"Les 'unités traumatiques' au cinéma." *Revue Internationale de Filmologie* (July–September).

"Une Histoire de la civilisation française." *Annales* (September–October).

"Ecrivains et écrivants." *Arguments* (Fall). (*CE*)

1961 "Préface." La Rochefoucauld, *Réflexions ou sentences et maximes*. Paris: Club Français du Livre. (*NCE*)

"Des Joyaux aux bijoux." *Jardin des Arts* (April).

"Le Théâtre français d'avant-garde." *Le Français dans le monde* (June–July).

"Le Centre d'Etudes des Communications de Masse–le C.E.C.MAS." *Annales* (September–October).

"Pour une sociologie de l'alimentation contemporaine." *Annales* (September–October).

"La Littérature, aujourd'hui." *Tel Quel*, no. 7 (Autumn). (*CE*)

"Le Message photographique." *Communications*, no. 1 (Fall). (*IMT*) (*OO*)

"*Les Etudes de motivation*." *Communications*, no. 1 (Fall).

"*Civilisation de l'image*." *Communications*, no. 1 (Fall).

"La Première Conférence internationale sur l'information visuelle." *Communications*, no. 1 (Fall).

"Savoir et folie." *Critique*, no. 174 (November). (*CE*)

"Témoignage sur Robbe-Grillet." *Clarté*, no. 39 (December).

1962 "Structure du fait-divers." *Médiations* (Summer). (*CE*)

"Le Dandysme et la Mode." *American Lines Paris Review* (July).

"Littérature et discontinu." *Critique*, no. 185 (October). (*CE*)

"Les Choses signifient-elles quelque chose?" *Figaro Littéraire* (13 October). (*GV*)

"A propos de deux ouvrages de Claude Lévi-Strauss: Sociologie et sociologique." *Informations sur les sciences sociales*. (December).

1963 "Préface." Bruce Morrissette, *Les Romans de Robbe-Grillet*. Paris: Minuit. (*CE*)

"Préface." La Bruyere, *Les Caractères*. Paris: Union Générale d'Editions. (*CE*)

"Préface." Jean Cayrol, *Les Corps étrangers*. Paris: Union Générale d'Editions.

"L'activité structuraliste." *Lettres Nouvelles* (February). (*CE*)

"Oeuvre de masse et explication de texte." *Communications*, no. 2 (March).

"La Vedette: enquête d'audience?" *Communications*, no. 2 (March).

"Le Message publicitaire." *Cahiers de la publicité* (July).

"La Métaphore de l'oeil." *Critique*, no. 195–96 (August–September). (*CE*)

"Entretien sur le cinéma." *Cahiers du cinéma*, no. 147 (September). (*GV*)

"Criticism as Language." *Times Literary Supplement* (27 September). (*CE*)

"Mythologie de l'automobile." *Réalités*, no. 213 (October).

"L'imagination du signe." *Arguments,* no. 27–28 (Fall). (CE)

"Les Deux Critiques." *Modern Language Notes* (December). (CE)

"Les Deux Sociologies du roman." *France-Observateur* (5 December).

1964 "Image, raison, déraison." In *L'Univers de l'Encyclopédie.* Paris: Libraires Associés, vol. 1. (NCE)

"Trois Fragments: 'Edipo,' 'I tre dialoghi,' 'Arte, Forma, Caso.'" *Menabo* (Turin) (February).

"Janson." Paris: Editions de la Galerie Weiller (February).

"Interview." *France-Observateur* (16 April). (GV)

"Entretien." *Image et Son* (July). (GV)

"Littérature et signification." *Tel Quel,* no. 16 (Winter). (CE)

"Présentation." *Communications,* no. 4 (November).

"Rhétorique de l'image." *Communications,* no. 4 (November). (IMT) (OO)

"Eléments de sémiologie." *Communications,* no. 4 (November) (ES)

"Les Sciences humaines et l'oeuvre de Lévi-Strauss." *Annales* (November–December).

"La Cuisine du sens." *Nouvel Observateur* (3–10 December).

1965 "Le Théâtre grec." In *Histoire des spectacles.* Paris: Gallimard "Pléiade." (OO)

"Préface." Chateaubriand, *La Vie de Rancé.* Paris: Union Générale d'Editions. (NCE)

"Réponse à une enquête sur le structuralisme." Catalogue général d'*Il Saggiatore* (Mondadori).

"Culture de masse/culture supérieure." *Communications,* no. 5 (May).

"Témoignage sur le théâtre." *Esprit* (May).

"Drame, poème, roman." *Critique,* no. 218 (July).

"Une écriture dialectique." *Combat* (July).

"Au nom de la 'nouvelle critique,' Roland Barthes répond à Raymond Picard." *Figaro Littéraire,* (14–20 October). (GV)

"Préface." Catalogue de l'Exposition Emmanuel Pereire (November).

"Picard lecteur de la Nouvelle Critique." *Nouvel Observateur* (10 November).

1966 "Sémantique de l'objet." In *Arte e Cultura nella Civilita contemporanea.* Florence: Sansoni.

"Préface." Jean-Pierre Boon and Jean-Jacques Brochier, *L'analyse terminologique du langage des sciences sociales.* C.E.C.MAS.

"Le classement structural des figures de rhétorique." *Le Français Moderne* (January).

"Les Vies parallèles." *Quinzaine Littéraire,* no. 1 (15 March).

"Alain Girard, *Le Journal intime.*" *Année Sociologique 1964.*

"Principi e scopi dell'analisi strutturale." *Nuovi Argomenti* (April–June).

"Interview." *Aletheia,* no. 4 (May).

"Situation du linguiste." *Quinzaine Littéraire*, no. 5 (15 May).

"La Mode et les sciences humaine." *Echanges* (August).

"Introduction à l'analyse structurale des récits." *Communications*, no. 8 (November). (*IMT*)

1967 "Proust et les noms." In *To Honor Roman Jakobson*. The Hague: Mouton. (*NCE*)

"L'arbre du crime." *Tel Quel*, no. 28 (Winter). (*SFL*)

"Préface." Antoine Gallien, *Verdure*. Paris: Seuil.

"L'analyse rhétorique." *Littérature et société*. Brussels: Institut de Sociologie de l'Université Libre de Bruxelles.

"La Face baroque." *Quinzaine Littéraire*, no. 28 (15 May).

"Interview par Raymond Bellour." *Lettres Françaises* (2 March). (*GV*)

"Edoardo Sanguinetti." *Catalogue Feltrinelli* ("100 Narratori di Feltrinelli') (May).

"Le Discours de l'histoire." *Information sur les Sciences Sociales* (August). Reprinted in *Poétique*, no. 49 (1982).

"Le Match Chanel-Courrèges." *Marie-Claire*, no. 181 (September).

"Science versus Literature." *Times Literary Supplement* (28 September).

1968 "Società, immaginazione, publicita." In *Publicita e Televisione*. Rome: R.A.I.

"L'effet de réel." *Communications*, no. 11 (March).

"Flaubert et la phrase." *Word* (April–August–September). (*NCE*)

"Le Refus d'hériter." *Nouvel Observateur* (30 April).

"Leçon d'écriture." *Tel Quel*, no. 34 (Summer). (*IMT*)

"Structuralisme et sémiologie." *Lettres Françaises* (31 July).

"L'écriture de l'événement." *Communications*, no. 12 (November).

"La Mort de l'auteur." *Mantéia*, no. 5 (Fall). (*IMT*)

"Linguistique et littérature." *Langages* (December).

1969 "Alejandro." Prospectus de l'Exposition Alejandro. Galerie Maya (Brussels) February).

"La peinture est-elle un langage?" *Quinzaine Littéraire*, no. 69 (1–15 March). (*OO*)

"Dieci Ragioni per scrivere." *Corriere Litterario* (29 May).

"Comment parler à Dieu." *Tel Quel*, no. 38 (Summer). (*SFL*)

"D'un soleil réticent." *France-Observateur* (17 June).

"Un Cas de critique culturelle." *Communications*, no. 14 (November).

1970 "La linguistique du discours." In *Signe, langage, culture*. The Hague: Mouton.

"To Write: Intransitive Verb?" In *The Structuralist Controversy: The Languages of Criticism and the Sciences of Man*, ed. Richard Macksey and Eugenio Donato. Baltimore: The Johns Hopkins Press.

"Masculin, féminin, neutre." In *Echanges et communications* (Mélanges offerts à Claude Lévi-Strauss). The Hague: Mouton. (*S/Z*)

"Introduction." Bernard Minoret and Danielle Vezolles, *La Fuite en Chine.* Paris: Christian Bourgois.

"Ce qu'il advient au signifiant." Preface to Pierre Guyotat, *Eden, Eden, Eden.* Paris: Gallimard.

"Préface." *Encyclopédie Bordas,* vol. 8: *L'aventure littéraire de l'humanité.*

"L'analyse structurale du récit: A propos d'Actes X–XI." *Recherches de Sciences Religieuses.*

"Une problématique du sens." *Cahiers Media* (Bordeaux).

"Par où commencer?" *Poétique,* no. 1 (January). (*NCE*)

"Musica Practica." *L'Arc,* no. 40 (February). (*IMT*) (*OO*)

"Entretien." *Nouvelles Littéraires* (5 March).

"Ecrire la lecture." *Figaro Littéraire* (9 March).

"L'Etrangère." *Quinzaine Littéraire,* no. 94 (1–15 May).

"Interview par Raymond Bellour." *Lettres Françaises* (20 May). (*GV*)

"*L'Express* va plus loin avec Roland Barthes." *L'Express* (25–31 May). (*GV*)

"La Théorie." *VH 101,* no. 2 (Summer).

"L'Esprit de la lettre." *Quinzaine Littéraire,* no. 96 (1–15 June). (*OO*)

"Le Troisième Sens." *Cahiers du cinéma,* no. 222 (July). (*IMT*) (*OO*)

"Vivre avec Fourier." *Critique,* no. 282 (October). (*SFL*)

"L'ancienne rhétorique: aide-mémoire." *Communications,* no. 16 (December).

"Sémiologie et urbanisme." *L'Architecture d'aujourd'hui,* no. 153 (December 1970–January 1971).

1971 "Réflexions sur un manuel." In Serge Doubrovsky and Tzvetan Todorov, eds., *L'enseignement de la littérature.* Paris: Plon.

"Action Sequences." In Joseph Strelka, ed., *Patterns of Literary Style.* University Park: Pennsylvania State University Press.

"Style and Its Image." In Seymour Chatman, ed., *Literary Style: A Symposium.* New York: Oxford University Press.

"La Lutte avec l'ange: analyse textuelle de *Genèse* XXXII, 23–33." In *Analyse structurale et exégèse biblique.* Neuchatel: Delachaux ey Nietslé. (*IMT*)

"Préface." Pierre Loti, *Aziyadé.* Parma: Ricci. Reprinted in *Critique,* no. 297 (February 1972). (*NCE*)

"Conversation with Roland Barthes." *Signs of the Times.* Cambridge, 1971. (*GV*)

"Digressions." *Promesses,* no. 29 (Spring). (*GV*)

"L'éblouissement." *Le Monde* (11 March).

"La Mythologie aujourd'hui." *Esprit* (April). (*IMT*)

"Ha perso l'arte di vivere." *Espresso* (1 August).

"De l'oeuvre au texte." *Revue d'Esthétique* (Fall). (*IMT*)

"Ecrivains, intellectuels, professeurs." *Tel Quel*, no. 47 (Fall). (*IMT*)

"Réponses." *Tel Quel*, no. 47 (Fall).

"Une idée de recherche." *Paragone* (Florence) (October). Reprinted in *Recherche de Proust*. Paris: Seuil "Points," 1980.

"Languages at War in a Culture at Peace." *Times Literary Supplement* (8 October).

"Un très beau cadeau." *Le Monde* (16 October).

"Entretien." *Quinzaine Littéraire*, no. 130 (1–15 December).

1972 "Sémiologie et médecine." In Roger Bastide, ed., *Sciences de la folie*. Paris: 'Mouton.

"Préface." Eugene Fromentin, *Dominique*. Turin: Einaudi. (*NCE*)

"Entretien." *Politique Hebdo* (January). (*GV*)

"Plaisir/écriture/lecture." *Lettres Françaises* (9–15 February). (*GV*)

"Lettre à Jean Ristat." *Lettres Françaises* (29 March).

"Jeunes chercheurs." *Communications*, no. 19 (June).

"Préface." Catalogue de l'Exposition des Arts Décoratifs, "L'affiche anglaise: les années 90." (June–September).

"Le Retour du poéticien." *Quinzaine Littéraire*, no. 150 (16–31 October).

"Le Grain de la voix." *Musique en Jeu*, no. 9 (November). (*IMT*). (*OO*)

1973 "Texte: Théorie du." In *Encyclopédie Universalis*, vol. 15. Trans. Ian McLeod as "Theory of the Text," in Robert Young, ed. *Untying the Text*.

"La Division des langages." In *Une Nouvelle Civilisation: Hommage à Georges Friedmann*. Paris: Gallimard.

"Les Sorties du texte." In *Bataille*. Paris: Union Générale d'Editions.

"Diderot, Brecht, Eisenstein." *Revue d'Esthétique*. (*IMT*)

"Réquichot et son corps." In *L'Oeuvre de Bernard Réquichot*. Brussels: Editions de la Connaissance. Extracts in *Quinzaine Littéraire*, no. 164 (16–31 May). (*OO*)

"Analyze textuelle d'un conte d'Edgar Poe." In Claude Chabrol, ed., *Sémiotique narrative et textuelle*. Paris: Larousse "L." Trans. Geoff Bennington, in Robert Young, ed., *Untying the Text*.

"Postface." In Jean Ristat, *L'entrée dans la baie et la prise de la ville de Rio de Janeiro*. Paris: Editeurs Français Réunis.

"Aujoud'hui, Michelet." *L'Arc*, no. 52 (February).

"L'adjectif est le 'dire' du désir." *Gulliver*, no. 5 (March). (*GV*)

"Saussure, le signe, la démocratie." *Le Discours Social*, no. 3–4 (April).

"Sémiographie d'André Masson." Catalogue de l'Exposition Masson (Tours) (May). Reprinted in *Critique*, no. 408 (May 1981). (*OO*)

"Supplément." *Art Press* (May–June).

"Par dessus l'épaule." *Critique*, no. 318 (November). (*Sollers écrivain*)

"Un rapport presque maniaque avec les instruments graphiques." *Le Monde* (27 September). (*GV*)

"Les Fantômes de l'opéra." *Nouvel Observateur* (17 December). (*GV*)

1974 "Situation." *Tel Quel*, no. 57 (February).

"Premier Texte." *L'Arc*, no. 56 (Spring).

"Au Séminaire." *L'Arc*, no. 56 (Spring).

"De la parole à l'écriture." *Quinzaine Littéraire*, no. 182 (1–15 March). (*GV*)

"Pourquoi j'aime Benveniste." *Quinzaine Littéraire*, no. 185 (16–30 April).

"Alors la Chine?" *Le Monde* (24 May). (*Alors la Chine?*)

"Roland Barthes contre les idées reçues." *Le Figaro* (27 July). (*GV*)

"Modernité de Michelet." *Revue d'Histoire Littéraire de la France* (September–October).

"Que deviendrait une société qui renoncerait à se distancer?" *Le Monde* (15 November). (*GV*)

"Bloy." *Tableau de la littérature francaise, III; de Madame de Staël à Rimbaud.* Paris: Gallimard.

1975 "Rasch: sémiologie des *Kreisleriana* de Schumann." In J.-A. Miller, J. Kristeva, N. Ruwet, eds., *Langue, discours, société: Homage à Emile Benveniste.* Paris: Seuil. (*OO*)

"Littérature/enseignement." *Pratiques*, no. 5 (February). (*GV*)

"Untel par lui-même." *Tel Quel*, no. 61 (February). (*RB*)

"Vingt mots-clé pour Roland Barthes." *Magazine Littéraire*, no. 97 (February). (*GV*)

"Préface." Gerard Miller, *Le Pousse-au-jouir du Maréchal Petain.* Paris: Seuil.

"Barthes puissance trois." *Quinzaine Littéraire*, no. 205 (1–15 March).

"Lecture de Brillat-Savarin." In Brillat-Savarin, *Physiologie du goût.* Paris: Hermann.

"Les Surréalistes ont manqué le corps." *Quotidien de Paris* (May). (*GV*)

"Le Bruissement de la langue." *Vers une esthétique sans entrave: mélanges offerts à Mikel Dufrenne.* Paris: Union Générale d'Editions.

"Proust et la nouvelle critique: table ronde." *Etudes Proustiennes*, vol. 2. Paris: Gallimard.

"Roland Barthes interroge Renaud Camus." *Quinzaine Littéraire*, no. 209 (1–15 May).

"En sortant du cinéma." *Communications*, no. 23. Trans. B. Augst and S. White as "Upon Leaving the Movie Theater," in *University Publishing*, no. 9 (1979).

"Résurrection de Michelet: table ronde." *Michelet cent ans après*. Grenoble: Presses Universitaires de Grenoble.

"Brecht et le discours: contribution à l'étude de la discursivité." *L'Autre Scène*, no. 8–9.

1976 "La Crise de la vérité." *Magazine Littéraire*, no. 108 (January). (*GV*)

"Le Chant romantique." *Gramma*, no. 5. (*OO*)

"Science fiction: il n'existe aucun discours qui ne soit une fiction." *Quinzaine Littéraire*, no. 225 (16–31 January).

"Un grand rhétoricien des figures érotiques." *Magazine Littéraire*, no. 113 (June). (*GV*)

"Sur la lecture." *Le Français d'aujourd'hui*, no. 32.

1977 "A quoi sert un intellectuel?" *Nouvel Observateur* (10 January). (*GV*)

"Une sorte de travail manuel." *Nouvelles Littéraires* (3–10 March).

"Fragments d'un discours amoureux." *Art Press* (May). (*GV*)

"Le plus grand décripteur de mythes de ce temps nous parle d'amour." *Playboy* (French edition) (September). (*GV*)

"Interview with J. Rivette and M. Delahaye." *Filmkritik* 21, no. 4.

1978 "Propos sur la violence." *Réforme*, no. 2 (September). (*GV*)

"L'Image." In *Prétexte: Roland Barthes*. Paris: Union Générale d'Editions.

"Conclusions." In *Prétexte: Roland Barthes*. Union Générale d'Editions.

"Des mots pour faire entendre un doute." *Elle* (December).

"Ça prend." *Magazine Littéraire*, no. 144 (December).

1979 "Un contexte trop brutal." *Nouvelles Littéraires* (6–13 February). (*GV*)

"Entretiens sur Roger Laporte." *Digraphe*, no. 18–19 (April).

"Roland Barthes s'explique." *Lire* (April). (*GV*)

"Le Sexe passe." *Nouvel Observateur* (14 May).

with Frédéric Berthet. "Présentation." *Communications*, no. 30 (September).

"The Wisdom of Art." *Cy Twombly: Paintings and Drawings, 1954–1977*. (*OO*) New York: Whitney Museum of Modern Art.

"Osons être paresseux." *Le Monde-Dimanche* (16 September). (*GV*)

"Délibération." *Tel Quel*, no. 82 (November). Trans. Richard Howard as "Deliberation," in *Partisan Review* 47, no.4 (1980).

"Pour un Chateaubriand de papier." *Nouvel Observateur* (10 December).

1980 "Préface." Renaud Camus, *Tricks*. Paris: Mazarine.

"Note sur un album de Lucien Clergue." *Sud*, no. 31.

"Du Goût à l'extase." *Le Matin* (22 February). (*GV*)

"Sur la photographie." *Le Photographe* (February). (*GV*)

"Interview: 'Maigritude.'" *Playboy* (French edition) (March). (*GV*)

"La Crise du désir." *Nouvel Observateur* (14–20 April). (*GV*)

"Cher Antonioni." *Cahiers du cinéma*, no. 311 (May).
"On échoue toujours à parler de ce qu'on aime." *Tel Quel*, no. 85 (July).
"Le Dictionnaire est aussi un rêve et un combat." *Nouvelles Littéraires* (21–27 September).
"Archimboldo." In *Archimboldo*. Milan: Ricci. (*OO*)
1981 "Italo Calvino vu par Roland Barthes." *Le Monde* (20 February).
"Une Leçon de sincérité." *Poétique*, no. 47 (September).

III. Books and Special Issues on Roland Barthes

Tel Quel, no. 47 (1971).
Mallac, Guy de, and Eberbach, Margaret. *Barthes*. Paris: Editions Universitaires "Psychothèque," 1971.
Critique, no. 302 (1972).
Calvet, Louis-Jean. *Roland Barthes, un regard politique sur le signe*. Paris: Payot, 1973.
L'Arc, no. 56 (1974).
Heath, Stephen. *Vertige du déplacement: Lecture de Barthes*. Paris: Fayard, 1974.
Magazine Littéraire, no. 97 (February 1975).
Thody, Philip. *Roland Barthes: A Conservative Estimate*. Atlantic Highlands, N.J.: Humanities Press, 1977.
Visible Language 11, no. 4 (Fall 1977).
Compagnon, Antoine, ed. *Prétexte: Roland Barthes*. Paris: Union Générale d'Editions, 1978.
Burnier, Michel-Antoine, and Rambaud, Patrick. *Le Roland-Barthes sans peine*. Paris: Balland, 1978.
Fages, J.-B. *Comprendre Roland Barthes*. Toulouse: Privat, 1979.
Journal of Practical Structuralism, no. 1 (July 1979).
Studies in Twentieth Century Literature 5, no. 2 (Spring 1981).
Lund, Steffen Nordahl. *L'Aventure du signifiant: Une Lecture de Barthes*. Paris: Presses Universitaires de France, 1981.
Poétique, no. 47 (1981).
George R. Wasserman. *Roland Barthes*. Boston: Twayne, 1981.
L'Esprit Créateur 22, no. 1 (Spring 1982.)
Lavers, Annette. *Roland Barthes: Structuralism and After*. Cambridge: Harvard University Press, 1982.
Critique, no. 423–24 (August-September 1982).
Communications, no. 35 (October 1982).
Culler, Jonathan. *Barthes*. New York: Oxford University Press, 1983.

IV. *Other Sources Consulted*

Altman, Charles F. "Psychoanalysis and Cinema: "The Imaginary Discourse."
  Quarterly Review of Film Studies 2 (1977): 257–72.
Anquetil, Gilles. "Roland Barthes au Collège de France: La Saveur du savoir."
  Nouvelles Littèraires, 13–20 January 1977, p. 10.
Antonioni, Michelangelo. "Lettre à Roland Barthes." *Cahiers du Cinèma*, no. 311
  (May 1980): 11.
Aron, Jean-Paul. "Roland Barthes: *Le Plaisir du texte*." *Cahiers du Chemin*, no. 19
  (October 1973): 134–42.
Assad, Maria L. "La Lecture comme mythe." *L'Esprit Créateur* 14 (1974): 333–41.
Auerbach, Erich. *Scenes in the Drama of European Literature*. Translated by Ralph
  Manheim. New York: Meridian, 1959.
Bartkowski, Frances. "Roland Barthes's Secret Garden." *Studies in Twentieth
  Century Literature* 5 (1981): 133–46.
Bataille, Georges. *Oeuvres complètes*. Vol. 6. Paris: Gallimard, 1973.
Béguin, Albert. *La Conscience critique*. Paris: Corti, 1971.
Bellour, Raymond. *Le Livre des autres*. Paris: Union Générale d'Editions, 1978.
  (Reprinted in *GV*, 45–56 and 69–86)
———. "La Clé des champs." *Magazine Littéraire*, no. 97 (February 1975): 15–18.
Benveniste, Emile. *Problems in General Linguistics*. Translated by Mary Elizabeth
  Meek. Coral Gables: University of Miami Press, 1971.
Bersani, Leo. "From Bachelard to Barthes." *Partisan Review* 34 (1967): 215–32.
———. "Is There a Science of Literature?" *Partisan Review* 39 (1972): 535–53.
———. *The Death of Stéphane Mallarmé*. New York: Cambridge University Press,
  1982.
Black, Max. *Models and Metaphors*. Ithaca: Cornell University Press, 1964.
Blanchot, Maurice. *La Part du feu*. Paris: Gallimard, 1949.
———. *L'Entretien infini*. Paris: Gallimard, 1969.
———. *L'Amitié*. Paris: Gallimard, 1971.
Bonitzer, Pascal. "Le Hors-champs subtil." *Cahiers du Cinéma*, no. 311 (May
  1980): 5–7.
Bonnefoy, Claude. "Barthes en bouffées de langage." *Nouvelles Littéraires*, 21
  April 1977, p. 9.
Booth, Wayne C. *A Rhetoric of Irony*. Chicago: University of Chicago Press,
  1974.
Boulez, Pierre. "Le Statut de l'amateur." *Critique*, no. 423–24 (August-
  September 1982): 663–65.
Bouttes, Jean-Louis. "A travers et à tors." *L'Arc*, no. 56 (1974): 57–62.
———. "Faux comme la vérité." *Critique*, no. 341 (1975): 1024–52.

Brée, Germaine. "French Criticism: A Battle of Books?" *Emory University Quarterly* 22 (1967): 25–35.

Brenkman, John. "The Other and the One: Psychoanalysis, Reading, *The Symposium*." *Yale French Studies*, no. 55–56 (1978): 396–456.

Bruckner, Pascal, and Finkielkraut, Alain. *Le Nouveau Désordre amoureux*. Paris: Seuil "Fiction et Cie," 1977.

Burch, Noël. "Barthes et le Japon." *L'Arc*, no. 56 (1974): 40–44.

Calvet, Louis-Jean. "Une Sémiologie politique." *L'Arc*, no. 56 (1974): 25–29.

———. *Pour et contre Saussure: Ves une linguistique sociale*. Paris: Payot, 1976.

Caplan, Jay. "Nothing But Language." *Visible Language* 11 (1977): 341–62.

Champagne, Roland. "Between Orpheus and Eurydice: Roland Barthes and the Historicity of the Reader." *Clio* 8 (1979): 229–38.

Charles, Michel. "L'Amour de la littérature." *Poétique*, no. 47 (1981): 371–90.

Chevrier, Jean-François. Proust par Roland Barthes." In *Prétexte: Roland Barthes*, pp. 370–93.

Choay, Françoise. "L'Emploi des signes." *Quinzaine Littéraire*, no. 94, 1–15 May 1970, p. 5.

Compagnon, Antoine. "L'Imposture." In *Prétexte: Roland Barthes*, pp. 40–64.

Conley, Tom. "Barthes's *Excès:* The Silent Apostrophe of *S/Z*." *Visible Language* 11 (1977): 355–84.

———. "A Message without a Code?" *Studies in Twentieth Century Literature* 5 (1981): 147–56.

Coward, Rosalind, and Ellis, John. *Language and Materialism: Developments in Semiology and the Theory of the Subject*. Boston: Routledge and Kegan Paul, 1977.

Crystal, David. *Linguistics*. Baltimore: Penguin, 1971.

Culler, Jonathan. *Structuralist Poetics: Structuralism, Linguistics, and the Study of Literature*. Ithaca: Cornell University Press, 1975.

———. *Ferdinand de Saussure*. New York: Penguin, 1977.

———. *The Pursuit of Signs: Semiotics, Literature, Deconstruction*. Ithaca: Cornell University Press, 1981.

Dadoun, Roger. "Marches barthésiennes." *L'Arc*, no. 56 (1974): 37–39.

Dannhauser, Werner J. "On Teaching Politics Today." *Commentary* 59 (1975): 74–78.

Davidson, Hugh M. "The Critical Position of Roland Barthes." In *Criticism: Speculative and Analytic Essays*, edited by L. S. Dembo, pp. 93–102. Madison: University of Wisconsin Press, 1968.

———. "Signs, Senses, and Roland Barthes." In *Approaches to Poetics*, edited by Seymour Chatman, pp. 29–50. New York: Columbia University Press, 1973.

DeGeorge, Fernande, and DeGeorge, Richard, eds. *The Structuralists: From Marx to Lévi-Strauss*. Garden City: Anchor, 1972.

Delcourt, Xavier. "Les mille façons de dire 'je t'aime.'" *Quinzaine Littéraire*, no. 255, 1–15 May 1977, p. 4.

Derrida, Jacques. *Of Grammatology*. Translated by Gayatri Chakravorty Spivak. Chicago: University of Chicago Press, 1976.

———. *Writing and Difference*. Translated by Alan Bass. Chicago: University of Chicago Press, 1978.

———. "White Mythology: Metaphor in the Text of Philosophy." *New Literary History* 5 (1974): 5–72.

———. "Les Morts de Roland Barthes." *Poétique*, no. 47 (1981): 269–92.

Dort, Bernard. "Barthes: Un défi au théâtre." *Magazine Littéraire*, no. 97 (February 1975): 10–11.

Doubrovsky, Serge. *The New Criticism in France*. Translated by Derek Coltman. Chicago: University of Chicago Press, 1973.

———. "Une Ecriture tragique." *Poétique*, no. 47 (1981): 329–54.

Doubrousky, Serge, and Todorov, Tzvetan, eds. *L'Enseignement de la littérature*. Paris: Plon, 1971.

Ducrot, Oswald, and Todorov, Tzvetan. *Encyclopedic Dictionary of the Sciences of Language*. Translated by Catherine Porter. Baltimore: The Johns Hopkins University Press, 1979.

Duvernois, Pierre. "L'Emportement de l'écriture." *Critique*, no. 302 (1972): 595–609.

Ehrmann, Jacques. "L'Emprise des signes." *Semiotica* 7 (1972): 49–62.

Escoubas, Eliane. "Lapsus Linguae." *Disgraphe*, no. 17 (1978): 143–54.

Finas, Lucette. "Barthes ou le pari sur une nouvelle forme de raison." *Quinzaine Littéraire*, no. 3, 15 April 1966, p. 15.

———. "Entre les mots et les choses." *Quinzaine Littéraire*, no. 28, 15–31 May 1967, pp. 3–4.

Finkielkraut, Alain. "Savoirs-vivre." *L'Arc*, no. 56 (1974): 70–77.

Flahaut, François. "La Limite entre la vie et la mort: Dracula et Frankenstein." In *Prétexte: Roland Barthes*, pp. 65–86.

———. "Sur S/Z et l'analyse des récits." *Poétique*, no. 47 (1981): 303–14.

Foucault, Michel. *The History of Sexuality: An Introduction*. Translated by Robert Hurley. New York: Pantheon, 1978.

Freud, Sigmund. "The Interpretation of Dreams." *Standard Edition of the Complete Psychological Works of Sigmund Freud*. Edited by James Strachey. Vols. 4 and 5. London: Hogarth Press, 1953.

———. "Beyond the Pleasure Principle." *Standard Edition*. Vol. 18.

Funt, David. "Roland Barthes and the 'Nouvelle Critique.'" *Journal of Aesthetics and Art Criticism* 26 (1968): 329–40.

Fynsk, Christopher I. "A Decelebration of Philosophy." *Diacritics* 8, no. 2 (1978): 80–90.

Gallo, Max. "Barthes le Français." *L'Express*, 12 April 1980, p. 91.

Gallop, Jane. "B.S." *Visible Language* 11 (1977): 364–87.

Gelb. I. M. *Grammatology: A Study of Writing*. Rev. ed. Chicago: University of Chicago Press, 1963.

Genette, Gérard. *Figures I*. Paris: Seuil, 1966.

———. "Le Journal, l'antijournal." *Poétique*, no. 47 (1981): 315–22.

Genelle, Gérard, and Todorov, Tzvetan, eds. *Recherche de Proust*. Paris: Seuil "Points," 1980.

Girard, René. "Racine, poète de la gloire." *Critique*, no. 205 (1964): 483–506.

Goodheart, Eugene. "The Myths of Roland." *Partisan Review* 47 (1980): 199–212.

Granier, Jean. *Le Problème de la vérité dans la philosophie de Nietzsche*. Paris: Seuil, 1966.

GREPH. *Qui a peur de la philosophie?* Paris: Flammarion "Champs," 1977.

Guiraud, Pierre. *Semiology*. Translated by G. Gross. Boston: Routledge and Kegan Paul, 1975.

Guthrie, W. K. C. *Socrates*. New York: Cambridge University Press, 1971.

Hahn, Otto. "Barthes." *VH 101*, no. 2 (1970): 5–11.

Harari, Josué V. "The Maximum Narrative: An Introduction to Barthes' Recent Criticism." *Style* 8 (1974): 56–77.

———. "Changing the Object of Criticism: 1965–78." *MLN* 94 (1979): 784–96.

Hawkes, Terence. *Structuralism and Semiotics*. Berkeley: University of California Press, 1977.

Heath, Stephen. "Changer de langue." *Magazine Littéraire*, no. 97 (February 1975): 18–19.

———. "Le Corps victorien: anthologiquement." *Critique*, no. 405–6 (1981): 152–65.

Henric, Jacques. "Roland Barthes: *Fragments d'un discours amoureux*." *Art Press International*, May 1977, pp. 4–7.

Higgins, Lynn A. "Barthes's Imaginary Voyages." *Studies in Twentieth Century Literature* 5 (1981): 157–74.

Hirsch, E. D. *Validity in Interpretation*. New Haven: Yale University Press, 1967.

Hollier, Denis, ed. *Panorama des sciences humaines*. Paris: Gallimard, 1972.

Hough, Graham. "The Importation of Roland Barthes." *Times Literary Supplement*, 9 December 1977, p. 1443.

Jameson, Fredric. *The Prison-House of Language: A Critical Account of Structuralism and Russian Formalism*. Princeton: Princeton University Press, 1972.

————. "Ideology of the Text." *Salmagundi,* no. 31–32 (1975–76): 204–46.

Johnson, Barbara. *The Critical Difference*. Baltimore: The Johns Hopkins University Press, 1981.

Keane, Patrick J. "On Truth and Lie in Nietzsche." *Salmagundi,* no. 29 (1975): 67–94.

Kennedy, J. Gerald. "Roland Barthes, Autobiography, and the End of Ideology." *Georgia Review* 35 (1981): 381–98.

Kenner, Hugh. "Decoding Roland Barthes: The Obit of a Structuralist." *Harper's,* August 1980, pp. 68–71.

Kevelson, Roberta. "A Restructure of Barthes' Readerly Text." *Semiotica* 18 (1976): 253–67.

Klein, Richard. "Images of the Self: New York and Paris." *Partisan Review* 40 (1973): 294–301.

Koch, Stephen. "Melancholy King of the Cats." *Saturday Review,* 2 September 1978, pp. 32–35.

Kofman, Sarah. *Nietzsche et la métaphore*. Paris: Payot, 1972.

Kristeva, Julia. *Semiotikè: Recherches pour une sémanalyse*. Paris: Seuil, 1969.

————. "Comment parler à la littérature." *Tel Quel,* no. 47 (1971): 27–49.

Kristeva, Julia; Miller, Jacques-Alain; and Ruwet, Nicolas, eds. *Langue, discours, société: Hommage à Emile Benveniste*. Paris: Seuil, 1975.

Lacan, Jacques. "The Insistence of the Letter in the Unconscious." *Yale French Studies,* no. 36–37 (1966): 112–47.

————. *Le Séminaire I: Les Ecrits techniques de Freud*. Paris: Seuil, 1975.

Laclos, Choderlos de. *Les Liaisons dangereuses*. Translated by Richard Aldington. New York: New American Library, 1963.

Lane, Michael, ed. *Structuralism: A Reader*. New York: Harper and Row, 1972.

Laporte, Roger. *Quinze Variations sur un thème biographique*. Paris: Flammarion, 1975.

Lapouge, Gilles. "Voyage autour de Roland Barthes." *Quinzaine Littéraire,* no. 130, 1–15 December 1971, pp. 3–4.

Lavers, Annette. "En traduisant Barthes." *Tel Quel,* no. 47 (1971): 115–25.

————. "A Mode of Knowledge." *Times Literary Supplement,* 1 August 1975, p. 878.

Leenhardt, Jacques. "Interview." *Diacritics* 7, no. 3 (1977): 64–72.

Lelouche, Raphaël. "La Retraite: Propositions sur Roland Barthes." In *Prétexte: Roland Barthes,* pp. 222–43.

Lévi-Vareuse, Jacqueline, ed. *Les Critiques de notre temps et Camus*. Paris: Garnier, 1970.

Lévy, Bernard-Henri. "A quoi sert un intellectuel?" *Nouvel Observateur*, 10–16 January 1977, p. 64.

Lotringer, Sylvère. "Argo-Notes: Roland Barthes' Textual Trip." *Boundary 2* 2 (1974): 562–72.

Lyotard, Jean-François. "The Endurance of the Profession." *Yale French Studies*, no. 63 (1982): 72–77.

Man, Paul de. "Nietzsche's Theory of Rhetoric." *Symposium* 28 (1974): 33–51.

———. *Allegories of Reading: Figural Language in Rousseau, Nietzsche, Rilke, and Proust*. New Haven: Yale University Press, 1979.

Marin, Louis. "R.B. par R.B. ou l'autobiographie au neutre." *Critique*, no. 423–24 (August-September 1982): 734–43.

Marshall, Donald G. "Interpretation without Representation." *Partisan Review* 42 (1975): 469–73.

Mauriès, Patrick. "L'Anonyme parisien." *Critique*, no. 361–62 (1977): 574–78.

McGraw, Betty R. "Barthes's *The Pleasure of the Text*: An Erotics of Reading." *Boundary 2* 5 (1977): 943–52.

———. "Semiotics, Ertographics, and Barthes's Visual Concerns." *Sub-Stance*, no. 26 (1980): 68–75.

McGraw, Betty R., and Ungar, Steven. "R.B. Polygraphe." *Studies in Twentieth Century Literature* 5 (1981): 127–32.

Metz, Christian. *The Imaginary Signifier: Psychoanalysis and Cinema*. Translated by Celia Britton, Annwyl Williams, Ben Brewster, and Alfred Guzzetti. Bloomington: Indiana University Press, 1982.

Miller, Jacques-Alain. "Pseudo-Barthes." In *Prétexte: Roland Barthes*, pp. 201–21.

Moreau, Jean. "Heurs." *Critique*, no. 314 (1973): 583–95.

Mounin, Georges. *Introduction à la sémiologie*. Paris: Minuit, 1970.

Murdoch, Iris. *Sartre: Romantic Rationalist*. New Haven: Yale University Press, 1952.

Nadeau, Maurice. "Le Petit Kamasutra de Roland Barthes." *Quinzaine Littéraire*, no. 160, 16–31 March 1973, pp. 3–4.

Newhall, Beaumont. *The History of Photography*. New York: Museum of Modern Art, 1964.

Nichols, Stephen G. "Roland Barthes." *Contemporary Literature* 10 (1969): 136–46.

Pautrat, Bernard. *Versions du soleil*. Paris: Seuil, 1971.

Pettit, Philip. *The Concept of Structuralism: A Critical Analysis*. Berkeley: University of California Press, 1977.

Picard, Raymond. *New Criticism or New Fraud?* Translated by Frank Towne.

Pullman: Washington State University Press, 1969.

Pierssens, Michel. "Le *S/Z* de Roland Barthes: L'avenir du texte." *Sub-Stance*, no. 1 (1971): 37–48.

———. *The Power of Babel: A Study of Logophilia*. Translated by Carl Lovitt. Boston: Routledge and Kegan Paul, 1980.

Polan, Dana B. "Roland Barthes and the Moving Image." *October*, no. 18 (1981): 41–46.

Pontalis, J.-B. "*Le Degré zéro de l'écriture*." *Temps Modernes*, no. 96 (1953): 934–38.

Prendergast, Christopher. "Myth, Ideology, and Semioclastics." *Cambridge Review* 93 (1972): 170–74.

Raillard, Georges. "La Voix de Roland Barthes." *Quinzaine Littéraire*, no. 346, 16–30 April 1981, p. 13.

Rey, Alain. "Le Corps aux miroirs." *Critique*, no. 341 (1975): 1015–23.

Rey, Jean-Michel. *L'Enjeu des signes: lecture de Nietzsche*. Paris: Seuil, 1971.

Rice, Donald, and Schofer, Peter. "*S/Z*: Rhetoric and Open Reading." *L'Esprit Créateur* 22 (1982): 20–34.

Richard, Jean-Pierre. "Plaisir de table, plaisir de texte." In *Prétexte: Roland Barthes*, pp. 323–46.

———. "Nappe, charnière, interstice, point." *Poétique*, no. 47 (1981): 292–302.

Riffaterre, Michael. "Sade, or the Text as Fantasy." *Diacritics* 2 (1972): 3–9.

Rivière, Jean-Loup. "La Déception théâtrale." In *Prétexte: Roland Barthes*, pp. 110–28.

Robbe-Grillet, Alain. "Pourquoi j'aime Roland Barthes." In *Prétexte: Roland Barthes*, pp. 244–72.

Robin, Léon. *La Théorie platonicienne de l'amour*. Rev. ed. Paris: Presses Universitaires de France, 1964.

Roger, Philippe. "C'est donc un amoureux qui parle et qui dit." *Critique*, no. 361–62 (1977): 563–73.

———. "Roland Barthes: Le Texte, science, plaisir." In *Les Dieux dans la cuisine: vingt ans de philosophie en France*. Edited by Jean-Jacques Brochier, pp. 68–77. Paris: Aubier, 1978.

Rosenthal, Peggy. "Deciphering S/Z." *College English* 37 (1975): 125–44.

Roudiez, Leon S. "Roland Barthes: Recollections in Gratitude." *Studies in Twentieth Century Literature* 5 (1981): 197–204.

Runyon, Randolph. "Canon in U^bis." *Visible Language* 11 (1977): 387–427.

Said, Edward. "The Problem of Textuality: Two Exemplary Positions." *Critical Inquiry* 4 (1979): 673–814.

Scholes, Robert. *Structuralism in Literature*. New Haven: Yale University Press, 1974.

————. *Semiotics and Interpetation.* New Haven: Yale University Press, 1982.

Scholes, Robert, and Kellogg, Robert. *The Nature of Narrative.* New York: Oxford University Press, 1966.

Schwartz, Danielle. "Barthes, le langage et le pouvoir." *Nouvelle Critique,* no. 106 (1977): 55–57.

Sebeok, Thomas A. "The Semiotic Web: A Chronicle of Prejudices." *Bulletin of Literary Semiotics,* no. 2 (1975): 14–19.

Silverman, David, and Torode, Brian, eds. *The Material Word: Some Theories of Language and Their Limits.* Boston: Routledge and Kegan Paul, 1980.

Sollers, Philippe. "Roland Barthes." *Tel Quel,* no. 47 (1971): 19–26.

————. "Pour Barthes." *Magazine Littéraire,* no. 97 (February 1975): 9.

————. "Sur S/Z." *Quinzaine Littéraire,* no. 90, 1–15 March 1970, p. 23.

Sontag, Susan. "Preface." In Barthes, Roland, *Writing Degree Zero* and *Elements of Semiology,* translated by Annette Lavers and Colin Smith, pp. vii–xxv. Boston: Beacon Press, 1970.

————. "Remembering Barthes." In *Under the Sign of Saturn,* pp. 169–77. New York: Vintage, 1981.

————. "Writing Itself: On Roland Barthes." *New Yorker,* 26 April 1982, p. 122.

Starobinski, Jean. *Words Upon Words: The Anagrams of Saussure.* Translated by Olivia Emmet. New Haven: Yale University Press, 1979.

Sturrock, John, ed. *Structuralism and Since: From Lévi-Strauss to Derrida.* New York: Oxford University Press, 1979.

Thomas, Jean-Jacques. "Sensationalism." *Studies in Twentieth Century Literature* 5 (1981): 205–18.

Todorov, Tzvetan. "De la sémiologie à la rhétorique." *Annales* 22 (1977): 22–27.

————. "Reflections on Literature in Contemporary France." *New Literary History* 10 (1979): 333–51.

————. "The Last Barthes." *Critical Inquiry* 7 (1981): 449–54.

————. "Lire Barthes." *L'Esprit Créateur* 22 (1982): 5–7.

Turkle, Sherry. *Psychoanalytic Politics: Freud's French Revolution.* New York: Basic Books, 1978.

Ulmer, Gregory L. "Fetichism in Barthes' Nietzschean Phase." *Papers in Language and Literature* 14 (1978): 333–51.

————. "The Discourse of the Imaginary." *Diacritics* 10 (1980): 61–75.

————. "Barthes's Body of Knowledge." *Studies in Twentieth Century Literature* 5 (1981): 219–36.

Ungar, Steven. "RB: The Third Degree." *Diacritics* 7 (1977): 66–77.

————. "From Writing to the Letter: Barthes and Alphabetese." *Visible Language* 11 (1977): 390–428.

————. "Doing and Not Doing Things with Barthes." *Enclitic* 2 (1978): 86–109.

———. "Philip Thody, *Barthes: A Conservative Estimate* and Roland Barthes, *Image-Music-Text*." *Sub-Stance*, no. 22 (1979): 119–22.

———. "A Musical Note." *Studies in Twentieth Century Literature* 5 (1981): 237–44.

———. "Forwarding Addresses: Discursivity as Strategy in Barthes and Derrida." *Bulletin of the Midwest Modern Language Association* 14 (1982): 7–17.

———. "The Professor of Desire." *Yale French Studies*, no. 63 (1982): 81–97.

———. "Barthes via Proust: Circular Memories." *L'Esprit Créateur* 22 (1982): 8–19.

Updike, John. "Texts and Men." *New Yorker*, 4 October 1976, p. 150.

———. "The Last of Barthes." *New Yorker*, 23 September 1980, pp. 151–53.

Velan, Yves. "Barthes." In *Modern French Criticism: From Proust and Valéry to Structuralism*. Edited by John K. Simon, pp. 311–39. Chicago: University of Chicago Press, 1972.

Vlastos, Gregory. *Platonic Studies*. Princeton: Princeton University Press, 1973.

Vološinov, V. N. *Marxism and the Philosophy of Language*. New York: Academic Press, 1971.

Wahl, François. "Le Code, la roue, la réserve." *Tel Quel*, no. 47 (1971): 64–85.

———. "Les Fragments du sujet." In *Prétexte: Roland Barthes*, pp. 154–76.

———. "Gli amici." In *Roland Barthes: Carte segni*, pp. 21–23. Milan: Electa, 1981.

Wahl, François, ed. *Qu'est-ce que le structuralisme?* Paris: Seuil, 1968.

Warren, Susan, and Woodruff, Lori. "The Contract: A Stele for Roland Barthes." *Visible Language* 15 (1981): 320–27.

West, Philip J. "Barthes/Barthes: Textual/Sexual." *Salmagundi*, no. 37 (1977): 133–49.

Wilcox, John T. *Truth and Value in Nietzsche*. Ann Arbor: University of Michigan Press, 1974.

Wood, Michael. "Rules of the Game." *New York Review of Books*, 4 March 1976, pp. 31–34.

Young, Robert, ed. *Untying the Text: A Post-Structuralist Reader*. Boston: Routledge and Kegan Paul, 1981.

Zeldin, Theodore. *France 1848–1945*. 2 vols. Oxford: Clarendon Press, 1970–73.

Index

System), 21, 28, 64, 86, 89, 100, 127; *S/Z*, xii, xv, 10, 18, 21, 28–30, 40, 42, 43, 50, 54, 66, 69–73, 78, 81, 87, 90–91, 93, 95, 100, 105, 113, 114, 119, 125, 137, 145, 154–56, 162, 163, 166 n. 9; *Writing Degree Zero (Le Degré zéro de l'écriture)*, 4, 7–15, 18, 20–24, 26, 30, 38, 43, 66, 71, 86, 89, 91, 102, 103, 124, 126, 157
Bataille, Georges, 59, 62, 104, 168 n. 7, 170 n. 2; *Le Gros Orteil*, 58; *The Story of the Eye*, 103
Baudelaire, Charles, 60
Beckett, Samuel, 160, 174 n. 11
Beethoven, Ludwig von, 73–74
Bellour, Raymond, 105
Benjamin, Walter, 149
Benveniste, Emile, 4, 74, 79, 122, 127. *See also* Significance
Blanchot, Maurice, 12, 62, 159, 168 n. 7
Booth, Wayne C., 66
Bouveresse, Jacques, 171 n. 8
Brecht, Bertolt, 104, 138
Brée, Germaine, 167 n. 3
Brenkman, John, 171 n. 3
Brøndal, Viggo, 13
Bunraku, 53–54; *See also* Writing, act of
Butor, Michel, 69–71, 78

Calvet, Louis-Jean, 167 n. 17
Camera Lucida (La Chambre claire). See Barthes, Roland
Camus, Albert, 7, 12, 166 n. 5
Cerisy-la-Salle, 58, 93, 160
Collège de France, xv, 127, 137
Coluche, 166–67 n. 16
Combat, 7
Communications, 117, 124
Connotation, xiv, 13, 22, 24, 26, 39–

43, 45, 89, 156. *See also* Denotation
Coward, Roslaind, xiv
Critical Essays. See Barthes, Roland
Critique et vérité. See Barthes, Roland
Culler, Jonathan, xiv, 6, 30, 61, 63, 88

De Man, Paul, 62, 148
Denotation, xiv, 22, 26–27, 39, 42–46, 156. *See also* Connotation
Derrida, Jacques, xii, 3, 4, 56, 61, 79, 101, 143, 168 n. 8, 171 n. 8, 173 n. 9; *Of Grammatology*, 91; *Speech and Phenomena*, 142
Descartes, René, 22, 23, 108; *Larvatus prodeo*, 28, 81
Documents, 58
Durkheim, Emile, 100

Ecole Pratique des Hautes Etudes, xv, 103, 112. *See also* Pedagogy; Seminar, space of
Elements of Semiology. See Barthes, Roland
Empire of Signs (L'Empire des signes), The. See Barthes, Roland
Erté. *See* Tirtoff, Romain de
Erté. See Barthes, Roland
Existentialism, 23, 36, 55, 101, 159, 173 n. 5

Figuration, 38, 68–76, 78, 81, 85, 95–96, 122, 149, 152–56. *See also* Writing, act of
Figure (of speech), 14, 104, 120, 154–55
Finas, Lucette, 86, 167 n. 3
Fischer-Dieskau, Dietrich, 73
Flaubert, Gustave, 4, 12, 56, 60, 63; *Bouvard et Pécuchet*, 23, 93–94; *Dictionary of Received Ideas*, 93